Men, Women and Relationships

MAKING PEACE
WITH THE OPPOSITE SEX

John Gray, Ph.D.

Published by
Beyond Words Publishing, Inc.
13950 NW Pumpkin Ridge Road
Hillsboro, Oregon 97124
Phone: 503-647-5109
Toll-free: 1-800-284-9673

Editing: Julie Livingston
Art Direction: Principia Graphica
Typesetting: The TypeSmith
Cover Design: Jerry Soga
Photography: Le Photographer
First Printing: 1990

Printed in the United States of America by Arcata Graphics,
Kingsport, Tennessee.
Distributed by Publishers Group West

ISBN: 0-941831-93-0
Library of Congress Catalog Card Number: 90-080256

The case studies in this book are real; however, the names and
circumstances have been substantially changed to protect the
anonymity and confidentiality of all cases.

Contents

Preface

My father's death has become, in my mind, an allegory for the purpose of this book. My generous, compassionate father was robbed by a hitchhiker and then left to die in the trunk of his car of heat asphyxiation. He tried for several hours to get out. During that time his car was reported twice to the police by nearby residents who had noticed the abandoned car. The police responded to both calls, but didn't find the car because the directions to its location were not clear. After the third call they were able to find the car, but it was too late.

In some ways my father's death was symbolic, not only of his life, but of other's lives as well. He always gave help to other people but did not know how to really share himself or let anyone into his heart. Like him, so many people are dying of broken hearts, alone and abandoned. They are not being rescued because the directions are not clear. We do not know how to find them or help them. This book can help by dispelling the confusion in relationships and replacing it with clarity and hope.

There is still, however, another important part to this story. Returning home for the funeral, I went out to the car to see how my father died. I climbed in the trunk and pulled shut the hood to feel what he must have gone through. I ran my fingers over the dents where he had banged on the trunk top to get help. I felt his aloneness. Rarely in his life had my dad asked for help.

Still in the trunk, I saw where he had broken out the back light to get air. I instinctively stretched my hand out through the hole he had made. One of my brothers, who had been standing outside the car, said, "See if you can reach the button to pop the hood." I reached my hand out a little farther and opened the trunk.

If my dad had thought to open the trunk with his hand, he would have lived. I, too, being in the trunk and trying to get out, did not think to open the lid from the outside. It took my brother, who was already on the outside, to point the way

My father's death has inspired me in my life in a profound way. It has prompted me to see my responsibility to help those who may be locked within their hearts, by pointing to the "button" by which they can free themselves.

Men, Women and Relationships is dedicated to all who are imprisoned within their own hearts. I hope that in reading this book, you will discover some of those buttons that go unnoticed when you are locked up within yourself. May you be successful in opening your heart to love and compassion. I hope that by your example you will inspire others to come out of their own trunks and share their love.

This book is also dedicated to those light bearers who are already on the outside trying to help others free themselves. May these pages support your efforts and enhance your work.

Writing this book and testing out its new insights, skills, and strategies has been for me a rich and fantastic journey. It has taken me to many heights, through many valleys and storms, into lands of sunshine, beauty, love, and trust.

I thank Bonnie, my wife, for sharing this journey with me and for her continued love and support. In developing the material of this book, she has been my greatest teacher. Many of the concepts I have written about I learned directly from listening to her. Her love, vulnerability, and honesty has helped me to respect femininity and has inspired me to be a better and more loving man. Through her love I have learned to trust, accept, and appreciate my own masculinity. Most important, I have learned the transforming power of love.

My gratitude goes also to my daughter Lauren for teaching me to love in ways I could never have dreamed. I thank my stepdaughters Shannon and Julie for their acceptance of me and for their love.

I thank my younger brother Jimmy. His unconditional love has supported me throughout my journeys and his unfortunate suicide has taught me to value life. His suffering has taught me compassion, while his endless love fills my heart and motivates me to be of service to others less fortunate than I.

Heartfelt thanks go also to my mother, Virginia Gray, whose unconditional acceptance and continued support has helped me become the man I am. I thank her for her spirituality and for being an example of selfless giving. I could not imagine having a better mom. I also want to acknowledge Lucille for her continued devotion to my success and for always believing in me.

I thank my clients, whose stories I share in this book, and the many thousands of participants in my seminars, who have trusted the ideas in this book and have proven their effectiveness. To all of them goes my deep appreciation for sharing their stories and their wisdom. Most of the best examples and case histories in this book are taken from their heartfelt sharing. Their support has made this book possible and the many books to follow.

I thank Ann Weyman, Sara Steinberg and Julie Livingston for their expert assistance in editing this book. My thanks also to Richard Cohn and Cindy Black and the staff of Beyond Words Publishing for their gentle persistence in giving birth to this book.

In conclusion, I thank you for letting me make a difference in your life. Thank you for your courage and sincere commitment to find the light of love within your heart and to share that love, bringing light into the darkness of our world, bringing compassion to heal our collective hurt, and bringing joy to heal our sorrow. Always remember, you are special and your love does make a difference.

Introduction

A great relationship requires work, but it also requires vacation. It shouldn't be all work. Both things are equally important. Women intuitively understand that to have a good relationship, you have to work at it. Men, on the other hand, are born with the knowledge that "at your job, that's where you work." You go to work, do your job and when you come home, that's your vacation time. And we're experts at it. For thousands of years a man went out on his hunt, patiently waited and then with a burst of energy ran after the animal he was pursuing. The qualities that made a man a good hunter — waiting, watching, conserving energy — now look like hanging out and laziness. She doesn't understand this is his way of relaxing from the day. When a woman sees her man sitting in front of the TV, remote control in hand, she takes it personally and mistakenly assumes that he really doesn't care about the relationship.

Truly, we need a new job description for relationships. And I use the term *job description* particularly for men, because a man is conditioned to learn a job.

Historically, the way a man supported his family and showed love to the woman in his life, was to go away and bring something back. Today, that doesn't work as well, because in many cases, she's out hunting too, and when you get back there's more work to do — relationship work. At one time it might have been enough for men to support their woman by supplying their physical needs, but this is no longer true. Women now know that they are capable of providing for themselves in the material sense: they need their men to support them emotionally. That's the whole secret. Now, men want to be supportive and loving, but it is a process of adjustment. We are learning the art of communication that goes beyond the transfer of information to the expression of love. Generally, when a woman says we need to talk a man feels "Oh, oh, not talking, not that." It's the same reaction we had the first time we went on the hunt. "Oh, no. I have to kill that animal? I have to do it? What if it gets me?" So there was fear, apprehension, not knowing what to do. But we learned, and we still can learn what's required in a relationship — what's required for the new job description.

The problem in relationships today is not money, although sometimes we think it is. It's communication. Today's relationships are about nurturing each other's emotional needs — and a woman's emotional needs today are different than they were fifty years ago. A man's emotional needs are different today, too. We are a different generation of people. The world is a different place now and expectations have totally changed.

To a man, real love is when you don't try to change anybody. When he meets the "right" person, often after lots of interviews, he will let his heart come out and love this woman just as she is. A man wants the same in return, but most women don't know that.

When a woman is shopping for her partner, she looks for a man who makes her feel good, who she cares for and loves. But somewhere there's a feeling welling up inside. "He's got potential; I see it. What I could do with him. Love will overcome. I'll just love him. I'll just give to him and he will change."

Unfortunately, men, there's nothing you can do to change that about women. That's the way they are, but women can learn to work with that, just as men can learn to accept that in women. A woman is going to want to change us. In this book and in my book *Men Are from Mars, Women Are from Venus,* I talk about this trait in fun, friendly terms, and most importantly in a positive way. There is nothing bad about men or women, if we approach relationships positively and with a commitment to do our best to understand each other and to make things work. Ultimately, the objective I have in helping couples is for them to learn to respect each other's differences and become a little closer to each other as a result.

There's a fun way to look at our relationships. During those moments when you want to pull your hair out, when you wonder what's going wrong, why this isn't working out, and you think maybe we're just not right for each other, maybe we're just too different, that's the time to remember that maybe your partner is from another planet. Men are from Mars and women are from Venus and on these planets we have different customs. If you learn to honor and respect the customs of the different planets, then things go smoothly, but if you don't honor and respect the customs, you step on each other's toes.

I have found that the secret to success in helping couples is to look for the easiest things to change, rather than the difficult things. I recall asking a couple to talk about their problems. Like a good Venusian, the woman remembered every detail of their problems. They don't forget. The man, on the other hand, appeared to shrink down in his chair, because Martians are known for solving problems. What makes a man feel good on Mars is feeling competent and having other people recognize his ability. That is why men, as a rule, won't stop and ask for directions. "Look how competent I am, I can get us there." The last thing a Martian wants to hear from his partner is that he's lost. Remember, for thousands of years men were hunters and guides and moved the tribe around. They had to know where to go. Getting lost was not an option. So men have a very precise meaning around competence and women, if you want to recharge his batteries when he's feeling low, just give him some appreciation. Don't remind him that his batteries are low, or that he's been driving around the block for fifteen minutes. I promise you, he knows.

There are some little things that a Venusian can change about a Martian, but there is one big thing that women need to recognize, because men won't ever change this trait: When a man has spent the whole day solving this problem and that problem and is feeling stress, he will come home and, like the healthy man that he is, he will go into his cave. All Martians have a cave and on it there's a sign written in Martian. I'll give you the translation: "Do not enter, fierce dragon inside". Every man knows that sign, but women don't—and a man doesn't understand that he has to explain this aspect of himself gently to women. There is another sign on the cave and it says: "Be back soon." It is very important to know that he will come out and that he's not wasting time in there when he could be doing something meaningful to a Venusian, like talking.

For a Venusian, the way to feel better is to talk. So many women today, are putting on Martian suits, working and not getting their emotional needs met during the day. Now, more than any time in history, women need to talk in order to find balance and wholeness.

The difficulty you and your partner face is that if you talk to him about your problems, his inherent nature is to give you solutions. At that moment, getting solutions is not going to make a woman feel better. What she is looking for is empathy, someone to hear her.

When he comes out of his cave, you may be furious inside for having to wait so long to be with him. You may even walk off to build your own cave to punish him for not wanting to talk to you. When this happened in my own marriage eight years ago, I was just learning about caves and my wife's needs.

I came out of my cave and my wife went off. I thought, "Great, I can just watch TV." I didn't know I was being punished. Days passed and we were hardly talking at all. I thought, "Now this is really peaceful. It's like going on a fishing trip." A few days later when I approached her in a sexual way, I discovered that she had been silent because she was upset with me.

The gift we can give ourselves is to know that we are also human, that men and women sometimes forget these differences exist. We also need to remember that we don't change overnight. When people make mistakes, they just need another chance, particularly when you are dealing with the difference between the sexes. It is also important to know that you don't have to take everything your partner is saying personally. Knowing that I'm a Martian, my wife will say to me "You don't have to solve these problems, this isn't your fault. I just need to talk about this. I'm already starting to feel better." And I say, "You are?" and she says, "Yeah." And I think, "All right!"

I hope that this book will provide you with valuable insights and tools that you can use to better all your relationships, to gain greater self-esteem and to understand the changes that men and women are going through and to appreciate the unique qualities that make us who we are.

John Gray, Ph.D.
September 30, 1993
Mill Valley, California

CHAPTER ONE

THE ART OF LOVING AN ALIEN BEING

PEOPLE ARE DIFFERENT

Recognizing this fundamental truth is essential for creating positive and loving relationships.

In practice, however, we do not fully acknowledge that people differ from us. Instead we are bent upon changing one another. We resent, resist, and reject each other's differences. We demand that the people in our lives feel, think, and behave as we would. And when they react differently we make them wrong or invalidate them; we try to fix them when they really need understanding and nurturing; we try to improve them when instead they need acceptance, appreciation, and trust.

We complain that if only they would change, we could love them; if only they would agree, we could love them; if only they would feel the way we do, we could love them; if only they would do what we ask, we could love them.

What, then, is love? Is love accepting and appreciating a person only when they fulfill our expectations? Is love the act of changing a person into what we want rather than what they choose to be? Is love caring for or trusting a person because they think and feel the way we do?

Certainly this is not love. It may feel like love to the giver but not to the receiver. Real love is unconditional. It does not demand but affirms and values. Unconditional love is not possible without the recognition and acceptance of our differences. As long as we mistakenly believe that our loved ones would be better off thinking, feeling, and behaving the way we do, true love is obstructed. Once we realize that not only are people different but they are supposed to be that way, the obstacles to real love begin to fall away.

HOW WE ARE DIFFERENT

Once we accept that people are different we can begin to seriously explore *how* we are different. Ultimately all human beings are unique and it is impossible to categorize them. But by creating a greater awareness of our possible differences, these systems are immensely helpful.

The study of morphology divides people into three body types that are associated with three major psychological differences: action oriented, feeling oriented, and mind oriented.

Hypocrites, Adickes, Kretschmer, Spranger, Adler, and Jung classified our differences by four temperaments, generalized by some as "physical, feeling, thinking, and intuitive." The widely used Myers-Briggs indicator expands these four into sixteen.

The ancient practice of astrology describes twelve psychological types. Sufi teachings recognize nine basic psychological types called the enneagram. Many contemporary personal growth and business seminars describe the following four types: supporter, promoter, controller, and analyzer. It is proposed that the individual potentially possesses all of these qualities, and with a greater awareness he or she can choose to develop and integrate them.

Some, however, oppose categorizing people since this may limit them or box them in. To say one person is analytical while another is emotional may give rise to judgment. This fear arises because experience tells us that when we are being judged as "less than another," it is because we are being categorized in some way; we are being seen as different. Hence, we fear being different.

From one perspective, judgments and prejudice are associated with differences. But at a deeper level we can clearly see that the original cause of these judgments is nonacceptance and nonappreciation of our differences.

For example, a person might be judged as "too emotional" by an "analytical person" with the mistaken expectation that all people should be like him. This belief makes him incapable of truly appreciating or respecting an emotional person. In a similar way, an "emotional" person might judge an analytical person as "too analytical," because the emotional person is not appreciating their differences.

Though the acknowledgment of differences can be perceived as a threat, it is not. Through accepting that people are different we are freed from the compulsion to change them. When we are not preoccupied with changing others, we are free to appreciate their unique values. Ultimately, the recognition of differences among people allows us to release our judgments.

UNITY IN DIVERSITY

Accepting our psychological differences frees us to experience an underlying oneness that permeates our relationships. In an abstract way, we are all the same. In every spiritual teaching is an acknowledgment of that oneness. Deep within we feel a spiritual oneness with our fellow humans. When we read of children suffering from hunger, we feel in our hearts the pain we would feel if they were our own children.

Ultimately we are all motivated to break free from the chains that separate us and to realize our oneness. This opening of the heart is really an awareness that what is outside us is also inside us. The quest to open the heart takes a variety of forms: the path to enlightenment, the quest for God, the dream of happy marriage, finding one's soul mate, or creating a loving family. In each example, one is inexplicably drawn to something and someone else.

The seeker of enlightenment is drawn to a teacher because the teacher embodies something within the student that the seeker is to realize. Through loving and understanding the teacher or the teaching, the seeker is indirectly loving and accepting those very qualities within himself. Gradually the seeker finds what he seeks within his own being. In this way we are inevitably drawn to that which we need to awaken within ourselves.

A man separated from his female qualities becomes detached and cold. He seeks relief through union with a woman's softness and warmth. Their innate differences create an attraction or chemistry. As he blends his male energies with her female energies, he momentarily experiences the bliss of his own wholeness. Through touching the softness of her femininity with love, he becomes soft and gentle, yet maintains his masculine strength and drive.

We may seek to find yet a deeper union with our soul mate, a special person with whom to share our lives, as if ordained by the heavens. We are drawn to this person not because they are similar to us but because they are different. Our soul mate embodies qualities and attributes that we unconsciously seek to find within ourselves. Through loving this person, we begin to accept and awaken those same qualities hidden within our own beings. This discovery of self brings us greater fulfillment.

Although love allows us to integrate within ourselves the qualities of the loved, its prerequisite is an awareness of difference. We are drawn to that which is different. Our challenge is to understand, accept, and appreciate those differences, and then they will naturally emerge within ourselves.

This is a challenge because the process is not always easy. Intense attraction to someone is a sign that there are many differences to harmonize, many conflicts to resolve. Attraction is not under our control. We can be sure, however, that when there is attraction, there are lessons to learn and discoveries to be made. Because we are attracted to people who are unlike ourselves, the fundamental basis for enriching relationships is the acknowledgment that people are different.

This book will explore the common differences between men and women. Through respecting, accepting, and appreciating these differences, many of the problems that plague our relationships can be solved.

Certainly all women are not the same, nor are all men the same. But in very general ways, men and women differ from each other. Through increasing your awareness of these differences and the ways they apply to the people in your life, confusion between the sexes begins to clear up. Important questions can be answered, judgments can be released, and conflict can be more successfully resolved, and eventually avoided.

UNDERSTANDING OUR DIFFERENCES

Kathy, age 32, is a successful musician and composer. Her career has taken off with opportunities opening in all directions. Like so many successful career women, she is not married and at times wishes she were. "I don't know what I do to turn men off," she says. "Somehow I am pushing them away. Maybe I make too many demands. What can you expect from a man? Men are very confusing. Relationships are confusing. I don't even know what a good relationship looks like."

Alise, age 36, is a business consultant, and Henry, age 40, is a land developer. They have been married six years. "When we got married Henry was attentive, considerate, and so romantic," Alise explains. "Now everything is routine and boring. We don't even talk. Sometimes at night, after Henry has fallen asleep on the couch, I cry myself to sleep remembering how much I loved him and how special he made me feel. I don't understand why everything is so difficult now. We can't even have a conversation together. Occasionally he will open up and share, then something happens and he clams up. I wish I knew why."

Patrick, age 42, a restaurant designer, is frustrated with his live-in girlfriend Jennifer, age 36, who is an artist. He loves her and thinks about marrying her, but is unsure because they fight so much of the time. "Whenever I say something constructive or try to help her," Patrick says, "Jen reacts as though I am attacking her. Then when I explain myself, she gets more upset. I have no idea what to do. I feel frustrated because I really want to support her. I love her but when she overreacts to everything I do, I become mean and defensive. I don't know how long I can take it."

What is missing in each of these relationships is a deep understanding of how men and women are different. Without this understanding it becomes nearly impossible to fully appreciate and respect the differences that make each sex special and unique. Keeping this in mind, let's review the three examples listed above:

KATHY WANTS TO SHARE, TOM WANTS HIS "SPACE"

Kathy is frustrated because she is unable to fulfill her wants and needs with a man without offending him. For example, when she and her partner Tom get together after work, she wants to talk about their respective days, while he wants to forget his day and read a magazine or watch TV. The more she attempts to have a conversation and the more he resists, the more tension they both feel.

She says, "How was your day?" He says "Fine" while inside he thinks, "Ah . . . , now I can sit down, watch the news, and zone out."

She asks, "How did your meeting go?" He says "OK" while inside he thinks, "Oh no. Here we go again. She wants to interrogate me about my day. I don't want to talk about my day. If I did, I would talk about it. I just want to forget the day and watch the news."

She says, "Did you remember to renew your car registration?" He says "Yes" while inside he thinks, "I remembered it, but I didn't renew it yet. I can't believe she keeps track of everything I do. I feel so smothered. Doesn't she trust that I can handle my own car registration?"

She tries again, "How was the traffic to town this morning?" He answers "The usual" while inside he thinks, "Who cares about the traffic. Why is she trying to bother me this way? Maybe she is trying to tell me I should leave more time to get to work. I hate it when she tries to improve and reform me. Give me a break, I just want to watch TV."

"Did you get to your meeting in time?" His response is "Yes." He thinks, "Get off my back, will you. You never trust me. Sure, I missed part of the meeting, but the last thing I want to hear from her is a lecture on how I should give myself more time. I bet she is waiting for an opportunity to say 'I told you so.'"

Kathy senses Tom's irritation but has no idea why he is angry. She feels hurt and asks, "Are you angry with me?" He says "No!" while inside he thinks, "I just want to have some peace, and now she wants to talk about feelings. I hate it when she does this. Now I can't even enjoy watching the news, because she is upset with me. I was feeling fine about her until she did this to me. Why can't she just support me when we get together? Can't she tell that I've had a hard day? I don't bother her with a bunch of questions!"

Tom doesn't realize that Kathy *is* trying to support him, by treating him the way she wants to be treated. She is not trying to improve him with her questions; she is just trying to make conversation. Ultimately she wants him to support her by asking her caring questions. Unfortunately, he thinks he is supporting her by *not* asking questions and giving her "space," and doesn't understand why she is not respecting his "space."

On the other side, Kathy feels unloved, ignored, and taken for granted. She thinks, "I can't believe he doesn't want to share with me. He used to talk to me. He just doesn't love me the way he used to. Maybe I am boring to him. It hurts not to feel special anymore. I am so angry. He never listens to me. This is not the kind of relationship I want. Why can't I find a man who can love me? He knows I've had a hard day and I need to talk. I was so attentive to him, and he hasn't even asked me about my day. It's not fair."

Kathy doesn't realize how her attempts to support Tom actually make him feel unsupported. In various ways she mistakenly treats her male partner the way she wants to be treated, and then doesn't understand why it doesn't work. Kathy wrongly assumes that men will respond the way she or another woman would.

ALISE TRIES TO PLEASE, HENRY NEEDS APPRECIATION

Alise is upset because she feels everything she does to help Henry is unappreciated and rejected. In truth, much of what she does is appreciated, but when it causes her to burn out and resent her relationship, then Henry would prefer she do less.

For example, before Henry gets home Alise will do a variety of things to please him. She takes out the trash, she straightens up his desk, she cleans the house, she washes and folds his T-shirts and underwear, she thinks about his favorite foods and prepares a meal, she picks up after him and washes their dishes, she takes messages off the answering machine, and does anything else she can think of to please him and make his life more fulfilling. In short, Alise anticipates Henry's every need and tries to attend to it. She then resents him for not doing the same in return.

Henry comes home from work already tired; when he feels his wife's resentment he becomes even more exhausted. He does not fully appreciate all that Alise does, because it makes her so resentful of him. He would rather she do less and be more appreciative for what he is doing to make her life easier. He needs her to be happier and have warmer responses to him. Henry is turned off by her martyr-like approach to their relationship.

Alise is confused because she is behaving in a way she knows would please her. In short, she is "doing unto him as she would have him do unto her." Unfortunately she doesn't ask Henry for more support. She assumes that because she is working so hard to please him, he should give back to her without her having to ask. She also assumes that if Henry loved her, then he would anticipate her needs. She does not understand that her doing more in the relationship, while resenting, makes him want to do less in the relationship. When she does ask for help — generally in a demanding tone — Henry just gets mad and smolders in silence.

Rarely do they talk except about practical matters. Whenever Henry does share about his day, Alise, in another attempt to please, tries to help him feel better. This turns Henry off; then he doesn't want to open up further to Alise about his day. For example:

Henry says, "We didn't get that new account at the office. I have to lay off about half of my crew. It's really a hard decision."

Alise, in an enthusiastic tone, says, "Well, now you have to decide who your best workers are and let the others go."

Henry's responds with silence. He is turned off. Inside he thinks, "I wasn't asking her for advice. I am quite capable of handling this problem. Of course I will keep my best workers. Why can't she just listen and appreciate how hard I work. And why is she so enthusiastic?"

Alise is perplexed. She wants to help and doesn't grasp that Henry feels insulted by her effort to solve his problem. She is enthusiastic because she wants so much to please him, and this appeared to be an opportunity. At times like this she hasn't the faintest notion of what he really needs. She doesn't understand that he just wants her to listen and appreciate how hard he works. Just as she wants to feel special, he wants to feel as though he's her hero.

PATRICK INVALIDATES JENNIFER'S FEELINGS

Patrick is frustrated because he doesn't understand Jennifer's angry reactions at times when he thinks he is supporting her. For example:

When Patrick comes home the first thing he does is to read through his mail. Then he listens to his messages and pets the dog. After looking at the newspaper for a while, he wanders into the kitchen where Jennifer is making dinner. The first thing Patrick says to Jennifer is, "Why are you mixing those spices together?"

Feeling angry and criticized, Jennifer retorts, "I feel like it, that's why." Inside she grumbles, "He hasn't even said hello and already he is criticizing me. He is ignoring me. He would rather read his mail than talk to me. He's not even excited to see me. I've been waiting to see him all day. I feel so embarrassed. He doesn't even want to give me a hug or kiss. He could care less. What a creep. He would rather pet his dog. And then he has the gall to come into my kitchen and complain about my cooking."

Patrick detects her upset and tries to make Jen feel better. He says, "Well, it's no big deal, but I just think those spices don't go well with red snapper. I think you should leave out the pepper." Inside he thinks, "Why is she defensive about a little suggestion? What's the big deal? She is so temperamental! Can't she take a little feedback?"

Jennifer says, "If it's no big deal, then why do you always insist on criticizing me when I've asked you not to! You are so mean. You don't even care how I feel. You don't love me anymore. Why should I even bother? All you care about is yourself."

Patrick then says, "That's ridiculous. I wasn't criticizing you. I can't believe you. Why do you make such a big deal out of everything? Of course I love you." Inside he adds, "I hate having to put up with your irrational outbursts. I wish you would grow up."

Patrick doesn't understand the valid reasons for Jennifer's feelings. He doesn't realize that comments like "that's ridiculous" or "I can't believe you" or "you're making such a big deal out of this" invalidate her feelings and make her feel worse. Even the phrase "Of course I love you" implies that Jennifer is insecure for doubting his love.

Jennifer overreacts to his suggestions because she feels neglected in the relationship. She is no longer being treated as she was in the beginning. He takes her for granted, then makes her feel foolish for becoming upset. He doesn't attempt to understand the real reasons for her sensitivity. His lack of respect for her feelings makes her feel invalidated, and her defensiveness increases.

Patrick is not an unloving man. He is willing to respond to Jennifer's needs. The problem is that he doesn't know what her needs are, because they are different from his. Likewise, he doesn't respond well to her reactions because they make no sense to him. Since he would not be upset were he in Jennifer's place, he reasons, then she shouldn't be upset either. Not realizing how condescending he sounds, he invalidates her feelings. As a result, they start to fight.

Patrick mistakenly assumes that Jennifer would be happier if she were like him, so he tries to change her rather than explore her needs and fulfill her. Like most men, Patrick does not understand that women are different and that they are supposed to be the way they are.

REEVALUATING OUR ASSUMPTIONS

Relationships are so puzzling because we mistakenly assume that our partners are like us. To some extent they are, but in many important aspects they are different. Let's look at four common ways that assuming men and women are alike negatively affects our relationships:

IT IS DIFFICULT TO NURTURE

When we expect another person to react as we would, we inevitably feel frustrated if they react differently. Out of frustration, we may automatically begin to invalidate our partner's feeling reactions even though our original intent was to nurture and support them.

When Jennifer and Patrick experience a crisis, it is difficult for Patrick to understand why Jennifer is getting so emotional. Under stress, he naturally becomes more detached. Jennifer, however, usually becomes emotional.

This particular difference between men and women is quite common. But their failure to understand this difference creates new problems. Patrick takes her emotional reaction personally, assuming that Jennifer doesn't trust his ability to handle things. He thinks that by saying "don't get upset" he is helping her, because his way of dealing with crises is to detach and not get upset. Instead, Jennifer gets *more* upset because Patrick doesn't share his feelings or validate hers. She cannot believe that he really cares because he seems so withdrawn.

IT IS DIFFICULT TO ASSIST

We also may offend our partner by treating him or her the way we want to be treated. We mistakenly assume that "what is good for me is good for you."

For example, Alise commonly irritates her husband Henry by becoming overly caring. She is not trying to irritate him; as a matter of fact, she has no idea why he is annoyed. She is confused because she would welcome more caring from him.

By assuming that he would gladly welcome her caring influence, Alise unknowingly offends her husband. She thinks she is helping when, in truth, she is only making matters worse. It is nothing personal. Simply because he is a man, Henry feels smothered by her love. It is quite normal for men to feel smothered by too much caring. She cannot succeed in assisting him unless she first understands how his needs differ from hers.

IT IS DIFFICULT FOR WOMEN TO APPRECIATE, ACCEPT, AND TRUST

Problems arise when we expect another to think, feel, and behave the way we do. Women frequently misinterpret a man's love by evaluating his behavior according to their feminine standards. For example, Patrick customarily prioritizes his problems and ignores those objectives (or commitments) that are not at the top of his list. When Jennifer's needs are then overlooked, it is hard for her to appreciate, accept, and trust that he loves her.

From his point of view, if her need were urgent, he would put it at the top of his list because she *is* so important to him. However, because Jennifer doesn't understand Patrick's thinking and behavior, it is hard for her to believe him when he explains how important she really is to him. He doesn't understand that his way of handling problems frustrates Jennifer and doesn't support her needs.

This mutual misunderstanding arises because of one very fundamental difference between men and women. When under stress, men tend to prioritize and focus on what is most urgent. The drawback to this kind of stress reaction is that they forget other responsibilities or attach little importance to them. When Jennifer's needs are thus minimized, it does not feel very good to her. She cannot understand this reaction because she reacts differently under stress.

Under stress, women tend to become more acutely aware of the variety of problems and demands being placed upon them. To become oblivious to the needs of someone she cares about in order to fully focus on solving a problem at work is not one of her common experiences. Thus, it is hard for her to trust that he really does care about her.

IT IS DIFFICULT FOR MEN TO
CARE, UNDERSTAND, AND RESPECT

It is hard to respond in a caring, understanding, and respectful way when you assume that your partner *should* think and feel the way you do.

Patrick has a difficult time respecting Jennifer when she feels unloved or unsupported. He knows how much he loves her, so when she doesn't feel his support, he takes it personally. He loses respect and judges her as ungrateful or irrational.

When she has had a long day and reacts emotionally by feeling overwhelmed and hopeless, he feels as though she is complaining that he isn't helping enough.

From her point of view, Jennifer just needs to unwind and be heard. She merely needs to share; he assumes she needs him to solve her problems.

Because Patrick doesn't have the same pressing need to share his feelings, it is hard for him to respect her need to share. When he is upset he deals with it through problem solving. When she is upset, he assumes his strategy will help her too. Instead of listening, which is what she needs, he continually interrupts her with "solutions" to her problems. Jennifer doesn't get what she needs — simply to be heard — and Patrick doesn't get appreciated for trying to help. Because of faulty assumptions, they both end up frustrated.

No matter how committed we are to improving our relationships, it is impossible to make significant advances without reevaluating our hidden assumptions. The vast majority of conflicts between men and women stem from one basic misunderstanding: We assume that we are the same when, in many ways, men and women are as different as aliens from separate planets would be. Without an understanding of how we are different, all our efforts to unravel the mysteries of keeping love's magic alive cannot even begin to bear fruit.

WHAT IF . . .
MEN CAME FROM MARS AND
WOMEN CAME FROM VENUS?

The communication gap between men and women can be so vast that at times our partners seem as different from us as beings from outer space. Let's pretend for a while that this is true. Let's pretend that men come from Mars and women from Venus.

Imagine that one day long ago Martians, looking through their telescopes, discovered the planet Venus. They had been getting pretty bored hanging around on Mars, but as soon as they spotted the strange Venusians, they started feeling quite excited. Quickly they built spaceships and flew to Venus.

When they arrived they were amazed by the way they felt in the presence of these beautiful beings. The Martians began to feel powerful and more alive. A new sense of responsibility and purpose pulsed through their Martian muscles.

The Venusians reacted just as strongly to the arrival of the Martians. They had intuitively known that this day would come. When they saw the Martians, they felt a trusting love in their hearts that they had never felt before. Some said they felt like flowers opening to the warm rays of the sun; others felt centered and clear, aware of their inner wisdom.

Together the Martians and Venusians decided to fly off in their spaceships and live happily ever after on the most beautiful planet in the solar system, Earth. For some time they lived in harmony, free from conflict.

The secret to their success was the tremendous appreciation and respect they had for each other's differences. Neither Martian nor Venusian tried to change the other. They did not view their differences as superior or inferior, but greatly appreciated the way their differences complemented each other. Through their loving interactions they all felt more powerful and fulfilled.

One morning, when the effects of Earth's atmosphere had finally taken hold, they all woke up with a peculiar kind of amnesia. They forgot that they were from different planets.

In an instant, they forgot that they were supposed to be different. They forgot that they spoke languages that sounded similar but were actually quite distinct. When they tried to communicate they were inevitably misunderstood.

The Martians and Venusians forgot that their needs and wants were different. They forgot that they had different motives, purposes, aims, values, drives, impulses, urges, and reactions. They forgot that they had divergent ways of thinking, feeling, recognizing, conceptualizing, perceiving, understanding, deciding, and concluding. They forgot that they had contrasting manners of acting and responding.

In one night, they lost the awareness necessary to respect each other's unique qualities; differences were now interpreted as flaws and afflictions — temporary manifestations of stupidity, sickness, craziness, meanness, immaturity, stubbornness, selfishness, weakness, or badness. Immediately, a host of problems arose. Differences between the Martians and Venusians had become a source of conflict instead of joy, appreciation, and wonder.

In a similar way, men and women feel compelled to fix or change the other instead of supporting, nurturing, and validating. Needless to say, it becomes increasingly difficult to give and receive support. Relationships lose their magic and are filled with confusion and struggle. The bond of love diminishes when men and women are unable to understand, respect, appreciate, and accept their differences.

CONFLICTS IN HANDLING UPSETS

When men and women fail to understand how different the sexes are, a host of problems will arise. Take Jennifer and Patrick, who experience a conflict that is quite common between men and women.

When Jennifer is upset she needs to talk about and explore her feelings, to have her feelings validated. Next, she needs to be touched, held, and comforted by someone she trusts and loves.

Patrick, however, handles upsets quite differently. When he is upset, he must have some space. He needs to pull away so he can think about what happened. In his mind he has a private cave where he withdraws to mull over what's bothering him. During this pulling-away stage he doesn't like to be touched.

When Patrick and Jennifer try to support one another without an awareness of or respect for how they are different, unnecessary problems are sure to result.

One day Jennifer becomes very upset. She needs to talk about what is bothering her. But, when Patrick realizes she is upset, he gives her some space by leaving the room. Remember, for him, that is the loving thing to do.

Because Jennifer would never even think to walk away when someone she loved was upset, she misinterprets his behavior and thinks perhaps Patrick doesn't care about her.

Since the relationship is new, Jennifer excuses his behavior by imagining that he didn't notice she was upset. She begins to cry, making sure to sob loudly enough for Patrick to hear. When he hears her crying, Patrick, again out of respect for her privacy, leaves the house.

Jennifer is now thoroughly confused. She wonders how this man, who appears to love her so much, could act in such an uncaring and inconsiderate way.

After some time Patrick returns. Jennifer decides to give him another chance and approaches him in an attempt to talk about her original upset feelings. But now she is even more upset, because she is afraid that Patrick's leaving the room and then leaving the house means he doesn't care about her anymore.

Patrick listens attentively for a few moments, and then decides that by his standards, she is too emotionally involved with the problem.

"You're getting upset over nothing," he says. "How could you think I don't love you?" With a laugh he adds, "This is ridiculous, you must be kidding."

Patrick truly thinks he is giving some helpful advice. Jennifer, of course, finds his attitude anything but loving. Instead, she feels abandoned, insulted, and hurt. "I can't believe you love me," she responds. "Why do you treat me this way?"

Patrick, who has reached out to help, is naturally confused and frustrated. He feels unappreciated and gets upset. In typical male fashion, he silently retreats to his secret cave of the mind to figure out what just happened.

Now both Patrick and Jennifer are upset, confused, and frustrated. Each has tried the best way he or she knows to solve a problem, but the situation has only gotten worse. Neither of them has any idea of what really happened; both think the other is a bit crazy.

Neither Patrick nor Jennifer is crazy. They are just different.

MEN SHUT DOWN EASILY

As Patrick walks away, Jennifer begins to feel guilty for offending him, even though she has no idea how she did it. She knocks on his door and in true female style says, "I understand you're feeling upset, Patrick. Let's talk. Tell me how you're feeling?"

He responds in typical male fashion. "I'm not feeling anything. I just want to be alone!"

Jennifer persists in her attempt to assist him in exploring his feelings, which women commonly do to help each other.

"I can tell you're angry with me," she says. "It's OK. Let's talk about it. I want to know what you are feeling." Jennifer is treating Patrick exactly as she would want to be treated.

Patrick, however, is offended and irritated by her concern. He needs space and she is crowding him. He barks, "Just leave me alone!"

Jennifer finally leaves him alone, terrified that she has lost his love.

In reality, Patrick is not nearly as upset as Jennifer imagines he is. He just needs a little time to cool off. Jennifer assumes something terrible has happened, because she would have to be extremely resentful to shut down as he has just done. She does not understand that shutting down happens to Patrick when he is just a little upset.

In fact, men tend to "shut down" completely in an instant and then open up just as quickly. Women do not understand this; once they open up to a person it takes them a long time to close down completely.

Because Patrick and Jennifer are unaware of their natural differences, they end up misinterpreting, fighting, and resenting each other. Even though they love each other very much, they do not understand how to support each other. Their real problem is that they do not understand their divergent needs.

HOW WOMEN LOSE SELF-WORTH

Henry and Alise love each other very much. However, after being married for six years, Alise is doubting her self-worth and resenting her husband, while Henry is no longer motivated to share in the relationship. He generally comes home, eats dinner while watching TV, and then goes to sleep. Occasionally they go out, but they don't talk much.

Alise, like many women, has a particular vulnerability when she falls in love. When Alise is being loved, cherished, and treated with respect, she feels really good; from these good feelings come feelings of self-worth. But if her partner begins to treat her in a less respectful way and she doesn't feel loved, her attitude changes — she begins to feel as if she doesn't deserve to be loved after all.

The logic of this vulnerability sounds like this: "If I am being loved and respected, then I feel worthy of love and respect. Conversely, if I am not being loved and respected, then I have done something wrong and I am unworthy of love and respect." In order to compensate, the logic goes on, "If I am not receiving what I need, then I must give more before I deserve to ask for what I need."

This is exactly how Alise started feeling in her relationship with Henry. After the first year of their marriage, Henry became overly focused on his problems at work and gradually began to ignore her. When Henry came home from work, he didn't mention any problems. That was his male way of communicating that everything was fine. Each day, however, he became increasingly more distant. Alise assumed that something she had done offended him deeply and was causing him to retreat and to withhold his love. She imagined that he was secretly resenting her, because for her to clear up an upset, talking is generally essential; if you don't talk a problem out, you can't give up the resentment.

Out of fear of making things worse, Alise tried to be extra loving and giving to Henry. Ironically, the less Henry fulfilled Alise's needs, the more compulsively she tried to please Henry and the more she would give.

Occasionally, Alise would explode and demand that he be more loving. Henry's reaction was generally to become quiet and withdraw.

This would scare Alise even more. From her point of view, she had tried everything to win back his love and was failing.

Since Alise could recognize that Henry was uncomfortable with her feelings and demands, she began to suppress them and tried to behave in a detached, reasonable, and nonemotional way. From time to time, however, she would lose control and overreact emotionally.

When Henry pulled away, Alise would feel guilty for her emotional reactions and try harder to suppress her feminine nature in compliance with what she believed to be his wishes. As her guilt and shame intensified, her compulsion to give more grew even stronger.

As this pattern repeated over the years, Alise gradually lost her sense of self as a woman. As a result, the couple got along, but she was unhappy. Henry occasionally wondered what had happened to the glow in her face and the sparkle in her eyes. Alise had lost her self-worth while Henry had lost touch with his loving feelings. Bored and unmotivated in his relationship, Henry had no idea what had happened.

HOW MEN LOSE MOTIVATION TO GIVE

Like most men, Henry over prioritizes his attention to such extremes that he appears to have tunnel vision. When there is a big problem at work he is apt to forget Alise's needs altogether and can only be motivated by the biggest or most urgent problems that are presented to him. After six months of marriage he started to feel that he had successfully solved the problems of the relationship — men tend to assume that once they please a woman, she will stay that way — and now he was drawn to and consumed by the problems of work. He gradually became unconscious of his partner's ongoing needs.

Unfortunately the problem does not stop here. Just as being feminine has its weaknesses, so does being masculine. Feminine vulnerability causes Alise to give more when she receives less. Masculine weakness causes Patrick to give less when he receives more.

The logic of this common male weakness sounds like this: "If she makes certain sacrifices for me, I must have already done something to deserve it, so I can relax and receive for a while. If I am receiving more, then I don't need to give more, I can give less."

This is one of the reasons why, after winning or earning the love of a woman, men may become lazy in the relationship. As long as she continues to give with a smile on her face, he assumes that he is giving enough. He doesn't feel motivated to give more.

After a while, Henry's and Alise's relationship begins to look very lopsided. When Henry gives less Alise gives more, because she wants more. Alise assumes that her sacrifices to please Henry will naturally motivate him to give more back to her. Unfortunately her sacrifices have the opposite effect.

Henry is not encouraged or motivated to give more when he experiences receiving more by giving less. The price Henry pays in this cycle is that he loses Alise's genuine appreciation and acceptance. The price Alise pays is that she sets herself up to receive less and resent more.

Each time Alise gives in order to win Henry's love and Henry does not return her gift, she accumulates a degree of resentment. No matter how hard she tries to be loving, she cannot escape feeling resentful when she is giving from emptiness instead of giving from fullness. With each passing day her ability to appreciate, accept, and trust her partner diminishes; she is unable to give him the love he needs.

To a great extent, even Alise is unaware of this buildup of resentment. From time to time it slips out. Ironically, it comes out when one would least expect it. Whenever Henry goes out of his way to do something special or nice, her accumulated resentment prevents Alise from feeling her natural appreciation for his loving gesture. Or when she is asking for his help, her resentment intrudes, turning her request into a demand.

WOMEN, THE GREAT SCOREKEEPERS

What Henry doesn't know is that women have an incredible capacity to give without getting back. They can give and give and appear happy— because inside, they are keeping score. Women are great scorekeepers. They can keep giving because they assume that one day the score will be evened out. They assume that at some point their partner will be so grateful that he will return all that support. She will then be able to relax and be taken care of for a while.

A man generally has little conception that the score in the relationship is uneven. This is because when he does something for his partner, he expects something in return before he gives more. A man won't let the score get uneven. When the score is 3 to 1 he will begin to grumble about giving more or simply refuse.

A woman has the capacity to let the score reach 20 to 1 before she will begin to grumble. When Alise finally begins to complain about how unfair things are, Henry resents her because he has been thinking that the score is even. He resents her for withdrawing her appreciation, because he mistakenly assumed that she must have really appreciated him; otherwise, why would she have continued to give? He feels offended by her accusations. Henry feels she owes him an apology, when in truth he has been giving less in the relationship.

To resolve this kind of dilemma, the man must take responsibility to give more through understanding his partner's needs. He must also forgive her for not appreciating him and for storing up her resentment. The woman must take responsibility for being a martyr and allowing the score to get so uneven. Together, they can start a new score card.

IF ONLY WE KNEW

These examples reveal very clearly how not understanding our differences creates problems in our relationships. With an awareness of their differences men and women can begin to construct new solutions to age-old conflicts.

Let's look back at our examples: Patrick could begin learning how to support Jennifer by listening to and exploring her feelings when she is upset. He would realize that treating her as though she were a man invalidates her and makes her even more upset.

If Jennifer understood their differences, she would be less threatened by his male reactions, knowing that he isn't trying to be mean or intending to withhold his love. Jennifer could come to understand and support Patrick's need to pull away when he is under stress, while Patrick could learn ways to reassure Jennifer when he is withdrawing. Jennifer could find ways to share her upsets with Patrick without sounding to him as though she is blaming him.

Henry and Alise could discover new ways to handle their problems. If Alise understood men, she would know that men are like firemen: if there is a fire they give their all to put it out; otherwise, they get extra sleep to prepare for the next fire. Knowing this, she would know that if she doesn't continue to communicate her needs, he will assume that everything is fine and give less to the relationship. She could then share her needs without resentment, in a way that Henry can understand.

If Henry understood how women are different, he would recognize that when women are not feeling centered, they give of themselves to the point of exhaustion. The next time Alise was overwhelmed he might not automatically blame her for taking on too much. Instead, he could be compassionate and fulfill her need to be centered by listening to her.

Alise could understand that men react to resentment by becoming passive and lazy. The next time Henry was overly passive, rather than trying to rehabilitate him, she could take responsibility for her own resentment, come back to a loving place, and share her feelings of appreciation for the things he does do for her.

Having released her resentment, she would then ask for support. A man is much more responsive to a request that is not backed by resentment, sacrifice, or suffering.

Henry would also understand that women tend to give more when they feel unloved. The next time Alise appeared especially interested in his day, he might get the message that Alise is unconsciously wishing for him to be more interested in her day. He could then respond by expressing his interest.

The next time Henry felt resentful because he wasn't being appreciated, he could remember that Alise really would be appreciating him if she weren't experiencing an accumulation of her own resentment. He would understand that she just needs to share her emotions in order to feel her love and appreciation again.

The next time she resented him, she could remember Henry would give more if he really understood her needs. She would take responsibility for communicating her needs in a way he can hear. She would realize that men don't change their ways of doing things as quickly as women, but when they do change, it is solid. On the other hand, women don't change their feelings as quickly as men. Henry must learn to be patient in listening to Alise as she shares her upset feelings.

A way, then, to rekindle your desire to understand instead of judge is to imagine that your partner or loved one is an alien from a far distant planet. Certainly if you met an adorable extraterrestrial, you wouldn't try to change him. You would probably feel an intense curiosity to understand his differences. In seeking to understand, you would be patient and tolerant. This desire to understand another with an attitude of acceptance is the basis of a positive and loving relationship. Giving your loved ones permission to be different opens a new dimension in which love can blossom.

In the next chapter we will explore four keys for creating cooperative and harmonious relationships.

CHAPTER TWO

BUILDING A RELATIONSHIP

There are four keys to creating mutually supportive and rewarding relationships:

1. *Purposeful communication* — Communicating with the intent to understand and be understood.

2. *Right understanding* — Understanding, appreciating, and respecting our differences.

3. *Giving up judgments* — Releasing negative judgments of ourselves and others.

4. *Accepting responsibility* — Taking equal responsibility for what you get from the relationship and practicing forgiveness.

These four keys can unlock the potential within you to create loving relationships and fulfill your hopes and dreams. They will help you to realize why your relationships have had problems in the past, and provide a foundation to build stable and life-enriching relationships in the future.

PURPOSEFUL COMMUNICATION

Communication is essential if we are to learn about and respect each other's differences. In my first book, *What You Feel, You Can Heal,* I explored in great depth the importance of telling the truth in our relationships, especially the truth about our feelings. Intimacy thrives on the communication of truth. But without an understanding of the underlying purpose of communication, even the best communication skills will inevitably fail.

What is this purpose and how can knowing it affect our communication? To answer this question, I will share with you how I experienced it one day. My wife and I were waiting in a restaurant during a lunch break at one of my relationship seminars. I told the waiter we were in a hurry. He quickly seated us, brought us the menu, and we ordered. So far my communication seemed to be working well.

While we were ordering, another group was seated at the table next to us. As my wife and I waited for our food, we watched the new group leisurely order their meal and, within ten minutes, receive it. Even though we had ordered first, our food was nowhere in sight.

My temperature started to rise. After another five minutes passed and we still hadn't gotten our food, I began to boil.

I hunted down our waiter and with calculated restraint said, "I want to remind you that we are in a hurry. The people next to us ordered after we did and they've received their food." And then I blurted, "Where's our food?"

The waiter said, "Your food is coming, sir."

His answer didn't help, so I repeated myself, "The people next to us have already gotten their meal — where's my food?"

The waiter replied again, "Your food is coming."

Needless to say, I was furious. All of my compassion and good nature was gone, along with all my communication skills. I went back to the table wanting to start a war. As we continued to wait for our lunch, we watched the people at the next table finish their food and pay their check.

At this point, it was too much to bear. On the way to find the manager, I saw our waiter and approached him again. After explaining I was on a tight schedule, I asked again, "Where's my food?"

In a panic he repeated, "Your food is coming, sir."

Then fortunately, I asked, "*Why* is my food taking so long? *Why* were those people served before me?" I was finally addressing the real cause of my upset.

This time, the waiter explained, "Sir, those people ordered from our sandwich menu, which goes to a different kitchen. You ordered from our entree menu, which goes to the main kitchen. Although you can't see it from here, we're swamped by a graduation party in the next room. The cook has promised me your order is coming. I'm truly sorry it's taking so long."

In a flash my tension and distress were gone. They were gone because I could *understand* the situation. With this understanding I could feel compassion for the waiter. I could relax and choose to wait for my meal without feeling tense, resentful, and uncomfortable. I actually began to take pleasure in the view from our table and, most of all, I began to enjoy spending the time with my wife. You see, my communication with the waiter had been useless until I used it to seek more *understanding*.

Had I not taken the direction of *communicating to understand*, I could have made matters worse by communicating to manipulate or control. I could have said "I can't believe this has happened; it is disgraceful. I want to talk to your manager" or "If my food is not here in three minutes, I am leaving this restaurant and I will never come back."

When we feel upset or threatened, communication often becomes twisted and manipulative. When we communicate to intimidate, threaten, disapprove, hurt, fault-find, or make someone feel guilty, we are misusing communication. We may succeed in controlling, but inevitably we will create resentment. True and effective communication has the intent to share our understanding and more thoroughly share another's understanding.

RIGHT UNDERSTANDING

Ultimately, it's not just communication that makes relationships work. Communication is but a vehicle through which we can understand each other. Right understanding enriches our relationships, while misunderstandings ruin them. Purposeful communication allows us to increase right understanding.

How many times have you argued with someone you loved, and then found out later it was just a misunderstanding? One of the common problems in relationships is that after we get to know someone, we have a strong tendency to believe that the meaning we give to their words and gestures is accurate. We think we know what they mean, yet we frequently misunderstand their intended meaning. We jump to the wrong conclusions.

Many times in counseling couples, I take on the role of interpreter. He says something and she hears it in a different way. She says something and he says she's wrong. In an instant they are arguing. It is as though they are speaking two different languages. By rephrasing his meaning into words and expressions that she can understand, and vice versa, the conflict is resolved.

I remember once asking a client what she needed from her husband. Martha took a deep breath and began to cry, saying, "I just need him to listen to me . . . to hear me. I feel he doesn't love me."

As her husband Joe listened to what she said, I watched him appear to go cold. Then he silently shrugged his shoulders. I saw Martha's frustration and disapproval increase as he silently exhaled.

Next, I asked her what her husband's response had meant to her. She said, "It means he doesn't care. He's telling me that I'm wrong, that I'm too needy, and that if I had something interesting to say he might listen."

Joe started to defend himself, saying she was wrong about his response. I stopped him and asked him what was actually going on inside when his wife was feeling and expressing her need to be heard.

He said, "I was feeling frustrated. I was thinking about the things I did this week to let her know how much I love her. I was beginning to feel inadequate and disappointed because I don't know what to do. Then when she told you how she felt about my reaction, I got angry and started to make her wrong."

Martha had misunderstood Joe's detached reaction. She assumed that he didn't care and was judging her. Ironically, her misunderstanding of his reaction provoked him into actually feeling uncaring and judgmental — even though in the previous moment he had begun to soften in response to hearing her original hurt feelings. Without the assistance of a therapist, they would have continued to argue.

The original positive, caring, and vulnerable feelings we all have when we fall in love can be quickly forgotten due to simple misunderstandings and faulty assumptions. Wrong assumptions may actually provoke the behavior that, in the beginning, is imagined.

Most of the emotional tension in relationships arises from misunderstandings. Good communication lessens the chances of misunderstanding and ensures more positive relationships. Learning some basic communication skills will help, but what really makes communication work is the *intent* to understand.

There are many levels of understanding necessary for communication to succeed in a relationship. They are:

- A deeper understanding of ourselves and others.

- An understanding of how men and women react differently to stress.

- A deeper understanding of the true feelings that underlie what we say and do.

- An understanding of the true feelings behind the actions and reactions of others.

- A greater understanding that appearances do not always reflect reality. (For example, when your partner shrugs her shoulders, it may mean something different from when you shrug yours.)

- An understanding that what may be easy for you to ask, may be difficult for others to ask.

- An understanding that what may be easy for you to hear, may be painful for others to hear.

- An understanding that what you think should be helpful to others may not be — even if it is helpful to you.

- An understanding that people speak different languages, which may only sound the same as ours.

Right understanding starts with realizing that we are all individual and unique and that it is very easy to misunderstand each other. By understanding and respecting our differences we can truly build bridges that will unite us.

FEAR OF BEING DIFFERENT

One of the reasons we fail to acknowledge our differences is that while we were growing up, being different meant being laughed at or rejected. To become popular or powerful we needed to become like those who were already popular or powerful. As kids, we spent a lot of time trying to be like other kids.

Even though we're adults now, and even if we were very fortunate in having parents who could truly support us in our uniqueness, we're still apt to think being different means risking rejection and failure. To various degrees, most people are insecure about appearing different. We are afraid that someone will come along and correct us or judge us as wrong, bad, or inadequate. Unfortunately, this is a valid fear. Insecure people are everywhere and quite automatically pounce on anyone who starts to step out and be themselves. For this reason, differences can be seen as a threat.

DIFFERENCES ARE MAGIC

Just like magnets, differences in people attract. As we grow in understanding, we can begin to appreciate these differences.

The true differences between men and women are actually complementary, giving each the opportunity to find balance. If I am overly aggressive, I may be attracted to someone who is more relaxed and receptive. Through relating with this more relaxed person, I am able to connect with the more relaxed qualities in my unconscious. These more relaxed and receptive qualities balance out, support, or complement my more developed aggressive qualities. These complementary differences are what draw us to each other and create the mysterious feeling we call love.

The magic of difference creates yet another dimension to loving relationships. As we accept and appreciate the differences between people, we begin to also see the similarities. Although each one of us is unique, we are also, in many ways, the same. This seeming paradox points to a wonderful truth about relationships: The right person to share your life with is generally a blend of complementary differences and similarities.

There are many ways to express this mysterious blend. Here are a few I have heard from people who are both in love and in relationship.

- "We are so different, but what keeps us together is that we are both so intense."

- "We are different in many ways: he is a night person, I am a morning person; he is a dreamer, I am practical; he doesn't worry about things and I worry about everything. Yet, on some other level, we are one. It is as though we are on the same wavelength."

- "Sometimes I love her and sometimes I hate her. When I am not loving her, it is because I am not capable of loving at that time; I am not feeling good about me. In my heart I know it is right for us to be together."

- "Many of our problems are completely different, but what we have in common is, we have a lot of problems! We've learned to help each other cope with our problems without making the other person feel bad or unworthy. I think if he were perfect and had no problems, I would feel as though I was bringing him down all the time."

- "For two years our marriage was perfect. Then we fell out of love; the romance was gone. I woke up one morning realizing that we were two very different people with little in common. It was depressing and disappointing. That is when I began to learn about genuine love. Through sharing our feelings and releasing our hidden resentments, we came to truly know and love each other. I began to love the real person rather than the person I wanted him to be."

In each of these examples, love was nurtured over time through acceptance and understanding. In this way, love fulfills its purpose to harmonize differences and create positive and lasting relationships.

GIVING UP JUDGMENTS

Releasing negative judgments, the third key to creating a supportive relationship, is the inevitable outcome of right understanding. As we become able to understand our differences and successfully communicate our feelings, thoughts, and desires, we can then begin to let go of our negative judgments.

Our negative appraisals of ourselves and the results of our actions inhibit us from fully expressing our talents. Ultimately, deprecatory judgments keep us from fully enjoying all we have and our lives in general. Judgment and criticism are symptoms of low self-esteem.

When we feel that we are not enough, we begin to feel that what we have or what belongs to us is not enough; i.e., we do not have enough time, money, love, etc. We begin to feel that friends or family are not enough. Negative judgments ruin our relationships.

Judgment will continue until we understand, appreciate, and honor the differences between people. When we are able to love, accept, appreciate, and respect others, quite automatically we begin to accept and appreciate ourselves. This is the true secret of releasing judgment. Through loving others we are able to love ourselves, and through loving ourselves we can love others. Our self-esteem and self-worth grow daily when we are creating loving relationships.

When we stand in negative judgment of others, it is a symptom of our own self-hatred. Most negative judgments are the projections onto others of the opinions we secretly have about ourselves.

FINDING OUR ONENESS

True relationship is born from an awareness and appreciation of how we are different. From the vantage point of understanding and respecting our differences, we can more clearly appreciate our similarities. Recognizing our similarities gives rise to positive attitudes like compassion, empathy, understanding, acceptance, tolerance, and oneness. Acknowledging our differences creates attraction, appreciation, interest, respect, purposefulness, and excitement.

As we succeed in understanding each other, through honest sharing and heartfelt listening, we begin to realize and release the negative judgments that separate us from each other. You see, it is not the differences that separate us, but our judgments around those differences — judgments born out of misunderstanding.

ACCEPTING RESPONSIBILITY

The fourth key to making relationships work is taking equal responsibility for what happens in the relationship and practicing forgiveness. Being responsible is the opposite of feeling as though you are a victim. Practicing forgiveness is next to impossible when you cannot see how you are equally responsible.

Have you ever felt "I gave and I gave and I got nothing back" or "I was having a great day until you ruined it." This is our victim side, a signal that we are not taking equal responsibility.

Victims think they are not responsible for what happens to them or for how they feel. Victims feel powerless to create change. Victims ignore their responsibility for provoking abuse in their relationships. The victim attitude not only ruins our relationships but also our lives.

Victims do not admit that had *they* handled things differently, they would have gotten better results. Victims are not willing to acknowledge how they contributed to their problem. Victims are not willing to see how they are misinterpreting a situation and making it worse. Moreover, they refuse to benefit in some positive way from a negative experience. They hold their past as an excuse for not being true to themselves.

A sign of a victim attitude is the feeling of resentment and blame; there is a denial of responsibility.

When we are resenting, in some way we are not willing to trust or accept the person we are resenting. We cannot trust, because we do not understand how we have provoked their behavior. We do not accept, because we mistakenly expect them to know what we need. Mind reading is sometimes easy from one woman to another, but it is almost impossible for a man to read a woman's mind, or vice versa.

When we are resenting someone, we do not take into consideration why they did what they did. We do not seek to validate why they may feel the way they feel. Simply put, we feel as though we are the victim and they, perforce, are the villain.

HOW WE UNKNOWINGLY PROVOKE

Without thoroughly understanding how we are different, it is easy to conclude that we will unknowingly step on each other's toes from time to time. Understanding that we are as different as Martians and Venusians opens us to seeing how we have offended others.

A close examination of what we do or do not do, in this context of respecting our differences, helps us to understand how our behavior affects others and why we get certain reactions. But taking responsibility for our behavior is not enough.

We are also responsible in less obvious ways. Just as our behavior provokes reaction, so do our thoughts and feelings. It is much more difficult to perceive how we affect others when our thoughts and feelings are doing the provoking, but they do have an effect.

When we openly or secretly judge another, they will tend to momentarily react in the way that we are judging them to be. If we judge them to be unloving, they may become momentarily unloving; if we judge them to be uncaring, they may react in an uncaring way, etc.

The more significant a person is to you, the more you are affected and provoked by their judgments. When you are dependent upon a person, your effect on their thoughts and feelings increases. Being sexually intimate with a person also heightens their impact on your behavior.

For example, when a woman judges a man as unloving and uncaring, he is apt to temporarily react that way. Even if she is pretending to appreciate what a caring person he is, if she secretly feels he is uncaring, the man will react to her in a more uncaring fashion. In that moment, his caring response is overshadowed by an uncaring reaction that is provoked by her negative judgments. The more bonded they are, the more he will be affected by her judgments and temporarily lose touch with his warm feelings.

When a man judges a woman as irrational and overly emotional, she will tend to become irrational and overly emotional. Even if the man pretends to be understanding while a woman is sharing her feelings, if he secretly thinks she is not making sense, then she will lose her balance, disconnect from her intuitive center, and become confused.

Being provoked, however, does not mean the provoker is responsible for our reactions. We are always accountable for our own actions and reactions. Blaming the provoker is just another way of being a victim, not a justifiable excuse.

Understanding how our thoughts and feelings can provoke a reaction does not mean we should condone or excuse the provoked behavior. It simply gives us a way to understand our partner's behavior; it creates an opening through which we can more fully relate to their reaction.

There is a still more powerful way that we provoke abuse. Just as *judgments* provoke *temporary* dysfunction, *resentments* provoke *continuous* dysfunction. A man who resents his wife's emotions may provoke her into being continuously hypersensitive. A woman who resents her husband's uncaring attitude may provoke him into being continuously indifferent.

It is not uncommon for a man to come home feeling affectionate toward his wife, and then, when he enters her presence, suddenly become uncaring. She may be acting in a perfectly acceptable manner, but her hidden and unresolved resentments provoke in him an uncaring response.

In a similar way, it is not uncommon for a woman to come home feeling affectionate toward her husband, and then in his presence become overwhelmed with negative feelings. Again, his behavior may be perfectly agreeable, but his unconscious resentments provoke in her a negative emotional response.

When we resent, we are holding on to our negative judgments. They stay firmly rooted until we experience some forgiveness. When we are unable to release our judgments, their power to provoke increases. No matter how good you think you are at disguising resentment, it is revealed in your actions, reactions, choice of words, body language, eyes, and tone of voice. It will seep out whether you are aware of it or not.

If you are free of resentment and you begin to negatively judge a person, it can easily be replaced minutes later with a positive judgment. But when you feel resentful, you are actually holding on to that judgment, either consciously or unconsciously.

Not only does resentment provoke negative reactions, but it also negates the effectiveness of communication. When you share your feelings and thoughts with an attitude of resentment, it is almost impossible for the person you are resenting to stay open to you. One of the reasons communication can be so easy at the beginning of a relationship is that there is no buildup of resentment.

Accumulated resentment undermines the growth of love in a relationship. The first step toward releasing resentment is to claim your responsibility; understand how you provoke the responses you get. Then, with a greater understanding of your partner and with better communication, forgiveness will become easier.

RESPONSIBILITY AND REPRESSED RESENTMENT

It becomes easier to take responsibility when we realize that by misjudging others as wrong, unloving, incorrect, or not good enough, we unknowingly provoke their dysfunction.

There is yet another serious obstacle to accepting responsibility in our relationships: repression. Both men and women easily repress their resentments. When a resentment is repressed, we become unconscious that it exists. Then it is very hard to accept responsibility for provoking dysfunction and abuse in our partners. The repression of resentments can make relationships very confusing.

When a person tries hard to be loving, understanding, and accepting without practicing good communication skills, they also become very good at repressing resentments. The harder some try to be loving, the more they repress their resentments. Then, when their partners react as if they are being provoked by judgments and resentments, it is very difficult to take responsibility. In this case, the good intention of trying to be accepting (and thus repressing negative resentments) makes things worse.

If a man hits his wife over the head with a club and she bleeds, it is easy for him to take responsibility for how he has affected her. She can blame him and he will easily take it, because he can see how he provoked her response.

But if his repressed resentments have hit her over the head and she is bleeding and blaming him, it is very hard for him to take responsibility. Her reaction to his unseen, unconscious abuse will seem unjustified and irrational.

GOOD INTENTIONS ARE NOT ENOUGH

You may wish to be loving — you may even try with all your might — but your love will never be pure unless you are free from resentment. When we are free of resentment, loving is effortless. When we have to try hard to love, this is generally a sign that we are repressing our resentments.

Think of a time when you felt deeply in love. Was it difficult to love? When I first met my wife, I certainly did not have to *try* to love or appreciate her. When my daughter was a baby and she fell off the bed, I didn't have to try to care about her; every cell in my body came alive to rescue and protect her.

Think of people you deeply respect, who have achieved many great things. Do you have to try to respect them?

If a positive attitude is not automatic and effortless, then it is fabricated. When we feel resentful, there is no way we can hide it from the listener. It will always put the listener on guard to protect herself from our blame.

With this knowledge about resentment, it is easier to be more responsible in our relationships. We become capable of taking responsibility when we recognize how our negative judgments, hidden or expressed, actually provoke much of the abuse or lack of support we get.

Linda, age 38, had been married for twelve years. After a few years of therapy, she realized how she was equally responsible for the problems in her marriage. For twelve years she had been feeling like a victim of her husband Bob's tendency to withdraw. She had resented that he was so cold, uncaring, and unloving. She now realized that her resentments had prevented him from hearing her feelings and needs. How could she expect him to be responsive when he was feeling her unspoken resentment?

Linda had believed that Bob would not feel her bitterness if she did not express it in her words or behavior. So from her point of view, Bob had no right to feel blamed by her, because she knew that she was not *openly expressing* her resentment. She did everything she could to cover it up, even to the point of making loving overtures toward Bob. When he didn't respond, her resentment grew.

Linda may have thought that her anger was hidden, but he could see it in the tightness of her jaw and hear it in the tone of her voice. As a result, his reaction, whenever she would ask for support, was to turn off and become uncaring.

Through therapy, Linda was able to see clearly how she was equally responsible for creating this problem. She realized that she had the power to change things and did. Once she stopped being the victim, her marriage improved dramatically.

This is not to say that her husband Bob was not also responsible. It takes two sticks to make a fire; it takes two people to create a conflict. However, Linda realized that her job was to be responsible by communicating her feelings and needs from a truly nonresentful attitude. She had a lot of work to do, discovering and releasing old resentments and learning genuinely to love him.

Through practicing a technique you will learn later, the love letter technique, Linda was able to explore her deepest feelings and release her resentments. As she learned to communicate in a responsible way, she was amazed to see how quickly her husband responded to her nonresentful feelings by giving her the support he had always wanted to give. They felt as if they were on a second honeymoon.

It is much easier to release our resentments when we thoroughly understand how we are responsible for what we get in our relationships. As long as we feel that we are doing everything right but are still not getting what we need, we will stay victims.

Knowledge is power. The knowledge of how we are different gives us the power to be more accepting, understanding, respectful, and appreciative. The knowledge of how our secret resentments provoke others frees us to be more responsible for what we get and better able to practice forgiveness. With greater understanding of our differences, we can release the judgments that compel us to change our partners rather than to appreciate and support them.

CHAPTER THREE

THE PRIMARY DIFFERENCES BETWEEN MEN AND WOMEN

The easiest place to start to understand the differences between men and women is with the physical. Most obvious, of course, is the difference in their reproductive systems. But ample research reveals other, equally significant physical differences. Look at these examples:

Men generally have thicker skin than women; thus, women tend to get wrinkles at an earlier age than men.

Women have shorter vocal cords than men, so men tend to have deeper voices than women.

Men have heavier blood and about 20 percent more red corpuscles than women. This means men get more oxygen and have more energy. Men also breathe more deeply than women, while women breathe more often.

By and large, men have larger bones than women. Women's bones are not only smaller, they're arranged differently. The feminine walk we men find so enticing is really a matter of bone structure. A woman's wider pelvis, designed for childbearing, forces her to put more movement into each step she takes — causing a bit of jiggle and sway as she walks.

Men have a higher ratio of muscle to fat, which makes it easier for them to lose weight than it is for women. Thanks to this extra muscle, men have quick start-up energy.

On the other hand, women have an extra layer of fat just underneath their skin, which keeps them warmer in winter and cooler in summer. This extra fat also gives women more energy reserves, so they have more endurance than men.

Although the physical differences are important, it's the psychological differences that give us new insight into the art of enriching relationships. These physiological differences set the stage for the deeper psychological differences.

GENERAL PSYCHOLOGICAL DIFFERENCES

Men and women are not only biologically and anatomically different, they are psychologically different as well. For example, it is universally observed that, compared to men, women are more intuitive, are more interested in love and relationships, and experience different reactions to stress. They also have different kinds of complaints and problems in relationships. To suggest, as many have, that these differences are entirely cultural and conditioned into us from childhood is absurd.

Certainly our cultural and parental conditioning affects how the sexes differ, but it is not responsible for our primary differences. From a pragmatic point of view these are determined physically by differences in our DNA programming. Then as children grow, they are further influenced by family and cultural conditioning.

In exploring our differences it would be absurd to assume that every male fits the description of a man and every female fits the description of a woman. Men are not all the same and women are not all the same in real life. Certainly, creating any stereotypical image of a man or woman ultimately would be misleading. A "real" man has a variety of qualities and characteristics that are both male and female. A "real" woman has a multitude of traits and attributes that are both male and female. There are, however, certain general differences that fit most men and most women. Men will generally relate to the masculine qualities, as most women will relate to the feminine qualities. These will be the focus of our exploration.

The problem with generalizing about the sexes is that people may begin to think something is wrong with them if they don't fit the description. But it is too cumbersome to continually qualify each generalization by stating that members of the opposite sex may equally relate if that particular side is more developed. To avoid this conflict, regard the generalizations about men to be descriptions of your masculine side and the generalizations about women to be your feminine side.

Initially, this categorizing necessary to our discussion may be confusing. Role reversal and gender confusion pervade our society. Women have denied aspects of who they are in order to develop aspects of their potential seen most commonly in men. In other words, they have rejected to various degrees their feminine side in favor of their potential to be more masculine. Likewise, men have rejected many of their masculine characteristics in favor of developing their potential to be more feminine.

Certainly, the development of our inner potential is a sign of growth. But to avoid creating new problems, we must learn to develop our potential without denying the primary qualities and characteristics of who we are as men and women (these primary male and female characteristics will be described in many contexts throughout this book).

Many women today are driven to be like men. They seek increased love, freedom, and respect at the expense of denying their own feminine values and qualities. Feminism has not only encouraged women to discover their potential to be like men, but has been mistakenly interpreted to mean that women *ought* to be like men. As a result, women have rejected, to a great extent, their essential feminine nature.

On the other hand, many men have responded by trying to be soft and sensitive in order to fulfill these women. This new sensitive man has been rejected by women as "wimpy" or "nice, but not desirable." In becoming more feminine, these men have denied much of their masculinity. They are frustrated because they recognize that the values of the old fashioned fifties have not worked, but have not found clear examples of what does work.

It is impossible to give a particular stereotyped image that works for every man or for every woman. In general, however, we can safely say that to nurture and value one's self while pursuing the development of one's potential is the answer to this continuing quest. Giving up one's primary qualities and characteristics in favor of another's is not.

The confusion we are experiencing today is due to the lack of acceptance of our differences. By accepting who we are and by embracing others' differences, we will learn to develop those complementary values and characteristics without compromising our true self.

For example, if a particular man tends to be rational in his assessments of the universe, he first needs to accept and appreciate that he is so rational. He will then be drawn to a more intuitive-type person, since intuition and rationality tend to be complementary. The masculine man tends to be more rational than intuitive. Through learning to love, understand, and respect the more feminine, intuitive person, he will naturally begin to develop his intuitive qualities without giving up his rational faculties.

On the other hand, another man may be predominantly intuitive. He needs first to accept and appreciate that in this respect he has more highly developed his feminine potential. Most likely, however, he has succeeded in developing his intuition through denying his rational, masculine side. To restore balance, he will be drawn to someone who tends to be more rational. Through learning to love, accept, and respect this person and her rational characteristics, he will naturally become more rational without giving up his developed intuitiveness.

As we explore common male and female differences through generalization, we should remember that these characteristics are based on what is "common" but not always the rule.

In some respects, the description of men and women needs to be a caricature of typical differences between the sexes. These differences tend to show up the most when we are under stress (varying reactions of men and women to stress will be covered in Chapters 6 and 7). When we are more at peace we tend to be more balanced in our expression of male and female values, qualities, and characteristics.

Even when a man appears primarily to have developed his feminine side, when he is under stress he will tend to react in a masculine way. He can safely assume that with some work, he can discover and develop the complementary masculine qualities within himself.

Likewise, a woman who primarily relates to the masculine qualities and characteristics described in this book can use the descriptions of feminine traits to validate and discover her rejected femininity. To whatever extent she has denied herself in order to develop her potential to be masculine, she can now work toward loving, accepting, and nurturing her female side.

COMPLEMENTARY DIFFERENCES

Take the example of a mirror to conceptualize how men and women can appear to be similar yet be so different. The psychological differences between men and women can be likened to the reflection in a mirror. When you look into the mirror, you see yourself. At least, you think it is you.

When you look a little closer you find that although the image looks like you, it is very different. Your mirror reflection is backward! Everything is turned around.

The feminine psychology is a mirror reflection of the masculine psychology. In many ways, men and women are like reflections of each other — different but complementary.

A fundamental way to understand this difference is in terms of two complementary forces that were defined by Newton. They are centripetal and centrifugal forces. Centripetal force moves toward a center. Centrifugal moves away from the center. These two apparently opposing forces are exemplified in male and female interactions.

In grade school you probably did a science experiment that involved filling a bucket with water and then swinging it around you in a circle by a rope connected to the handle. As you swung the bucket around you, quite mysteriously the water was held to the bottom of the bucket, even though the bucket was tilted on its side.

Centrifugal force tends to pull a thing outward when it is rotating swiftly around a center. It is an *expansive* force. If it were not for centrifugal force, the water would pour out of the rotating bucket. If you were to cut the rope, or let go, centrifugal force would cause the bucket to fly out, away from you.

On the other hand, centripetal force tends to pull a thing inward when it is rotating around its center. A restraining force, or a pulling back, it is the force that keeps the rope tight. In a sense, it holds things together through being *contractive.*

These forces are paralleled by male and female psychologies. Like the expansive (centrifugal) force, a woman's awareness moves out from her center. Her fundamental nature is to move out from her self and connect with others. When she falls in love, it is easy for her to forget herself completely. In relationships, it is easy for her to become overwhelmed by the needs of others.

Men, on the other hand, tend to contract in relationships. Once a woman accepts him, he begins to pull back into himself. He tends to focus on his own needs and not hers. Like the centripetal force, he tends to hold himself together and is less likely to lose himself. In relationships, it is easy for him to be self-centered and inconsiderate of others without even knowing it.

WOMEN EXPAND, MEN CONTRACT

One of the most common problems women have in relationships is that they forget their own needs and become absorbed in the needs of their partner. A woman's greatest challenge in a relationship is to maintain her sense of self while she is expanding to serve the needs of others. In a complementary way, a man's biggest difficulty is to overcome his tendency to be self-absorbed and self-centered.

While women tend to expand, men tend to pull back, or contract. Like the centripetal (contractive) force, men usually move toward a center or point. This explains why men are often frustrated in communicating with women. Women are apt to expand with a topic, while men want them to get to the point.

Generally, when a man speaks he has already silently mulled over his thoughts until he knows the main idea he wants to communicate. Then he speaks. A woman, however, does not necessarily speak to make a point; speaking assists her in discovering her point. By exploring her thoughts and feelings out loud, she discovers where she wants to go.

Just as men need to pull away to mull over an idea, women find greater clarity by expanding and sharing. When a woman begins sharing, she is not always aware of where it will take her, but she trusts that it will take her where she needs to go. For women, sharing is a potent process of self-discovery.

Many times men get frustrated with women simply because they don't understand this difference. They unknowingly interfere with this natural feminine process or they judge it as a waste of time. A man who understands this difference is able to nurture and support a woman through nonjudgmental listening.

CONTRASTING STYLES OF COMMUNICATION

For example, Harris came home and his wife Laura said, "Susie missed her soccer game for the second time. She was very disappointed. Your brother Tom called and said they were planning to come visit in June. I didn't know what to say. I don't know where we are going to be. We may want to visit my mother in June; right at the beginning of summer break. When is the summer break? I still can't find those pictures my mom asked for. Remember, the ones we took at Yellowstone Park? Did you read the article I left for you about not feeding the bears at Yellowstone? The parks just aren't what they used to be. I remember feeding the bears with my hands. I hope we can find those pictures. Sometimes I feel everything is completely disorganized in our life. I think we need to take some time to work out our summer schedule together."

By first sharing a variety of associated ideas, Laura was then able to feel more collected and discover the point she wanted to express, that they needed to work out their summer schedule.

Harris' approach is much different. Rather than share aloud his thoughts and feelings, he will mull them over inside and then express the bottom line.

For example, Harris receives an offer to do some work in June. He wonders if it merits rearranging his summer plans. He reflects on how much greater his income would be if he takes the job. He thinks about all the extra things he can do for his family with that money. He then reflects on various summer plans with the family if he didn't take the job. He considers doing the job and joining his family for the last part of the vacation. He realizes that's not a good idea. He wonders when the kids are getting out of school. He wonders if there is some way he can do this extra work without disappointing his family. He wishes he didn't have to give up part of his vacation time in order to earn the extra money, but he concludes that the extra gain is worth the effort and that somehow he will try to do both. He thinks, "I'll talk to Laura and see how she feels about it."

In this way, Harris ponders his problem inside his mind, then later expresses his conclusion or bottom line out loud. He comes home and says, "I'm thinking of doing some extra work in June. We should plan our summer schedule."

Because neither partner understands the other's approach, these contrasting styles of communication result in unnecessary tension. Let's explore Harris's reaction to Laura's expansive approach. Then we'll review Laura's inner responses to Harris's focused approach.

When Laura begins talking, Harris can sense from her tone of voice that something is bothering her. She needs something from him. When she begins by saying, "Susie missed her game and is disappointed," he thinks, "So this is what is bothering her. Why is she complaining to me about it? I wasn't supposed to take Susie to the game. She thinks it's my fault and I should be more attentive to the children. I feel so frustrated, I am already doing everything I can."

Then Laura talks about Tom's call. Harris's inner response is, "What does Tom's call have to do with whether I am a good father?"

Next Laura mentions not knowing whether they are going to be in town. Harris thinks to himself, "How do you expect me to know our summer schedule, when we haven't even talked about it. Are you saying I should call Tom and give him an answer right away? Look, we don't have to answer him yet."

When Laura asks about the date of the summer break, Harris broods, "How am I supposed to know when school ends. Do you think if I was a more concerned father that I would know? Why don't you call the school? I can't believe you are upset about this and you waited for me to come home instead of calling the school."

Then when Laura mentions the missing pictures, Harris responds inside thinking, "Why is she bringing up these pictures again. I told her before that I don't know where they are. How does this relate to Susie missing her soccer game? What is she trying to tell me? Sure I am forgetful, but I didn't tell Susie I would take her to the game. I wonder if she is comparing me to my brother Tom, thinking that he takes his family on vacations while I don't even take Susie to her soccer game. What a ridiculous comparison."

After Laura mentions the article about how the parks are not what they used to be, Harris wonders "What does this article about bears have to do with my being there for the kids. Is she implying that the kids are growing up fast and I am somehow missing out by not being a responsible parent? Why is she upset that she can't feed the bears with her hands anymore — what does she expect me to do about that? I am so confused. Why does she do this to me?"

Finally, when Laura mentions that her life is disorganized and requests a planning meeting, Harris reacts by thinking, "That's it! I can't believe she is blaming everything on me. She accuses me of being an incompetent father and husband. Now I don't even feel like going on a summer vacation with her. Why would she even want to go with me if this is the way she feels?"

In a burst of frustration, Harris exclaims, "I'm sick of your nagging. Why does everything have to be so complicated with you? Let's try being spontaneous for a change."

Harris' increasing defensiveness stemmed from his original misunderstanding of Laura's expansive approach. Unfortunately, Harris had no idea how Laura actually felt. Laura had been sharing a series of ideas that inevitably led her to what she wanted to say, i.e., the bottom line. Harris, however, wrongly assumed that Laura's bottom line was in her first statement. Having associated her upset tone with her remark about Susie missing the game, he thought everything that followed was an elaboration on that original point. Harris has completely misread Laura's feminine communication style.

Now let's explore Laura's inner responses to Harris's male approach of expressing the bottom line first, i.e., getting right to the point. When Harris comes home after being offered an extra job he says, "I'm thinking of doing some extra work in June. We should plan our summer schedule."

Instantly Laura's feelings are hurt and her pride is offended. She exclaims, "You are so inconsiderate. How can you make such decisions without first talking to me. Don't you care about your family? All you care about is your work. You would probably be happier if you didn't have a family. Don't you know the kids get out of school in June? Even if you are going to be so rigid about it, the least you could do is ask me how I feel. At least take me into consideration." Needless to say, they are now in the middle of a big argument.

Laura wrongly infers that Harris has made a final decision and is not open to hearing her thoughts and feelings. She feels excluded, unimportant, and taken for granted. She doesn't realize that he has thought a lot about her and his family. In truth Harris is open to discussion, but unfortunately he assumes Laura would know that.

WHY MEN APPEAR SELF-CENTERED

Another example of psychological contraction in men is a source of great confusion for women. It is hard for a woman to understand how a man can love her so attentively, and then suddenly shift and appear self-centered. Because this kind of shift is foreign to her, she takes it personally.

She does not realize how automatic it is for a man to become completely oblivious of everyone except his focus. When he is focused on pleasing her, he is very attentive to her. But when he thinks she is pleased, he finds a new focus, like a problem at work, and then directs all his attentiveness to that.

When under stress, men commonly increase their focus and become even more unmindful of others. This creates the appearance that they are self-absorbed or uncaring. At such times, they are not necessarily narcissistic or selfish, but may appear that way. They become absorbed in achieving their goal and forget everything else. To recognize that they really are caring, one can note that many times the goals they are absorbed in achieving are ultimately very altruistic or supportive of others.

It is hard for a woman to relate to this, because under stress a woman tends to expand her awareness and become even more conscious of others, especially the ones she loves. When a man is distressed at work he *appears* to forget that his family exists and focuses on solving the problem at work. Ultimately, though, he does care about supporting his family, and that is why he is so concerned about solving the problem at work.

A woman, distressed at work, compounds her upset, because she knows she is neglecting her family and may feel their needs even more strongly. Under stress her partner becomes more focused while she becomes more expanded.

As we have seen, automatic focusing is an example of the masculine, centripetal force. It restricts or contracts awareness in order to increase focus. A woman falsely assumes that if a man loves her, he will expand, which is her normal reaction. She needs to understand that the way a man reacts has to do with his inherent balance of masculine and feminine forces, and is not a measure of his love. A woman who understands this will not feel so resentful when a man ignores her, but will apply skills to get his attention when she needs it.

THE NEED FOR BALANCE

Every man and every woman has both male and female energies. We could not exist without a combination. The internal imbalance of these complementary forces determines many of the problems we experience in a relationship.

When a man has developed more masculine (contractive) tendencies than feminine (expansive) tendencies, at times he will appear self-centered and selfish when, in truth, he is just not focused on the needs of others. He will appear to be uncaring, but his real problem is his inability to access his feminine potential, through which he can easily be aware of the needs of others.

Similarly, a woman who has an excess of feminine energy will be overly concerned with others and have little awareness of her self. When experiencing the stress of not getting what she needs, she expands even more. She becomes more responsive to the needs of others but forgets herself. She sacrifices herself, without even knowing that she's doing it. At a time when she needs more, she is unable to assert herself or share her wishes, because she is unaware of them.

Just as a man under stress appears ungiving or uncaring because he contracts, a woman appears unreceptive or unsupportable because she expands. To avoid these extreme states, men need to explore, develop, and balance both their masculine and feminine sides, and women must do likewise. Through blending these complementary energies, not only do our relationships improve, but we become more creative.

To find greater balance within ourselves, we are naturally attracted to those qualities and characteristics that complement or balance what we have already developed. Male qualities are naturally attractive to the female, and vice versa. This is one of the secrets to understanding the "chemistry" of attraction between men and women.

Through learning to successfully love, appreciate, accept, and understand these differences, quite automatically we become whole within ourselves. Through loving the feminine, a man becomes more feminine while maintaining his masculine qualities. Through loving the masculine, a woman becomes more masculine without sacrificing her feminine qualities. By loving and respecting our differences we ourselves gain balance

THE MYSTERY OF ATTRACTION

If we look to how we are conceived, we can understand the creative process. The male is attracted to the female; the female ovum sitting stationary attracts the moving male sperm. When the two connect, the creation of new life begins.

Every creative action is the product of complementary forces. Because living is a constant process of creation, we are constantly attracting and being attracted to the complementary forces necessary for the creative process.

Chemistry happens when a person feels a complementary force or quality in another. The two people are naturally drawn to each other, just like the opposite poles of two magnets. In this magnetic field of love, all it takes to generate the electricity of desire, excitement, and attraction is interaction.

KEEPING THE PASSION ALIVE

When partners are able to keep their differences alive through loving and respecting each other, they can sustain the passion in their relationship. When men and women become too similar they lose the attraction or chemistry. It is boring to be with someone just like yourself. To maintain passion in a relationship we must work to preserve our differences while gradually incorporating the qualities of our partner.

Passion in the beginning of a relationship generally tells us that what we are attracted to in our partner is also within ourselves. If we are attracted to their warmth, then that very warmth is seeking to emerge from our potential or unconscious self, to be integrated into our conscious being.

Tom, who is very cool and detached, is attracted to Jane, who is warm and feeling. Unconsciously he is attracted to her because she reflects qualities of his undeveloped female side. Through loving her he discovers his own inner warmth and feelings, to balance his coolness and detachment.

By connecting with her he feels whole and experiences an immediate surge of fulfillment. In loving a partner who is different but who mirrors a part of his emerging self, Tom experiences the elixir of fulfillment that only a passionate relationship can stimulate.

For example, a certain kind of man is attracted to women who are warm, receptive, vulnerable, feeling, loving, and yielding. The type of man attracted to this more feminine woman tends to be in some ways cool, aggressive, assertive, reasonable, successful, and decisive. These are aspects of his male side seeking balance through union with her female qualities of warmth, receptivity, etc.

Through loving and accepting a woman's feminine qualities, a man automatically becomes more loving and accepting of his own feminine side. Through touching her softness he awakens to his own softness, and yet remains solid. His coolness is balanced by her warmth, his aggression is balanced by her receptivity, his assertiveness is balanced by her vulnerability, his power is balanced by her love, etc. By this process he is becoming whole. Through loving her, he discovers within himself his own feminine qualities. And as she loves him, her masculine qualities begin to be felt.

This paradox is integral to any loving and passionate relationship. By virtue of being different from our partners we are attracted to them. But through our inner potential to be like them, we are able to relate and have the possibility of intimacy, communication, and closeness. Without some differences there can be no relating; without some similarities there can be no joining.

HOW WE LOSE THE ATTRACTION

When partners do not respect and appreciate their complementary differences they lose their electricity, i.e., they are no longer turned on by each other. Without the polarity, they lose the attraction.

This loss of attraction can happen in two ways. We either suppress our true inner self in an attempt to please our partner, or we try to mold them into our own image. Either strategy — to repress ourselves or to change our partners — will sabotage the relationship.

When we succeed in changing our partner we may get some short-term need fulfilled, but ultimately there will be no passion. For example, Tom says to Jane, "Don't be so emotional, you're getting upset over nothing." If she represses her feeling side to please and accommodate Tom, he feels less friction with her and she wins his love. The short-term result appears to be a good and harmonious relationship, but now Jane and Tom will be a few degrees less interested, excited, or attracted to each other.

As this process of gradually suppressing their true selves continues, more and more degrees of passion and interest will be lost until they feel almost nothing for each other. They will be friends but experience no passion. The good news is that this process can be reversed; we can learn to find ourselves again without always having to change partners.

To whatever extent a partner must suppress his or her way of being, feeling, thinking, and doing to receive love or be safe in a relationship, the passion will fade. As we conform or reform, not only do we lessen the passion, but we also diminish the love.

Every time you suppress, repress, or deny yourself in order to be loved, you are not loving yourself. You are giving yourself the message that you are not good enough the way you are. And every time you try to alter, fix, or improve your partner, you are sending him the message that he does not deserve to be loved for who he is. Under these conditions love dies. By trying to preserve the magic of love through conforming or reforming, we only make matters worse.

When, in the name of love, you seek to repress yourself or change your partner, that is actually a kind of dysfunctional love.

WHY WE CONFORM AND REFORM

When men and women are attracted to each other a tension is produced. The two, each independent, seek to fuse together. By getting closer through relating, being together, doing things together, communicating, sharing, touching, and sex, tension is released and bliss, happiness, peace, inspiration, freedom, confidence, or fulfillment is immediately experienced.

These wonderful feelings are the result of awakening to our inner qualities, which in turn makes us feel whole. Unfortunately, however, this bliss is not lasting. It is but a glimpse of how we will feel when we are truly whole and balanced. But to actually become whole, these potential qualities must begin to emerge into our conscious being. To whatever extent we resist these emerging qualities, we will lose the pleasure and may even experience its opposite.

For example, when Tom loves Jane he becomes more considerate, compassionate, caring, and feeling. At first, this makes him feel happy and confident. But to whatever degree his past conditioning tells him,

"It is not OK for men to be feeling or considerate," his unconscious mind will automatically resist the emerging qualities of his feminine side.

Inner alarm bells go off, announcing, "Danger, danger, you are becoming a wimp. Watch out, do not proceed in this way. Pull back. ..." This inner resistance gives rise to a host of negative symptoms. He may suddenly feel resistant to his partner, dissatisfied, unhappy, distressed, oppressed, smothered, anxious, depressed, or empty.

What was so wonderful now becomes painful. To escape from these natural growth pains, Tom will seek to "avoid relationship." This is most easily accomplished by reforming or conforming — he may try to change his partner or give up being himself. In both cases he will find temporary relief, but in the long run the relationship will become less loving and passionate.

When a man is attracted to a woman, at some point he will resist his partner and may then seek to change her or deny himself in order to find relief. There are, of course, other means to obtain relief, like moving from one partner to another, having secret affairs, or developing any addiction that can numb the growing pains of resistance. In any case, to whatever degree he is resisting the emergence of the very qualities he was attracted to, he will seek to avoid true relating.

Reforming, one measure commonly taken to escape the distress of inner resistance, is an increasing demand for her to be like himself. He will expect her to want what he wants, feel the way he feels, and react the way he reacts. Out of his need to control or change her, he is unknowingly hurting her as well as reducing the original polarity and attraction.

She, on the other hand, may also contribute equally to this process. It is not all his fault; as the saying goes, it takes two to tango. As her own resistance to relating emerges, she may seek to ease her discomfort by denying herself.

Women who are attracted to controlling and reforming men tend to be equally good at conforming, complying, and denying themselves. They become overly dependent on their partners for a sense of identity. Of their own accord they offer up their sense of self to their partners, to earn love and create harmony.

For example, if Tom feels Jane is selfish or inadequate, she releases her own self-image and agrees with him. If he wants her to like the movies he likes, then she rejects her own preferences. If he thinks she is being unrealistic or demanding, she agrees and loses touch with her own values and needs. As he tries to change her, she yields to his control in order to be loved and feel lovable.

The opposite may also occur. A man whose female side is well developed may surrender overmuch to his partner's wishes. This type of man is generally considered the "sensitive type." The problem they often complain about is that women "like" them but are not attracted to them. They make great friends but women don't want them for an intimate relationship.

The woman who is initially attracted to this type has developed more of her masculine side. She is predominantly independent and aggressive. Unconsciously, she begins to control and dominate him and gradually, as he complies, she may lose interest.

When the independent type of woman begins a relationship with a sensitive man, after some time her suppressed female side begins to emerge. To whatever extent she has rejected her female side she will tend to reject her partner. She may begin to feel, "I need a real man," when in fact she needs to accept and develop her own feminine side. She is not really rejecting him, but her own female side, which he has already developed.

In a similar way, when a sensitive man rejects an aggressive woman, he needs to accept and develop his own male side. In rejecting her he may say that he wants a soft and vulnerable woman. In truth he doesn't need a woman to make him feel like a man; he needs to work on developing his emerging masculinity, which she is already helping him to find.

WHY WE RESIST OUR DIFFERENCES

This understanding of resistance helps us to understand why men and women typically seem so eager, loving, and giving in the beginning of a relationship, and then later pull back. Partners commonly put forth their best selves in the early stages of a relationship. As their resistance to each other increases, they tend to conform and reform. Knowledge about the underlying causes of this resistance unveils many of the mysteries of relationships.

The four basic categories and causes of resistance are:

1. *Macho man* (masculine resisting feminine)

2. *Martyr woman* (feminine resisting masculine)

3. *Sensitive man* (developed feminine, repressed masculine)

4. *Independent woman* (developed masculine, repressed feminine)

In the following sections we will look at examples of each of these types and some of their possible causes. Some people fit only one of these categories, while others may shift from one to another. Men commonly swing back and forth between being macho and sensitive, while women swing between martyrdom and independence.

MACHO MAN

Generally, a macho man is drawn to a woman because she reflects parts of his undeveloped feminine side. Through relating to her, he feels more whole and complete and thus turned on, excited, curious, or interested. This is the good part of getting closer to a person. But then the problems of getting close also emerge.

Through uniting with her, it is inevitable that he will begin to resist her differences. His loving union with her facilitates the emergence of his own feminine side. To whatever extent his past conditioning has rejected his own feminine qualities, as they begin to emerge he will begin to reject her.

For example, as a man loves his female partner, he may become more vulnerable, feeling, and in need of love and reassurance. These are qualities of his feminine side. If he has been conditioned to believe that feelings are a sign of weakness, he will resist this natural growth process.

This conditioning may have begun when he observed the way his father reacted to his mother's feminine side. If his father was judgmental or disrespectful of her feelings and vulnerability, then, unconsciously, the little boy may have resisted being vulnerable or expressive of feelings as he grew up. It could also be that his father didn't show his feelings, and so the little boy got a clear message again and again that men don't cry or show feelings.

These kinds of messages are unconsciously received thousands and thousands of times. Then as an adult, when macho man falls in love and his soft feelings begin to emerge, that early conditioning restricts the integration process. At such a time, he doesn't know what is happening. This inner resistance to his emerging feminine side is happening unconsciously. He experiences becoming uneasy, overly defensive, controlling, judgmental, frustrated, righteous, demeaning, condescending, impatient, or he simply shuts down — and doesn't know why.

Resisting his emerging feminine qualities, he rejects his female partner or tries to change her by "fixing" her or by invalidating her feelings and needs. Quite unconscious of the real cause of his discomfort, he imagines it to be his partner. To whatever extent he judges his own femininity, he will project those judgments onto his partner.

Without some kind of training manual like this book, it could take a macho man a very long time to understand his feminine side. To overcome his inner resistance, the macho man needs to practice respecting feminine qualities, values, and needs. Learning to listen to women with respect, caring, and understanding, and then patiently learning to accept his own feelings will help him to overcome the occasional resistance produced by early childhood conditioning. Compassion and empathy for women and children will emerge as he takes the time to understand what women really feel. He may even need to do some healing with his mother. Remember, before judging a woman he should try walking a mile in her high-heel shoes.

MARTYR WOMAN

Much the same resistance process occurs for women. For example, when a martyr-type woman loves her male partner, she may naturally become more assertive, strong, detached, and autonomous. These are qualities of her masculine side. Through loving, trusting, and accepting his aggression and assertiveness, she naturally begins to connect with those qualities within herself.

If she has been conditioned to believe that women who show strength will be rejected, she will unconsciously resist this natural integration process. She may have been programmed from early childhood on that women should not be assertive, women should stay at home, women are subordinate to men, women must never show a man that she is intelligent, women should be submissive, etc.

This kind of conditioning is most dramatic when a little girl watches her mother repressing her masculine qualities. When she sees her mother being a martyr, that is the feminine role she learns. When Dad treats Mom and her sisters one way, but he treats her brothers another way, she learns by example that her place is in the home, that she is subordinate and should wait on Dad, that she is to always comply with his wishes, that Mom's will is always subordinate to Dad's, that women should not be successful, etc. In thousands of ways she may get the message that it is not safe for a woman to act masculine.

In adulthood when she loves a man, her masculine side will begin to emerge. Because of her negative conditioning, she will not feel safe opening up to her male qualities and may become increasingly protective, critical, opinionated, mistrusting, manipulative, or resentful of the man she loves the most. All of the negative judgments toward her own masculinity get projected onto her partner. Although she is unconsciously resisting herself, consciously she compulsively begins to resist, resent, and reject her partner.

To overcome her inner resistance, the martyr woman needs to practice being autonomous and assertive. She needs, above all, to practice asking for support, and to give up expecting men to anticipate her needs just as she does for them. As her tendency in relationships is to keep score, she needs to take responsibility for her role in letting the score get too uneven. When it does get uneven she needs to practice forgiveness to release her resentments. She needs to honor and heal the repressed feelings of anger and resentment stored up from her past. She generally needs to do some healing with her father.

SENSITIVE MAN

As this sensitive-type man gets closer to a woman, his repressed masculine qualities begin to emerge into consciousness. At some point — if his conditioning says that aggression is destructive and not creative, or assertiveness is selfish and not positive, or that being reasonable is not loving — he will instinctively try to repress his emerging male qualities.

This kind of negative conditioning may occur in childhood. For example, by experiencing his father being abusive with his aggressive energy rather than being creative or productive, a young child may reject masculinity as hurtful and bond more closely with his mother. He may experience his father's assertive energy expressed in a selfish, controlling way and thus seek to repress his own assertiveness. He may observe his father justifying abuse and thus experience the power of the intellect as negative.

As a child, this sensitive man was powerfully affected by the examples set by his parents. He may also reject his masculinity when he perceives his mother being hurt by men. The mistrust she feels toward his father the boy begins to feel toward his own masculine side.

When a man has repressed his masculinity, he is generally attracted to women who have already developed those qualities. Again the union of opposites creates passion, but as his male energies begin to emerge a shift takes place. Due to negative conditioning surrounding masculinity, aggression, assertiveness, power, etc., he will begin to experience an inner resistance. This resistance gets projected onto his partner. He unconsciously becomes defensive, critical, mistrusting, manipulative, resentful, and disapproving.

To overcome his inner resistance, the sensitive man needs to practice giving up blame in his relationships and being completely responsible and accountable for what happens to him. He needs to practice being decisive, rational, and logical. He should rely less on his feelings and more on his mind to make decisions. He should practice doing little things to support his partner that require some extra effort. Most of all, he needs to practice following through and keeping his word.

To strengthen his masculinity, the sensitive man can do more things with men, hang out with men, see action movies, or participate in some competitive sport. Healing his relationship with his father is very important, as well as having male teachers, guides, or mentors.

INDEPENDENT WOMAN

When a woman who has repressed her feminine qualities becomes involved with a man who has developed more of his feminine qualities, inevitably her feminine traits will begin to emerge. Her conditioning brings up misleading ideas: that being soft and vulnerable is weak, or "feeling" people go crazy, or it is not safe to need others, or that people who need others are victims. As her feminine feelings, needs, and vulnerabilities emerge she panics inside and begins to resist her partner.

The overly independent woman doesn't feel it is safe to reveal her female side. She is afraid of being judged or hurt in some way. She may long for a more masculine man to "make her feel like a woman," when she really needs to heal the emerging woman in her. Out of resistance she may become judgmental, critical, controlling, demanding, and disappointed with her partner.

This conditioning to suppress her feminine side may have come from observing her mother being victim like or unfulfilled. The very same feminine vulnerability and softness that can make a woman so nonthreatening, attractive, and receptive, may have been distorted by her dysfunctional mother and expressed in a powerless, helpless, and unfulfilled way. To protect herself from turning out like her mother, she represses her feminine side. If, moreover, her father was rejecting, condescending, or invalidating of her mother's feelings, she probably concluded that feelings are irrational and unworthy of respect.

To overcome her resistance, the independent woman needs to practice being vulnerable and work on expressing her feelings and emotions in situations where she feels supported. She also needs to heal her relationship with her mother — in a sense she needs to accept the part of her that is like her mother, and acknowledge that it is lovable and worthy of support.

Trust is a major issue to overcome in her life. Trust means letting oneself be vulnerable, which involves being hurt from time to time. This woman must learn to feel her negative emotions and heal them as they gradually come up to be healed. Through persistent sharing of her feminine feelings she will overcome her shame and embarrassment around being feminine, and learn to respect her feminine qualities as she already values her masculine side.

She needs to recognize that even when she feels independent and strong, deep inside she fears that others will not love her. Secretly she may feel unworthy or not good enough. By opening up gradually, she will gracefully learn to balance her developed masculine side with her developing feminine side.

In a variety of ways, children are programmed to favor and reject different aspects of their masculinity and femininity. Deepening our understanding of our male and female sides frees us from the prison of negative childhood conditioning. Through learning to understand, accept, respect, and appreciate our gender differences, not only do we become more successful in loving and supporting our partners of the opposite sex, but also we learn to love ourselves. This kind of self-love liberates us to be all that we are.

MAINTAINING THE ATTRACTION

A relationship that sustains the magic of love is one in which we do not try to change the other nor deny ourselves. Through understanding our complementary differences we release the tendency to mold our partners into our own image. We are also able to accept and appreciate our own uniqueness without judgment, shame, or guilt.

A relationship blossoms, and attraction is sustained when we can both support our partners in being themselves and receive support for being ourselves. Just as we must learn how to give support according to our partners' unique needs, we must also learn how to receive support without giving up who we are. Learning to appreciate and respect our differences is essential if we are to have mutually supportive relationships. It is this growing love and respect of our differences that supports us through the inevitable periods of resistance, resentment, and rejection.

CHAPTER FOUR

HOW MEN AND WOMEN
SEE THE WORLD DIFFERENTLY

Men and women see the world as if each sex was wearing different glasses. In a generalized way, men see the world from a "focused perspective" while women see the world from a more "expanded perspective." Both perceptions are equally accurate.

Masculine awareness tends to relate one thing to another in a sequential way, gradually building a complete picture. It is a perspective that relates one part to another part, in terms of producing a whole.

Feminine awareness is expanded; it intuitively takes in the whole picture and gradually discovers the parts within, and it explores how the parts are all related to the whole. It places more emphasis on context rather than content.

This difference in orientation greatly affects values, priorities, instincts, and interests. Because "feminine open awareness" perceives how we are interrelated, women naturally take a greater interest in love, relationships, communication, sharing, cooperation, intuition, and harmony. Likewise, because "masculine focused awareness" perceives how parts make up a whole, men have a greater interest in producing results, achieving goals, power, competition, work, logic, and efficiency.

FOCUSED AND OPEN AWARENESS

Focused awareness can be conceived of in terms of a spiral moving toward a center or point. You could imagine an archer with his arrow pointed at the center of a target. Open or expanded awareness can be visualized as a spiral moving out from a point. To grasp open awareness, picture a satellite dish receiving from all directions and reflecting in all directions. Open awareness is like a floodlight, while focused awareness is like a laser. Each has its own unique value. Let's look at some everyday examples of how men are focused and women are open.

BOY SCOUTS AND GIRL SCOUTS

As her awareness expands out into the future, a woman is naturally concerned for what potentially could happen. She is motivated to prepare for the future. On the other hand, focused awareness makes men more concerned with efficiently achieving their goals. While the men are worried about getting to their destinations, the women are more concerned about what will happen when they get there.

This can be noticed quite clearly through observing Boy Scouts and Girl Scouts. While the Boy Scouts are busy figuring out how to get from point A to point B, the Girl Scouts are already preparing what they are going to eat when they get to point B.

When the Boy Scouts get to point B, one turns to the other and inquires, "Who brought the food?"

In response he hears, "I don't know . . . I forgot . . . I thought you were going to."

They were unprepared — oblivious of what they were going to do once they got there — because they were so focused on getting to the goal. Because they are born without an abundance of expanded awareness, Boy Scouts repeat daily as their motto, "Be Prepared!" It is even sewn into their uniforms. To mature properly little boys are trained to be prepared.

Little girls, on the other hand, need not be trained in this attitude; their open and expanded awareness makes them already preoccupied with being prepared. Like radar, their expanded awareness alerts them to all the possible things that could go wrong.

In preparing to such an extent, however, the Girl Scouts tend to be late in arriving, or they may feel the journey is too risky and let their fears hold them back. It is much easier to be courageous when you are unaware of the possible consequences of an action.

WALLETS AND PURSES

Contrasts in how men and women confront the world are most visually apparent when we compare a woman's purse with a man's wallet. Women carry large, heavy bags with beautiful decorations and shiny colors, while men carry lightweight, plain black or brown wallets that are designed to carry only the bare essentials: a driver's license, major credit cards, and paper money. One can never be too sure what one will find when looking into a woman's purse. Even she may not know. But one thing is for sure, she will be carrying everything she could possibly need, along with whatever others may need too.

When looking in a woman's purse the first thing you find is a collection of other, littler purses and containers. It's as though she carries her own private drugstore and office combined. You may find a wallet, a coin purse, a makeup kit, a mirror, an organizer and calendar, a checkbook, a small calculator, another smaller makeup kit with a little mirror, a hair brush and comb, an address book, an older address book for really old friends, an eyeglass container, sunglasses in another container, a package of tissue, several partially used tissues, tampons, a condom package or diaphragm, a set of keys, an extra set of keys, her husband's keys, a toothbrush, toothpaste, breath spray, plain floss, flavored floss (her children like mint), a little container of aspirin, another container of vitamins and pills, two or three nail files, four or five pens and pencils, several little pads of paper, a roll of film in its container and an empty film container, a package of business cards from friends and experts in all fields, a miniature picture album of her loved ones, lip balm, tea bags, another package of pain-relief pills, an envelope filled with receipts, various letters and cards from loved ones, stamps, a small package of bills to be paid, and a host of other miscellaneous items like paper clips, rubber bands, safety pins, barrettes, bobby pins, fingernail clippers, stationery and matching envelopes, gum, trail mix, assorted discount coupons, breath mints, and bits of garbage to be thrown away (next spring). In short, she has everything she could need and carries it with her wherever she goes.

To a woman, her purse is her security blanket, a trusted friend, an important part of her self. You can tell how expanded a woman's awareness is by the size of her purse. She is prepared for every emergency, wherever she may find herself.

Ironically, when she is being escorted to a grand ball she will leave this purse at home and bring a little shiny purse with the bare essentials. In this case, she feels that this night is for her. She is being taken care of by her man and she doesn't have to feel responsible for anybody. She feels so special and so supported that she doesn't need the security of her purse.

ENTERING A ROOM

Men and women will tend to enter a room differently. A man will walk into the room, pick a spot, move to it, then look out to one thing, then another, and yet another, until he gradually builds a picture of his environment (this may happen in just a few moments). His innate tendency will be to first focus, and then expand and open.

A woman, in contrast, will walk into the same room and in a quick glance, notice lots of things almost simultaneously. In a sense, she will take in the entire room before she is concerned about where her spot will be. She will notice the color of the walls, interesting people or pictures, friends or family members, how the room is set up, etc. Then, when she has a picture of the whole environment, she will find a spot in which to settle.

A more dramatic example is the behavior of men and women at an exposition or convention. You can observe the masculine focus as he very pointedly and purposefully moves from one display booth to another. A woman, on the other hand, seems to spontaneously flow through the convention as if taking everything in. For her, it is a process of exploration and discovery, while for the man it is a process of achievement and accomplishment.

He is focused on experiencing what he considers the most important or relevant booths; she is having a good time, eager to take everything in and, for that matter, eager to take things home with her. It is the feminine nature to shop and collect.

Shopping without a particular focus or deadline is very relaxing for women, but tends to be very draining for men. Conversely, men are energized if they maintain a sense of focus and purpose as they shop. With this perspective, let's observe how men and women behave differently in shopping malls and grocery stores.

SHOPPING

When a man is focused he is energized. A woman, on the other hand, can burn out very quickly if she is too focused, especially when she is in a very busy, expanded environment. Likewise, a man burns out or tires when he is too open and is not focused. For this reason, women generally enjoy shopping more than men.

A woman becomes more centered through shopping, because there are so many things to take into her awareness. This "taking in the environment" fulfills her need to expand and relate. As she experiences all the various items in the shopping arena, her awareness expands and yet is constantly related back to her self and loved ones. She sees a dress and her awareness soars, reflecting on the romantic occasions when she could wear it. She imagines herself in it. She tries it on. She enjoys its beauty, puts it away, and has had a fulfilling experience.

Thirty minutes of unfocused shopping is the maximum a man can take before he begins to tire. For women, a few hours of unpressured shopping can be relaxing, centering, and rejuvenating. Acknowledgment of this difference is steadily growing; notice that in most women's stores there are now chairs strategically placed for the husband or boyfriend to sit in.

Another shopping difference can be observed in grocery stores. Women are busy saving money by using discount coupons and buying what is on sale. Men certainly enjoy the conquest of a good deal, but in general they are more concerned with making money rather than saving it. Men are more concerned with getting to a goal, while women are more concerned with responsibly possessing what has been obtained. That is why a man is not instinctively motivated to carry a packet of discount coupons. When he grocery shops his goal is to buy food; when he is at work his goal is to make money.

PHONE CONVERSATIONS AND CAR TRIPS

Men don't like to be talked to while they are busy talking to someone else on the phone. Women are generally bewildered when a man resists being interrupted while talking on the phone. It is difficult for a woman to understand why he becomes so frustrated or irritable. She fails to realize that he does not easily keep track of two things at once.

Masculine energy wants to concentrate on one thing at a time; the interruption destroys his focus. Conversely, a woman is able to talk on the phone, keep dinner from boiling over, comfort a child, and understand what the man is saying to her — all at the same time. Her expanded awareness allows her to keep track of many things at once. Of course a man could allow his awareness to expand and do many things at once, but his general instinct is to focus on one thing at a time.

Driving the car is another situation that brings up these differences. Never try having an intimate conversation with a man while he is driving. He is so focused on getting to his goal in the most efficient way possible that it is difficult to keep his attention. Because his female partner doesn't readily relate to his focused awareness, she misinterprets his not listening to mean that he doesn't care. As a result, for many couples driving in the car can become a very tense experience. This little misunderstanding creates a resentment that causes conversations to turn into arguments and vacations into disasters.

These are simple, everyday illustrations of the masculine tendency toward focused awareness and the feminine inclination toward wide-open awareness. As simple as these examples are, they can provide the basis for resolving many of the difficulties in communication that can occur between men and women.

GETTING HIS ATTENTION

If a woman knows a man usually operates better when he focuses on one thing at a time, she can avoid conflicts by not distracting him. Or, if she needs his attention, this information can allow her to interrupt in a way that works. For instance, she can acknowledge the interruption and ask for his attention, which allows him time to change his focus.

Instead of just beginning to talk, she might say something like this: "Honey, I know you're busy, but I need some help right now. Would you take a minute?" This gives him a choice and a chance to switch his attention fully to her.

With this understanding she knows that if a man is not giving her his full focused attention, it is not because he doesn't care, but because his attention is already focused somewhere else. For example, if a man is watching the news, it is unrealistic to seek his full attention while the TV is on. Instead you could ask, "When would be a good time to talk?" If he says "We can talk now" and doesn't turn off the TV to listen, then he is also unaware of his limitation. He may honestly believe that he can watch TV and give you his full attention. Don't be fooled and then resent him later for not fully listening.

STRESS AND THE EMOTIONALLY ABSENT MAN

Under stress, focused awareness becomes more focused while open awareness becomes even more open. This simple difference can give rise to a host of misunderstandings. For example, when a man is under stress at work, it becomes difficult for him to release his focus. His mind fixates on a particular problem and it is hard for him to think about anything else. He comes home but his mind is still at work. When approached, he seems distracted and is thus inattentive and emotionally absent.

The more stress a man has at work, the more detached he may be at home. When spoken to, he may pick up a magazine and begin to read it. This is not a conscious insult, nor does it mean that he is not interested in you. He is unconsciously picking up the magazine to distract him from listening to you, because most of his mind is still focused on the problems of work. It can help if you politely ask for his full attention. If he gets distracted, pause until he notices that you are waiting for his complete attention.

For his part, a man can begin to realize that he is not giving a woman what she needs when he listens to her with a distracted mind. The deliberate decision to give her his full attention and remove all distractions will assist him in shifting his focus from work to his partner. Without a conscious decision to remain focused and give her the attention she needs and deserves, he will be easily distracted.

I suggest that men get in the habit of putting down the newspaper or magazine — not just in their lap but completely out of their hands — when listening. If there is a TV on, it is best to turn it off until the exchange is complete. These little physical actions increase your ability to turn off work and shift your focus to the family or relationship. If you have children it is important to realize that they too need to be heard.

MISINTERPRETING A WOMAN'S OVERWHELM

Because women have open awareness, they are more easily overwhelmed by the needs of others. Just as a man becomes absorbed in one problem, a woman becomes overwrought by a multitude of problems. One of the ironies of being overwhelmed is that when it happens to a woman, she temporarily loses her ability to prioritize, which leads to more overwhelm. She feels overly responsible, even compelled, to do "everything" and then feels powerless to do it all. This gives rise to the ancient adage, a woman's work is never done.

Without an understanding of this feminine vulnerability, men react to overwhelmed women by becoming frustrated. A man feels that he is being blamed for her unhappiness or that he is somehow responsible for the upset feelings she is experiencing. He defends himself by making her wrong for being so overwhelmed, judging her as "making a big deal out of nothing."

Men need to understand that when women are overwhelmed they are not necessarily trying to accuse or blame: they are just trying to talk about their problems in order to feel better. At times like these, a woman really needs to be heard. Unfortunately, most men don't know this secret. Instead, they try to make their partner feel better by explaining to her that she shouldn't be upset, or they suggest solutions to her problems. This attempt to fix her only makes matters worse.

For example, one afternoon on his way out the door, Tom hurriedly asks Jane, "Would you pick up my dry cleaning? I'm running a little late."

Jane responds in an upset and overwhelmed tone by saying, "I can't pick up your dry cleaning; I'm already in a hurry. I have to pick up Mary at school, make two bank deposits, return Timmy's library books, buy groceries for tonight's dinner, and try to get home in time to do my exercise program. I just don't know how I can do it all. Our bank account is almost overdrawn and the bills are piling up. There are so many things I have to do. I still need to give you your phone messages."

Hearing Jane's upset, Tom gets frustrated. In a rather judgmental and angry voice he says, "Look, it's no big deal, I'll pick them up myself." This is Tom's instinctive response to solve the problem of her being upset. He thinks that by saying this he has made everything all right. But it is not. Not only does he feel blamed, but she feels judged.

As he walks out the door with a frown on his face, Tom thinks to himself, "Why does she have to make such a big deal out of saying no. Couldn't she just have said it in a pleasant tone, instead of giving me a lecture on all that she is doing? Is she trying to make me feel guilty or something? I'm not making her do all those things today. All I did was make a simple request. It's not my fault that she is so overwhelmed. She acts like I am 'so-o' lazy and she is 'so-o' responsible. Just because I don't complain about all my problems, it doesn't mean that I am doing nothing."

In this example, Tom's response ("It's no big deal . . .") made Jane feel worse. He thought he was being nondemanding and thus supportive. Jane, however, assumed that he thought she was wrong for being upset about her day. This made her feel as though Tom didn't care about her distress. She ended up feeling unloved and unsupported.

In truth, Tom is upset about Jane being upset, but for different reasons than she imagines. Tom is resentful because he thinks she is making him wrong for asking her to pick up his cleaning. He thinks she is saying his request is unfair and demanding and has caused her to feel overwhelmed. Tom is not upset that she is upset; he is angry because he thinks she is blaming him for her upset.

Tom has misunderstood Jane. She is not trying to make Tom responsible, she is just trying to be heard. She is not trying to tell Tom that he is lazy and demanding. His asking her to pick up his cleaning has merely given her an opportunity to express how overwhelmed she is. She unconsciously seeks relief by sharing everything that is overwhelming her.

As a result of this misunderstanding, Jane is not only upset about her day, but is even more upset because she thinks Tom doesn't care about her feelings. She also feels bad because Tom, who was feeling fine before, is now leaving for work in a frustrated and angry mood. Neither Tom nor Jane feels loved or supported. They do love and desire to support each other, but because they misunderstand each other they are at odds.

FEELING BETTER DIFFERENTLY

When they are under too much pressure, men and women help themselves feel better in different ways. Women undergoing stress feel better by talking about their problems and being heard, while men feel better by prioritizing their problems, focusing on one, and then developing a plan of action or a solution.

Let's look at an example of how, when a woman attempts to share and feel better, but her partner keeps interrupting with solutions, they both end up frustrated.

HOW HE INVALIDATES HER

One day Mary is looking for the form to register her children at the local pool. As she searches she is also beginning to doubt whether they can afford to pay for pool memberships at this time. Because there is a limit to the number of pool members, if she pays in advance her children will be assured acceptance, but if she waits, they might miss out. As she looks through the mail she finds a $1,400 Visa bill. She becomes even more concerned and wonders whether this is the right time to pay for pool membership.

By the time Bill arrives home, Mary is rather upset. She says, "We got our Visa bill today. It's $1,400. I just don't know how we are going to pay it."

He says, "We'll manage. We've got plenty of time to pay it." He assumes she will feel better now that he has offered a solution to the problem, and he mistakenly thinks the only thing bothering her is the $1,400 bill.

Then Mary says, "We already owe on our American Express bill and the mortgage is coming up soon." She is continuing her attempt to share her various worries.

Bill responds in an annoyed tone, "Don't worry, we still have ten days." Irritated because she hasn't accepted his solution, he now begins to feel a little attacked. He wonders inside, "Is she upset with me for spending too much money or for not making enough money? She spends just as much as I do."

What Bill doesn't know is that Mary is just airing her feelings about money so she can feel good about buying the kids swimming passes.

At this point in their conversation she is feeling hurt and invalidated by his comment not to worry. Saying "don't worry" is Bill's attempt to help her feel better or to "fix" her. It is his way to solve the problem and feel better. What he doesn't understand is that this approach only makes matters worse for her.

The last thing Mary needs is to be told not to worry. What she hears is that she doesn't have good reasons to be worried and is thus foolish, unworthy of respect, irrational, or inadequate in some way. She feels that he is condescending to her and that he doesn't care about her feelings. She needs him to understand her worries, but instead of feeling heard she feels put off and put down.

In spite of her hurt she continues sharing her financial concerns and says, "You know we promised the kids that we were going to Disney World this summer."

With increasing frustration Bill says, "I know, I know. It will be fine." Misunderstanding her hurt tone of voice, he thinks, "How dare she accuse me of being a lousy dad. I keep my promises to the kids. Is she saying I am not a loving father? Is she criticizing me? Why is she bringing all this up?"

Bill feels attacked and rejected. What he doesn't know is that Mary thinks he is a great father. She is just concerned about their finances and needs to be heard.

Mary, feeling brushed off, continues to share her concerns. "We even owe for Laurie's hospital bill."

He says with increasing annoyance, "Look, I told you before that I am getting a bonus this month. Don't make such a big deal out of this." He is annoyed and irritated because he thinks she is accusing him of being irresponsible and undependable. He is taking her upset personally.

Mary responds in a mistrusting tone, "What if you don't get a bonus?"

He says, "You worry too much."

She says, "You promised your parents you would visit home. When are you planning to go?"

He barks, "Get off my back, will you." By this time Bill feels persecuted and interrogated as if he is the bad guy. He does not feel loved or appreciated. Indignantly he thinks, "Why is she telling me that I don't keep my promises?"

She persists, "Taxes are coming up in two months. Have you thought about how we're going to pay them? How much are we going to owe this year?"

He says defensively, "Of course I've thought about it. It will work out fine. It always does." He grumbles to himself, "Does she think I am an idiot? Of course I've considered my taxes."

She says, "I hope we can afford a membership at the pool this summer. But I think I lost the registration form. Have you seen it?"

By this time Bill is so angry that he doesn't want to talk to her. In a moment of frustration he says, "No, I haven't seen it . . . but if we are so broke, why are you thinking of new ways to spend money!"

As a result of this conversation, Mary's feelings are hurt and Bill is unwilling to talk to her. What could have been a very simple conversation turned into tension and conflict.

If Bill had understood that Mary needed to talk for a while to feel better, he wouldn't have been in such a hurry to identify and solve her problem. Let's see how they could have had this conversation turn out in a positive way.

Mary says, "We got our Visa bill today. It's $1,400. I just don't know how we are going to pay it."

Bill nods and says, "Um hum. Gee, that's a lot." Inside he thinks, "I wonder if this is the problem that is upsetting her. Generally the first thing she says is a warm-up to what is really bothering her. She probably needs to talk for a while. I'll just practice listening without interrupting.

Mary then says, "We already owe on our American Express bill and the mortgage is coming up soon."

Bill nods again and says, "Um hum. You're right." Inside he thinks, "I guess she needs to talk about our finances. Remember, don't interrupt. I'm sure I can support her if I minimize my comments and try to understand how she is feeling."

"You know we promised the kids that we were going to Disney World this summer. We even owe for Laurie's hospital bill."

Bill nods again and says, "We owe a lot."

She says, "What if you don't get a bonus."

Bill says, "If I don't get my bonus . . . we are in big trouble." With each response Bill remembers to not minimize her worries. If he wasn't being diligent in his support he could have easily slipped back into a put-down statement like "Oh, you worry too much" or a Mr. Fix-it statement like "If I don't get the bonus, then we'll get it next month or the month after . . . the bills will just have to wait." Fortunately, after much practice in listening, Bill has learned not to interrupt her flow with solutions or invalidating comments.

Mary then says, "Taxes are coming up in two months. Have you thought about how we're going to pay them? How much are we going to owe this year?"

He says, "I know it's a lot." In each case he is prudent in his comments. Bill recognizes that she just needs some time to be upset. He knows that his every comment is helping her to gradually feel better as long as he doesn't try to fix her.

She then remarks, "I hope we can afford a membership at the pool this summer. But I think I lost the registration form. Have you seen it?"

"Humm, no, I haven't seen it around," he says thoughtfully.

She then asks, "Do you think we should buy the membership now or wait?"

"I'm not sure," he says. "Maybe we should wait till I get my bonus. That will still give us time to register in advance." Bill is careful not to sound too confident in his response. One part of him actually feels that the swimming passes are a minor expense and can easily be purchased now. But another part, having listened to her concerns, realizes it would be a much better idea to wait.

Mary then says, "That makes sense." She gives him a hug. "Thanks for listening to me. I feel like you really understand. I just love you." To himself Bill thinks, "Wow, it really worked. I did it again. Once you get the hang of it, listening sure makes things easier."

In this example Bill has learned the secret to improving communication — listening. It is a skill that takes time to learn, just as learning to speak did. Mary, too, needs to learn the art of listening; otherwise she can make the same mistake, offending him when he speaks.

HOW SHE OFFENDS HIM

Just as well-intentioned men mistakenly try to "fix" women, women tend to misguidedly "improve" men at those times when a man talks about what is bothering him. All it takes is one or two objectionable comments and he will fall silent. At such times a woman generally has little idea of how she antagonized him. She doesn't realize that any attempt to "help" or "improve" him will be offensive. Let's look at four examples.

Bill and Mary: Bill is worried because he went into debt while remodeling his home. Now he is trying to figure out how he is going to pay his tax bill. When he comes home, he says in a rather defeated tone, "I don't know how we are going to pay our taxes this year."

Mary responds by saying, "I knew we should have spent less on our remodel." Bill now becomes silent and won't talk anymore. Mary feels bad and has no idea of how she hurt Bill.

If Bill was centered and not upset, he probably would not have been bothered by Mary's comment. He would have said, "You're right, we blew it." But because Bill is already upset and feeling defeated, her mentioning the remodel makes him feel as though she is trying to teach him a lesson on being responsible. He is also hurt and offended because he reads additional meanings into her remark.

"I can't believe she would say that," he thinks. "Does she think I am an idiot? Does she think I don't already know we overspent on the remodel? How dare she imply that I am irresponsible with money. Everybody overspends on a remodel. What's the big deal? I hate it when she treats me like a child and tries to change me. This is the last time I'll talk to her about my worries. Why can't she just listen and support me? Every chance she gets to criticize me she takes it."

Since men can shut down after just one wrongfully taken comment, let's look at more examples of the innocent ways a woman can hurt a man.

Joe and Martha: Joe, frustrated with low sales at the office, comes home silent and withdrawn. Martha asks, "What's the matter, Joe?"

Joe says in a depressed tone, "We didn't make our sales quota this month."

Martha responds, "Well, every business has its ups and downs. I don't think it would be so bad if we would plan for such times."

At this point, Joe stops talking. He feels unsupported and angry. Inside he thinks, "I didn't ask for her advice. I hate it when she gives me a lecture on how I could be a better businessman. Does she think I'm stupid? I already know every business has its ups and downs." Joe needs Martha to just listen and let him talk. Any unsolicited advice will be offensive.

Even advice that attempts to broaden a man's understanding can backfire, as the following scenario demonstrates.

Steve and Janet: Steve comes home and is very quiet. He seems tense and irritated. Janet, hoping to soothe him, says, "What's the matter?"

He says, "Oh, nothing. I'm just having a hard time with my secretary. Her resistance to my requests is driving me nuts."

Janet understands his frustration, but she also understands his secretary's frustration in dealing with Steve. She feels he will be able to handle the situation better if he understands his secretary's point of view. She is right, but this isn't the time to tell him. He needs her to be sympathetic to his side of the problem.

Hoping to help, Janet says, "You know, I bet your secretary would respond better to you if you would take some time to listen to her. You rarely talk to her. Tell her what you are really feeling."

Immediately Steve goes quiet. He is first stunned and then angry. He feels betrayed by his wife. "How dare she take sides with my secretary," he thinks. "My own wife thinks I am the problem. She never thinks I talk enough. I talk with my secretary — that's the problem. She doesn't listen. I was already furious with my secretary; now I am furious with my wife too."

In her attempt to help Steve by expanding his understanding, Janet unknowingly turned him off. Let's look at one more example of the type of comment that men find unsupportive.

Rick and Sharron: Rick took his wife Sharron out to a nice restaurant. During a forty-five-minute wait for their table, Rick got increasingly annoyed. Several times he spoke to the maitre d' in an attempt to speed up the process. A number of people who came in later were seated before him. Each time Rick would become more upset, even though he knew the recent arrivals had reservations and he didn't.

Sharron eventually mentioned the unmentionable. Rick was grumbling about how terrible the service was at this restaurant. He said, "I can't believe they are so slow here!" Sharron countered, "Do you think we would be waiting this long if we had made reservations?"

Rick's response was anger in his eyes and immediate coldness. He mumbled, "No!" and then fumed inside.

All of his anger at himself for not making reservations, which he had displaced onto the restaurant, was now displaced onto Sharron. Furious at her comment, he thought, "What a stupid thing to say. I can't believe her. If she's so smart, then next time she can take me out to a restaurant. If she wants reservations, let her make them. I'm not going to bother. I hate it when she picks at me. Does she think I don't realize that I forgot to make reservations? She acts as though I am supposed to remember everything. I don't even want to talk with her."

Rick had wanted Sharron to be on his side, not to take this opportunity to improve him. Her comment was intended to reveal to him how he could avoid waiting in the future and to help him be more responsible. Instead, it annoyed him because it started the obvious. What he needed her to say was, "Yes, they are slow."

In each of these examples, the man was looking to feel emotionally supported by his partner, and was turned off by any attempt to help, offer advice, or improve him. It is important to note that in each example the man wasn't asking for advice or help. He was just talking, and wanted his partner's passive support. Instead, she tried actively to help him be a better person in some way.

This is a mistake that women commonly make, having no idea of how they offend the men in their lives. Men have a feminine side, and from time to time need to share their thoughts and emotions to feel better. When this happens, women mistakenly shut their men down. All it takes is a few such experiences and he will stop sharing what he needs to share.

WHEN HE DOES WANT ADVICE

There are, however, times when a man *is* looking for advice and a woman's attempt to help may still unknowingly turn him off. When he has thought a problem through but has not found a solution, he may talk about it. After he has presented the problem he will say something like "What do you think?" This is a signal that he is asking for a solution. A male listener would suggest something the man could do to solve his problem. This is what he is looking for, and he will feel supported.

A woman, on the other hand, may make a number of mistakes when trying to help a man who is looking for a solution. She may try to nurture him, which turns him off, or she may try to help him see the bigger picture, which can upset him.

Women listeners often offend men inadvertently because women, as a rule, instinctively approach their problems in a feminine way. Women may talk about the way a problem was created or how to avoid the problem or even make the problem bigger by describing the way it affects them. In each of these ways, a woman may turn a man off so that he doesn't want to discuss his problems with her.

In addition, a woman may frustrate a man by wanting to explore how the problem makes him feel, and by listening in an overly concerned and sympathetic way. If a man is asking for a solution by saying "What do you think," he doesn't want to be nurtured with caring understanding of what he is going through. What he wants is a concrete suggestion.

Let's replay the above imagining that the men are coming to their partners not for emotional support, but for a solution.

Bill and Mary: Bill comes home and says to his wife Mary, "I don't know how we are going to pay our taxes. I didn't get my bonus and the house remodel has put us too far in debt. We could spend less on our vacation or take another loan against the house. What do you think?"

Mary responds, "If only we hadn't spent so much on the remodel. Henry warned us that it would cost more. We should have planned to pay a lot more." Bill is now intensely frustrated. Mary is sharing her feelings about what caused the problem, while Bill wants to focus on a solution.

To himself he thinks, "I know. I know we spent too much. I got that a long time ago. Why does she do this to me? We can't talk about anything!"

Bill has signaled his desire for a conversation to solve the problem. He wants Mary to say something like "I think we should try to spend less on our vacation and try to avoid going further in debt" or "I don't know what to do. Are there any other options?" Mary could also offer a new option by saying, "Maybe we should try selling our boat. We've talked about that before."

In short, when Bill asks what Mary thinks, he wants her to focus on ways to solve the problem as he presented it.

Let's look at another example.

Joe and Martha: Joe comes home frustrated, wondering why he didn't make his sales quota. "I don't know what's happening," he tells Martha. "I didn't make my quota this month. I even expected to do better this month. Why do you think this is happening?"

Martha replies, "Well, I think we should have planned on this happening. Every business has its ups and downs. We should have a backup fund to carry us through times like this."

Joe's response to Martha's good advice is frustration. She has not responded to the problem as stated with a suggestion regarding why sales were low this month. Instead, she has brought up another issue that she is worried about, namely, how can the couple better prepare for lean times. Rather than answering Joe's question, Martha has replied to an unasked question, "How do you think we could avoid being affected by job setbacks?"

Joe needs Martha to give a specific answer to his question, such as "Well, that new product line you introduced may have overwhelmed some of the buyers" or "I just don't know why (little pause), you have worked so hard and your products are so good. Maybe it is the economy" or "I read an article yesterday that said we have recently entered a recession. Maybe that's why."

These comments are all directed at the immediate problem. To be supportive of him, Martha needs to stay focused on the issue as he has described it.

Let's look at how another wife's advice addressed her husband's question, but still fell short of the mark.

Steve and Janet: Steve comes home and says to his wife Janet, "I've been having a hard time with Phyllis (his secretary). She is resisting my requests, and it is driving me nuts. What do you think I should do?"

Janet responds by saying: "I think she is resisting you because you are so closed. You need to be more open. You never sit down and really talk with her. If you understood her point of view, I don't think she would be resisting you."

Steve is frustrated and offended by Janet's response. He feels blamed and judged as incompetent. He thinks, "Well, that's the last time I'll ask you for advice. Why do you have to blame me for not being open? I talk with my secretary. . . ."

Janet has given Steve good advice, but has worded it in a way that makes him defensive. She has told him how he could have avoided the problem, instead of telling him what he can now do about it. Steve could have heard and appreciated the same suggestion had Janet worded it in terms of what action he can now take, instead of focusing on what he did wrong.

Steve would be more open to Janet's advice if she focused not on the cause of the situation, but on its resolution. She might say, "I think you should sit down and have a talk with Phyllis. Schedule some time and really listen to what she is feeling. Take the time to listen to her and I think she will want to listen to you."

Finally, when a man asks for an opinion or advice, the last thing he wants is consolation or sympathy. Here's an example of the way kind words can backfire.

Rick and Sharron: While Rick and Sharron are waiting for their table at a restaurant, Rick says, "I can't believe this place is so slow. What do you think we should do? Should we try another restaurant?"

"I know you've had a hard day," Sharron responds. "We've been waiting at least 45 minutes. It must be pretty difficult to wait this long. You're probably really hungry. Did you eat lunch today?" Sharron has responded to Rick's feelings instead of the problem, because that is the way she would want him to console her if she was upset about waiting.

Rick is now even more furious. He feels as though Sharron is treating him like a child. Inwardly he gripes, "Don't mother me this way. I can't believe that you are not furious with this restaurant too. Who cares if I ate lunch. . . ." He does not want her to console him. He wants her to respond directly to his question with an answer.

Sharron might reply, "Well, we've waited this long. We might as well wait a little longer" or "I think we should stay but get the menu, so at least when we get seated we can order right away" or "I think that's a good idea. What about going to that new restaurant along the freeway?"

Each of these responses will feel supportive to Rick, because his problem is being addressed instead of his feelings.

With the help of the above examples it is easy to see some of the common ways men and women unknowingly create tension and conflict when they are simply trying to help each other to feel better.

MEN NEED SOLUTIONS, WOMEN NEED TO SHARE

Men instinctively look for solutions. When a man has a problem, the first thing he does is to go to his "cave" and try to find a solution on his own. If he can find a solution or plan of action, he will feel better. If he doesn't find a solution, then he will come out of his cave, find another man whom he respects, and talk about it.

When he shares a problem with another man, he is generally looking for another opinion to solve his problem. If he receives a good solution, he will immediately feel better. Thus, when a woman is upset and starts talking, he assumes that she is looking for a solution to her problems. He has no reference point to let him know what she really just needs to be heard for a while. So he tries to help by solving her problems, which usually ends up invalidating and frustrating her.

When a woman is upset, her first need is for it to be OK to be upset for a while. She needs him to listen to her feelings without trying to fix her. Through sharing her problems in a nonfocused way, she will naturally feel better. Her feeling of overwhelm will diminish even if all the problems remain unsolved.

A man mistakenly assumes that all of a woman's problems need to be solved before she will feel better. This is why he gets so frustrated and exhausted when listening to her talk about all the things that are bothering her. He feels he is being expected to solve all of these problems, but he feels powerless to help her.

He especially becomes frustrated when she is bothered by problems that nothing can be done about, or that have not happened. Some common masculine attitudes toward getting upset are:

1. "Why get upset if there is nothing you can do . . . what good will it do to feel upset?"

2. "Don't get upset until you know for sure it has happened."

3. "Since it's already happened, there is no sense in getting upset . . . there is nothing you can do about it now."

These three mottoes keep men mainly in their heads and out of their feelings. Being in your head is useful for solving problems, but it is not always good for your health and emotional well-being. Women instinctively understand that feelings need to be shared if we are to successfully release the tension produced when our desires and expectations are frustrated. Even if there is nothing you can do about a situation, it is important to talk about the feelings involved. Sharing feelings is essential if we are to create and sustain intimacy.

When he understands this difference, a man can relax when a woman is sharing. Instead of feeling responsible for solving all her problems, he can simply focus on solving one problem: he can fulfill her need for a fully focused listener, which will help her to feel better even if none of her problems are solved.

MALE FORGETFULNESS

Focus is necessary to get a job done, but it's possible to have too much concentration. When masculine energy isn't balanced with feminine energy, it tends to focus on one thing to the exclusion of everything else. In the pursuit of one objective, nothing else gets done. This pattern is especially troublesome in relationships.

For instance, even though a man may love his wife very much, if his masculine and feminine awareness is out of balance, he may forget important dates like their anniversary or her birthday, or simple things like picking something up at the store or taking phone messages. It is not that he doesn't care, but his awareness is focused in another direction.

This forgetfulness is understandably hard for women to accept. A woman assumes that forgetfulness connotes lack of caring or interest. It's hard for her to believe that a man who forgets birthdays and anniversaries could really love her. After all, this kind of behavior is so foreign to her experience of loving someone. Men prioritize in the context of achieving their goals, while women prioritize according to the importance of their relationships. With this perspective, it is easy to see how men can unintentionally hurt the feelings of women.

SPINNING OUT AND SPACING OUT

One of the biggest areas of conflict and frustration between men and women is communication. This is because men listen and talk for different reasons than women. Men listen to gather information in order to solve problems, while women listen in order to relate or share. Men talk when they have a specific point to make, or when they are helping someone else to solve a problem. Women talk in order to explore a topic as well as to discover themselves.

From this simple perspective, it is easy to see why men get frustrated when listening to women. A woman expands in search of the point she wants to make, whereas a man expects her to get right to the point, the way a man would. He assumes something is the matter with her for rambling on, or he feels that she is wasting his time. Neither is true.

Women explore their thoughts and feelings *as* they share them, gradually discovering the point they want to make. Men tend to be intolerant of this because men generally don't speak unless they have a specific point to make. When they do speak they try to come to the point as efficiently as possible.

When a conversation is underway and the man falls silent, the woman often mistakenly assumes that he is slow, stupid, withholding, or just unconcerned. None are true. He is doing what is natural for him. He is mulling over his thoughts, to formulate a point to make. This is hard for her to recognize because she processes her thoughts and feelings through sharing them outside herself.

Men occasionally need to mull things over, just as women need to talk out their thoughts and feelings. As a result, the man comes back clearer and more directed, and the woman comes back more centered.

The drawback of both these approaches is that men can sometimes "space out" and forget that they are mulling over a problem, while women can "spin out" and lose themselves in exploring tangents, getting far off the subject.

When a man spaces out he can easily forget what he considered to be important. For instance, he may forget birthdays, appointments, promises, his schedule, his priorities, etc.

When a woman spins out she loses the ability to discern what is really important to her, tending to make everything equally important. She may become overwhelmed and overreact to situations. She feels as though the needs of others are as important or even more important than her own. She may make her children's every need more important than her spouse's romantic needs. She may overreact to his shortcomings by displacing all her frustrations of the day onto him. While sharing her thoughts and feelings, she may spin out and never make an actual point.

Because we are not perfectly in balance at all times, it is realistic to expect men to space out occasionally while mulling things over, just as it is perfectly normal for women to spin out occasionally while sharing their feelings. This understanding is important because it helps women to be more tolerant of men when they space out and forget things. It also helps men to realize that women are not crazy when they spin out and become overwhelmed.

Without this understanding, when a man detects that a woman is "spinning out" he panics and worries that she could go on forever. In most cases, she just needs to talk for a while, and then she will find her center again.

Sometimes a woman will spin out and become confused when she doesn't feel safe enough to explore and share what she is really feeling, or if she has shared it but it has not been heard. Ironically, the very process of sharing that can lead her to greater self-awareness can also create confusion.

On the other hand, when a woman realizes that a man has spaced out, she panics and worries that he doesn't care. Generally what has happened is that he didn't have enough information to arrive at a solution to the problem at hand; he has spaced out and forgotten everything, unconsciously waiting for more information.

To remember what he was mulling over, he just needs some more information. If he feels judged or made wrong for spacing out, he loses touch with his positive intent to serve or support. He may become defensive. To find his focus again, a man needs to feel trusted, needed, and appreciated.

When a man spaces out and may even forget what his partner wants or forget what she is talking about, she has to work hard to continue to trust his caring intent to serve her. If she gets frustrated she can say to herself, "I *can* trust that he cares; his forgetting does not mean he doesn't care. I *can* trust him to remember more and more as he feels more loved, accepted, trusted, and appreciated."

Likewise, a man must work hard to not judge a woman when she is spinning out. He needs to listen with patience and remember that she needs more caring, understanding, and respect at such times.

If he starts to become too frustrated, the male partner could say, "Would you please pause for a moment. I need some time to think about what you are saying." Or he could say, "I want to hear what you are saying, but I need some time to think about what you have already said." In most cases he won't even need to ask her to pause; as she expresses herself she will pause. During those times, he should practice saying nothing and continue trying to understand her point of view. He can say to himself, "She has a right to her emotions. As I understand her feelings, she will feel better and her emotions will become more positive. I *can* find the good reasons for her feelings. I *can* listen without making her wrong. She needs my silent support."

As he is able to more fully understand her feelings, he can more effectively focus on her. His attentiveness and focus will help her to become more centered.

A PROCESS OF UNFOLDING

Regarding communication the male motto is: "Don't speak unless you have something to say." This intimidates women, because for them communication is not just a means of conveying a point, but a means of discovering a point.

When women need to share, they don't know exactly what they want to say. Sometimes they have so much to share, they don't know where to start. Or they may need time to share a progression of feelings and thoughts before they discover the point they want to make. A man also goes through this preparation process, but in a different way. He ponders things within, comes to a conclusion, then shares it outwardly.

A woman, on the other hand, just wants to share and connect. She wants to enjoy being together. For her, communication is not just a sharing of information, it is a sharing of her self. It is a basis for intimacy. It is fulfilling and centering.

For a woman, sharing is a gradual unfoldment and she may need to be drawn out. She may not know exactly what she wants to say, but (1) she wants to connect and feel in a relationship, and (2) communication is her major means of connecting and relating.

When an upset woman shares her feelings, it is as though she is sharing the contents of her purse. She needs time to clean out that purse without being judged for having so much in it, or for not knowing exactly what and how much she has inside. So if she begins to spin out, a man can imagine that she is just taking everything out of her purse. When it is all out, she will feel much lighter and he will have served a very important role.

When a woman is sharing what's inside of her, if she has a respectful, attentive, and caring listener she will feel safe to empty out her purse (her inner feelings). Once everything is out, she will feel much more centered and loving. She will greatly appreciate the support.

MIND READING

Throughout this book, we'll see that faulty communication between the sexes is largely due to mistaken assumptions. One of the most common of those assumptions manifests itself as what we can call "mind reading." Because men and women do not realize how different they are, they assume that they know what the other is thinking or feeling before it has been clearly stated.

True, women are quite accurate when mind reading other women, because they are already so similar. Likewise, men can accurately read the minds of other men. But when men and women start mind reading each other, trouble is inevitable.

A man prematurely decides that he knows what a woman is saying. His error lies in assuming that she started out making the point she wanted to make, as a man would. He may be listening and then, before the speaker is finished, says, "I got it, I got it." This works fine with another man, but to a woman, his statement is preposterous. She knows that he can't know what she intends to say, because many times *she* doesn't even know. While sharing, she is *in the process* of finding out what she feels, thinks, or wants.

Men need to understand that if a woman needs to talk, and if his desire is to support her, then his purpose in listening is not just to get the gist of what she is saying, but to help her get it out. As she gets it out, without being interrupted, her view might change midstream or she might completely change the subject. She may ask questions and then start answering them.

By expecting this to happen, he can avoid feeling frustrated. He needs to remember that just as he has to mull over his problems before talking about them, a woman needs to talk about her problems before she will have a definite opinion. If she feels overwhelmed by difficulties, just by talking about them she may feel better.

Sometimes she will even find out that there is no problem. But the last thing she needs when she is upset is for a man to tell her that there is no problem. The next-to-last thing she needs is for him to offer a string of solutions to whatever she is saying. Finally, the next-to-the-next-to-the-last-thing she needs from him is "OK, I got it!" To be interrupted by "I got it" sounds like "OK, OK, will you shut up, I don't want to hear it anymore."

Women also mind read, but in a different way. They tend to attribute negative interpretations to a man's behavior patterns. When he is quiet, she assumes he doesn't care. When he is distracted, she assumes he doesn't love her. When he is late, she assumes that she is no longer important to him. When he forgets to do things, she assumes he is getting even. When he shuts down, she assumes he is leaving her.

Because she is not a man she has no reference point to help her understand why he does what he does. It is hard for her to trust his love. But she could look for the real and positive reasons for his behavior; she could share her fears in a way that avoids blame but asks for reassurance. In later chapters we will explore how she can more successfully ask for this kind of support.

It is important to work at new ways to communicate that take into account these differences. Just as women are especially vulnerable to being interrupted, men are particularly sensitive to being doubted or mistrusted. When a woman is interrupted again and again, or subjected to an impatient listener, she will close down and become unwilling to share her feelings. Her love is replaced with doubt and mistrust.

When a man is mistrusted by his female mate, he tends to react in a most confusing way. If he is being blamed and punished for a crime he didn't do, his reaction is to commit the crime to get back at the punisher. If she assumes that he is uncaring when he is trying to be caring, at least in his male way, then eventually he becomes cold, impatient, and uncaring.

As you can see, this negative pattern fuels itself. The more uncaring he becomes, the more untrusting she becomes. The more untrusting she becomes, the more uncaring he becomes. This is a major communication trap, but we can end the cycle by increasing our understanding of each other with respect, trust and compassion.

Another female form of mind reading is the expectation that others already know and anticipate their needs. It is very unrealistic to expect a man to anticipate a woman's needs. With this expectation she will surely end up disappointed. On the other hand, men expect women to know their loving feelings by looking at what they do. Women need to be reassured again and again that they are loved and special. In a similar way, men need to be reminded again and again of the woman's needs, wishes, and wants.

MALE TUNNEL VISION

Their focused awareness can make men incredibly determined and efficient, but it can also make them oblivious to other's needs and to priorities not directly related to their primary goal. Consequently, when a man is focused on a particular task or problem, he may not notice the signs of growing distress in his environment, family, relationship, or even within his own body. He does not feel pain or hurt, nor does he acknowledge this in others. He unconsciously negates the importance of needs that are not directly related to his focus. If his wife and children are hurting and upset, his reaction is that they shouldn't hurt and they shouldn't be upset. This kind of invalidation and denial is very hurtful to others and destructive to relationships.

Thus, it is quite common for a man to get sick on the first day of vacation or when a major project is completed. He may have ignored his body's needs until the job was done, and now the body cries for help through falling ill. Or he may become emotionally depressed because he has not been creating the emotional support he needs.

A man can also begin to feel his inner emotional poverty if he fails at his task, or if he retires from it. Statistically, most men die three years after they retire. They have been running on empty without knowing it. When the job is complete, their debt to their bodies and to others must be paid.

The solution is not finding another job in which to bury oneself, nor masking the problem through drinking or drugs. The cure for this man's physical or emotional pain is to create the emotional support he needs and to reassess his priorities and values. He needs something to work for, a new goal and a purpose, to live. He needs to balance his work needs with his emotional and health needs.

Another consequence of tunnel vision is that men tend to neglect the needs of others — not because they don't care, but because they are unconscious of the part of them that does care. He, his wife, and their children all suffer from his neglect. Many a man, after his kids have grown up, says, "I didn't realize how quickly time passes. I feel that I missed out on something very precious." Guilt, regret, sorrow, and shame often accompany this realization.

HOW WOMEN CAN DEAL WITH TUNNEL VISION

Women are naturally gifted with an intuitive awareness of the needs of others. But open awareness can be a mixed blessing when her partner is experiencing tunnel vision. While the man thinks everything is fine in the relationship, the woman is burdened by her awareness of all the problems.

When he is not sharing this burden, she mistakenly assumes that he is happy with the relationship. When he acts as though everything is fine, while she sees problems, she gets the message that she is much too demanding or that he doesn't care and thus will never do anything to change.

This feminine awareness of a relationship's problems becomes a burden to her when he is not willing to hear and validate her awareness. When he denies the validity of her needs and perceptions, she then feels the burden of the relationship and the family rests on her shoulders. She feels alone and unsupported. No wonder women become frustrated when men act as though everything is fine.

With this new understanding of tunnel vision, a woman can correctly conclude that her partner appears satisfied only because he is unconscious of the problems. She can realize that in most cases if he was aware of the problems, he too would be upset or would be motivated to improve things.

Both partners are equally responsible for creating a good relationship. However, their roles are different. The woman will naturally be more aware of the relationship's needs and problems.

She should remember that he is more easily distracted from relationship needs by the demands of his work. She cannot realistically expect him to know when her needs are going unfulfilled unless she communicates them to him. Sometimes he will not even know if his *own* needs are not being met.

For relationships to work, women need to be aware of this male vulnerability, recognize the importance of good communication skills, and persist in communicating their needs and wishes. They must be willing to ask for support — and continue to ask.

This is probably the most difficult task for women in having positive relationships with men. Women don't want to ask. They expect men to anticipate female needs and to feel obliged to fulfill them. Women commonly fall prey to the negative myth, "If he loves me, then he will know what I want." This kind of expectation is destructive to relationships.

Even with good communication techniques, a man may at first tend to minimize the importance of her needs and wishes. This resistance is not from lack of caring; it occurs because he does not readily relate to and therefore cannot understand her needs. Tunnel vision has turned off his awareness of emotional needs. If she wrongly thinks that he does not care, she will give up trying to communicate her needs and the needs of the family. She may stop asking just when it is beginning to work. Understanding his tunnel vision can help her to accept his valid need for her to be gently persistent in asking for his support.

This kind of responsibility, however, must not be misinterpreted. Women in general already take on too much responsibility for the feelings and needs of others. Just as a man becomes resistant to fulfilling the needs of others, she feels compelled to fulfill the needs of others at the expense of not fulfilling her own needs.

Furthermore, I am not implying in this discussion that it is a woman's responsibility to fulfill the needs of the relationship. I am saying, however, that she carries a responsibility to herself to persist in communicating those needs, striving to do it in new ways that don't make him wrong.

For example, he needs to be reminded of how important time shared with him is to her. This is hard to do, as we have said, because she believes that if he really loved her as much as she loves him, then she wouldn't have to ask. The truth is, if he were a *woman*, then she wouldn't have to ask him for more participation in the relationship. As she learns to ask for his participation without secretly resenting him, he can more readily remember his and her needs for relationship. He can recall how much better he feels when he is receiving her love and giving his.

A woman's biggest mistake in a relationship is to give up communicating her needs and to start doing everything by herself. In the short term this is easier, but in the long run she is not developing the necessary communication and understanding in her relationship. Ultimately she will feel a consuming compulsion to do everything, while wrongly assuming that her partner doesn't care to help or participate.

If, instead, she persists in communicating, she can help a man become aware of the relationship problems that his tunnel vision prevents him from seeing. Tunnel vision is like a spell that can take over a man. He is released from that spell when he is able to *hear* the needs of others. When he is not mistrusted and rejected for his tunnel vision, but loved, trusted, and talked to in a positive way, he can come back to his caring self. This kind of loving communication frees him from the spell.

Transformation is possible. Through accepting and understanding each other's differences with love, our relationships can be transformed. We become more of who we truly are: loving and caring beings.

A MAN'S RESPONSIBILITY

For a man to enjoy a good relationship with a woman, he must adjust his expectations. Instead of thinking his work is over when he comes home, he must realize that having a relationship is also a part of his work. There will always be obstacles to overcome in sustaining a loving relationship. Too often men assume that once they are married, the work of having a relationship is over. Realistically, that is when it begins.

A man's major responsibility is to counteract his tendency to be overly focused and strive to be caring, respectful, and committed to understanding his partner's feelings and needs, while maintaining his masculine sense of self. Through gradually learning to hear her feelings, he will become more motivated to support her and will become aware of his own needs in the relationship.

A WOMAN'S RESPONSIBILITY

Even though a woman is more aware of the needs in a relationship, that does not make her solely responsible to solve its problems. But she is responsible for getting her own needs fulfilled — in two main ways. First, she must communicate her needs and wishes without resenting her partner. Second, she must get her needs fulfilled from a variety of sources, and not make her partner the source of her dissatisfaction, or the sole source of her fulfillment.

Consider the woman who tries to improve a suffering relationship by giving to the man, while expecting him to give back to her in the same way. She takes on the responsibility of pleasing him, but ignores herself until it is too late. By denying her own needs, she prevents him from being able to support her. Men are drawn to where they are needed, trusted, and appreciated. A man runs from the needs of a woman when it appears that he cannot satisfy her needs. The signal that he has failed is her resentment.

Women typically do not communicate their needs until they have sacrificed for so long that resentment has set in. Then, no matter how they communicate their needs, it will sound like nagging, complaining, bitching, blaming, or demanding. This just increases a man's resistance to hearing that he must continue to work on his relationship.

It is very difficult for a man to react in a positive way to resentment or a "guilt trip." He cannot contribute to the relationship when he is considered the "bad guy." To enrich the relationship, a woman's major responsibility is to share her feelings, thoughts, and needs without secretly harboring resentments, but with a loving, accepting, trusting, and appreciative attitude. She also must not expect him to meet all her needs, creating instead many avenues of fulfillment in her life. With this extra love and support from family and friends, she is not as needy for his love and reassurance, and can be more accepting of his particular limitations.

Men commonly expect there to be no more problems once they are in a relationship, and women expect the men to fulfill their needs without having to be reminded again and again. When these mistaken assumptions are corrected, communication improves. He can more easily hear about problems, and she can share her needs in a more supportive way. With better communication, they are then able to share more equally the burdens — and the joys — of the relationship.

MAKING DECISIONS

Just as a man can be too focused, women can be too open. Being too open or too focused greatly influences how men and women make decisions. Overly open women tend to be aware of so many possibilities that they can't focus on one and make a decision. For example, they may spend days looking for *exactly* the right birthday present for their spouse, seeing so many possibilities that they are unable to make a decision.

A man might find such behavior incomprehensible. Instead, he would concentrate on buying a gift and get it done quickly, perhaps missing a better present because he didn't take the time to explore at least some of the options.

Because women are more relationship-oriented, they tend to include others in the decision-making process. Before a decision is made, they talk with others, including everyone affected by the decision, and then finally they reach a conclusion together. In contrast, men first make a decision on their own, and then are open to changing it according to feedback from others. First a man makes his decision privately in his "cave," and then he checks it out with others. If his first conclusion is not accepted, then it is back to the drawing board.

Without a true understanding of these different decision-making styles, conflict, confusion, and resentment are sure to follow. When he makes decisions before exploring how she feels, she ends up feeling excluded, disrespected, and unimportant. In reality, he is not aware that she is waiting to be included. He mistakenly assumes that if she has something to say, she will just say it. He does not realize her need to be included and drawn out.

She does not offer any feedback because she assumes that he has rigidly made his decision and excluded her. She does not realize that he has come up with his best decision on his own, and now he is open to feedback. This is confusing to a woman because she first collects all the information and then makes a decision — one that is much more final than the kind of decision a man makes.

For example, a man might say to his wife, "I think we should take a vacation in June for ten days. We can go camping and have a great time." Hearing this, she is stunned. She can't believe that he hasn't even asked her if, when, and where she would like to have a vacation.

He assumes that she will speak up if she doesn't like his idea. So when she doesn't respond, he thinks his idea has been accepted. She, however, is still recovering from the shock of someone else being so selfish as to make a major decision without including her before the final say. It sounds to her as though he is saying, "I've decided that we are going camping for 10 days in June and I don't care what you want to do. My mind is made up." It is important to note that this is not what he is saying, but in feminine language that is what it sounds like. Emotionally she will react to his decision as if he is not willing to include her, when he is, in truth, open to feedback.

Some women understand this; when a man makes a decision, they know that he is open to feedback and open to change. Most women, however, do not understand this difference. They either resent him for it, or they are intimidated by it. If he is resented or mistrusted, then he becomes fixed and rigid, but if he is appreciated for making a decision, then he is open to changing it. Women don't get a lot of chances to see this flexible male side, because as soon as he makes a decision alone, women feel they have to fight to be heard. When they start fighting, men lose their openness to change and protect themselves through righteousness and rigidity.

On the other hand, men get frustrated with a woman's more democratic decision-making process. It seems long and tedious. A woman generally wants to explore by asking lots of questions before she makes a decision. Often the man assumes she is pretending not to know what she wants, when in truth she needs time to explore all possibilities and various points of view before making a decision. He may become furious because he feels controlled through her lack of knowing.

For example, Joe has decided that he would like to go camping with the family during the summer. He says, "I think it would be a good idea for us to go camping this summer." Martha responds, "I don't know. I haven't thought about our vacation yet."

"I don't know" is a very creative state of mind. From this state of mind Martha is able to access her intuition as well as be open to many sources outside herself. Free from being locked into the limits of her mind and logic, she can respond to her inner feelings.

Joe, however, thinks that "I don't know" means she is rejecting his suggestion. In frustration he thinks, "I hate it when she stalls me. She takes such a long time. If she doesn't want to go, why doesn't she just say so? She is so controlling."

To ease his discomfort at her needing more time to make a decision, Martha could say, "I think it's a good idea, but I need some time to think about it. I appreciate your patience" or "That sounds like a good idea. Let's talk to the kids and see if they also want to go" or "We haven't been camping in several years. What a good idea. Before we decide, would you give me a few days to think about it?"

These kinds of responses can help him to be more patient. He can make her life easier if he respects her need for more time to make decisions.

SEX AND DECISION-MAKING

Sex is one area in relationships where the decision-making process is particularly important. Generally a man knows when he is open to having sex. A woman however, may be open to having sex but may need more time to discover whether she really wants to. Men don't readily understand this because when they are open to having sex, they also simultaneously want it.

When a husband asks his wife whether she would like to have sex that night, if she says "I don't know," it is very easy for him to mis-interpret and think she is saying "no." While he thinks he is being rejected, she is just warming up to the idea. She may be quite open to having sex, but needs some time for her inner feelings to emerge before she can make the decision.

For example, Bill says to Mary, "I'm in the mood to make love tonight. Would you like to?"

Mary, starting to experience rush of feelings, says, "I don't know." Inside her are various layers of feelings yet to be discovered: "How nice, making love sounds good, but I am tired tonight, I still have to make those calls, I'm not sure I want to get sexual tonight, I don't know if I have the energy, I may just want to be cuddled, another part of me would love to have sex, you are such a wonderful lover, I would love to have sex tonight. . . ."

But when Bill hears "I don't know" he hears rejection. Feeling hurt and defensive, he says, "Oh well, forget it. Tonight is probably not a good night." Inside Bill thinks, "I hate it when she rejects me. If she doesn't want to have sex, why doesn't she just say it! Well, that is the last time I am going to ask. If she doesn't want to make love to me, I'll just take care of myself."

If he understood this difference between men and women, he could remedy the situation. To her statement, "I don't know," he could respond, "Is there part of you that wants to make love?" Then she might say, "Part of me would love to. I just need a chance to feel whether this is the right time."

If Mary understood how men hear "I don't know," she could respond to his suggestion by saying "I love making love with you. I need some time to discover whether tonight is the right night for me" or "Making love sounds like a wonderful idea. I don't know if tonight is the right time for me. Give me a little time to see."

After she responds in one of the above courteous but still indefi-nite ways, she will want him to be reassuring and patient and to gently persist in his interest. He could say "OK, we'll just take it as it comes" or "You take all the time you need, Honey" or "I understand. We could just cuddle for a while and see if anything happens" or "Do you want to talk about anything?"

With sex, as with many other areas of life, it is essential for men to understand that when a woman says "I don't know," she is not saying no.

FORMING OPINIONS

Similar to the decision-making process, men and women form and express opinions differently. Understanding these differences can avoid much conflict.

Similar to the process of making decisions, women take longer to form opinions. They take additional time and care to consider various points of view and to gather all available information. Even when they express their opinions they tend to be open to other points of view, and are careful to let others know that they do not claim to be absolutely right.

When she is centered, a woman has a gracefulness and flexibility that leave a door open for others to have differing beliefs. She uses phrases such as, "It sounds to me like, I feel as though, it could be that, it looks to me like, what I see is, what I hear is, it seems to me that, etc." Her style of expression reveals that she is open to seeing the value or truth in other points of view.

Men form and express opinions in an opposite way. A man quickly forms an opinion or conclusion based on what he already knows. Then he tests it out by proclaiming it *as if* he were absolutely certain. Through experiencing various reactions to his opinion, he then reassesses its accuracy. If others agree with his opinion, he feels more definite. If others have differing opinions, he may weigh their merits against his own and then change his view.

When a woman hears a man's opinion she may react negatively, because she does not realize that he is open to hearing others. It sounds as though he thinks he is absolutely right, and that any other view is foolish, irrational, or unintelligent. Because her conclusions are the result of careful consideration, she tends to be intimidated or offended by a man's quick conclusions and opinions. To her, he appears narrow-minded, arrogant, and unwilling to hear others.

This man, however, may be quite open to changing. He merely appears rigid because his process of forming conclusions is different. He is quick to form conclusions, but he is also quick to change if presented with more information. Although he is not absolutely certain, he appears that way to women.

For example, Bill says in a definite tone, "Our children are completely spoiled." Dismayed, Mary says, "They are not. I can't believe you would say that." They are now headed in the direction of an argument.

Mary assumes that Bill is not open to changing his point of view. She prejudges him as a righteous, opinionated, and self-centered person. To her, having a discussion after Bill has voiced such a definite-sounding opinion is out of the question. If she wants to be heard she thinks she faces the formidable task of *convincing* rather than *sharing*.

Without a prior understanding of how men reason things, Mary interprets Bill's statement as arrogant and rigid. Because she fears she must fight him to be heard, she becomes opinionated and aggressive. This aggressive attitude, in turn, makes him defensive and resistant to her point of view. Her fear becomes a self-fulfilling prophecy.

If, however, Bill said to his friend Tom, "My children are completely spoiled," Tom might respond, "I know what you mean. Kids today are very different from our generation. I don't think they are spoiled, I think they are just more assertive. In the long run I think they will do fine."

In this case, Tom heard Bill's point of view, but Tom knew instinctively that Bill was also open to other opinions. Thus, Tom was able to express his differing point of view without defending his own or attacking Tom's. He trusted that there was room for him to differ in his opinion. Tom knew that Bill would compare the merits of the differing ideas and possibly form a new opinion.

With this understanding, Mary would have responded to Bill in a nondefensive manner. When Tom said, "Our children are completely spoiled," she could respond in a supportive and open way, saying, "They sure do make a lot of demands, but I don't think they are spoiled. They are very responsible in getting their homework done. They're just different from our generation." In this example, Mary felt safe to express her point of view; the couple could have a conversation and not an argument.

Through understanding our differing styles we can respect and integrate them both. By forming opinions and then making decisions, truly balanced men and women understand the creative value of openly sharing thoughts and feelings, yet they also respect the value of self-reflection and thinking a problem over before seeking input from others. The intention to be open to and respectful of our partner's style of reasoning is very helpful to avoid conflict.

These differences of awareness not only style our thinking processes but even affect our sexual experience. Let's look at some examples of how our focused and open awareness is manifest in the sexual needs and experiences of men and women.

FOCUSED/OPEN AWARENESS AND SEXUAL EXPRESSION

During sex, men tend to skip foreplay in favor of reaching the goal of orgasm, whereas women favor the pleasurable process of foreplay. Even their physiologies express this difference. Men need two or three minutes of genital stimulation to reach climax, statistics show, whereas women need an average of eighteen minutes. These figures are staggering: she needs six times as much duration and attention to reach climax.

If a man doesn't understand this difference, he can easily and mistakenly assume that his partner does not enjoy sex as much as he does. Most important, if he does not know that she needs six times as much foreplay, then he will not be motivated to give it to her. Without this foreplay, she certainly will not enjoy lovemaking as much. When she is not fulfilled in sex, it stops being fun and energizing, and becomes difficult and tiring for both.

Because a woman has open awareness, it takes more time for her to relax and open up to enjoy sex. If a woman doesn't understand and accept this difference, she can easily believe that something is wrong with her. She may even imagine that she is frigid or unable to be aroused, when in reality she is not getting the relaxed foreplay that she needs.

In many cases, because a woman takes longer to experience intense arousal, she will fake arousal to give her man a sense of accomplishment and also to avoid appearing inadequate. This sets up a negative loop. When a woman appears satisfied without enough foreplay, a man gets the wrong message. He thinks what he is doing works and will continue doing the same thing. Rather than give more foreplay, he may give even less foreplay. This is certainly a delicate subject to talk about, but if a woman is pretending or exaggerating her pleasure, she is setting herself up not to get what she needs.

GETTING TO THE GOAL VS. ENJOYING THE RIDE

When a woman is overwhelmed from her day, it is more difficult for her to relax enough to have a sexual climax. At these times, what she needs is to be cuddled. She needs lots of hugs, affection, and intimate embracing. Through being held and loved in a nonsexual way, she can just relax without any demands being made of her. This is a heavenly experience for her and is closely related to how men feel after they have a climax.

It is important to understand this feminine need; otherwise, men don't take the time to give this kind of loving support to their partners. This nonsexual, non-goal-oriented physical touching is highly valued by women in ways that men do not understand. Touching is as important to women as sex is to men.

This does not mean that women don't like sex. They love it just as much as men. The difference is that when women are tense they relax through non-goal-oriented hugging and cuddling, yet when men are tense they feel a compulsion to intensify that tension through goal-oriented sex. Open awareness wants to expand the process of pleasuring each other, while focused awareness wants to get to the goal as efficiently as possible.

Because men are goal-oriented in sex, they sometimes get impatient with foreplay. Women sometimes need a lot more than eighteen minutes of foreplay to have an orgasm. In fact, sometimes sex can be quite satisfying to a woman even if she doesn't have an orgasm. This nonorgasmic experience is much different from what a man would suspect.

It is hard for a man to understand how a woman can sometimes feel sexually satisfied without having an orgasm. One way men can relate to this is by comparing her nonorgasmic sex to his "quickie." Just as a man can be satisfied by getting right to the goal (a five- to ten-minute quickie), a woman enjoys the ride or the process of moving toward the goal. Arriving at the goal (orgasm) is not primary to her fulfillment just as the process of getting there (foreplay) is not primary to a man.

Of course, this does not mean that women don't enjoy orgasm. In general, though, she does not fully enjoy orgasm unless she first enjoys foreplay. Sometimes she is not even interested in orgasm, but rather wants to savor the sensuality of enjoying and pleasing each other. At times she may be very goal-oriented and at other times she may just enjoy the process of getting closer.

A man also experiences different desires in his sexual experience. Sometimes he wants to take time and enjoy tantalizing his partner. Gradually his whole body is filled with pleasure, and then when he climaxes, he experiences the joy, sensuality, and ecstasy of a full-body orgasm.

This full and ripe experience is contrasted by having a quickie. In a quickie — five to ten minutes of foreplay — he focuses on getting to climax as fast as he can. Although he is satisfied by either, the quickie is not as deeply fulfilling as indulging in the sensual pleasure of foreplay. It is like comparing fast food to gourmet food. Sometimes we want fast food and other times we want the finest.

At times a woman just wants to cuddle. She wants to be held and touched and doesn't care about having an orgasm. Understanding this makes it easier for a man to feel successful in lovemaking if his partner does not have an orgasm. He will also be more motivated to create times when they can just cuddle without having to be sexual at all. This is very important to women.

In a similar way, sometimes a man just wants a release and he is satisfied. It is important to men to forget all the foreplay and experience quickies from time to time.

This balanced understanding relieves a woman from feeling pressured to perform as a sex goddess whenever they make love. He does not demand that she have an orgasm each time. She does not expect him to relish long, drawn-out lovemaking every time. During quickies, a woman doesn't have to resent not getting foreplay if she knows that at other times they will cuddle and sometimes, when they are both feeling more balanced, they will enjoy gourmet sex.

Our sexual needs change in cycles like the weather or the phases of the moon. These cycles are then interrupted by the varieties of stress in our daily lives. A healthy sexual relationship demands flexibility and tremendous acceptance of our differences.

THE LOGISTICS OF FOREPLAY

Because their awareness is so expanded and open, women are easily distracted or affected by their environment, especially when it comes to their own needs. When it is her time to relax and enjoy, a woman may find herself worrying about unpaid bills or wondering if the house is safe.

Men need to recognize that for women, environment is essential to the lovemaking process. Beautiful surroundings go a long way. Lighting a candle, sweet smells, low light, soft music, all can make a tremendous difference.

For an overly open woman to relax (and remember, most women become overly open after a stressful day), she may need her whole body touched before she is focused enough to enjoy direct stimulation of her erogenous zones.

When a man is tired he can be sexually satisfied by a quickie; a woman may be equally satisfied by a loving massage all over her body. By feeling throughout her whole body, she is brought back to her center.

Understanding different kinds of awareness helps us to identify some of our common differences, but it doesn't determine how sex or making love should look. Styles of making love are very personal and it is not possible to say what is right for everyone. At most, this discussion can help you explore your partner's needs and be more open to looking for and accepting his or her differences.

LIVING IN THE PROMISE

Open awareness is capable of recognizing the potential of someone or of a situation. The ability to see what one could be is a great virtue, but can create a variety of problems when it is out of balance. When a woman is too open she can fall in love with a man's potential. If she lacks focus, she will react today to things she expects to happen in the future — she imagines she is happy today because she expects her needs to be fulfilled in the future.

Certainly it is normal to be happy when you expect something good to happen. This becomes a problem, however, when anticipatory happiness masks the unhappiness in the moment. It is hard for an overly open woman to have enough focus to experience what she is feeling in the present when she is borrowing her happiness from an unrealized future.

She may even be in a relationship with a man whom she does not love, imagining that one day her love will change her man. She imagines he is her ideal partner. Through perceiving his potential to be loving, supportive, understanding, etc., she begins to feel as if he has already changed. She lives in a fantasy world. She sees what she wants to see rather than what is.

For example, imagine that someone offered you a check for a million dollars. That would be quite exciting. The only hitch is that you have to wait a month before the check will clear. Even though you have to wait, you will probably be very happy and excited. In much the same way, being in a relationship with someone who holds a lot of promise can excite you and make you very happy, regardless of what you are getting at present.

As you go home with this check for a million dollars, even though it will take a month to clear, you will feel like a millionaire. If you have any credit cards you will probably start spending your money before it comes in. This living in the future is like counting your chickens before they hatch. It leads to certain disappointment, especially if the check never clears.

Let's look at an example of one couple "living in the promise." Daniel, 32, a writer, married Susan, 33, an executive secretary. Daniel was never sure that he wanted to be married to Susan. He also loved another woman. But Susan was sure that he was perfect for her. She even left her previous husband, who was quite famous, to be with Daniel. She said, "I have never met a man as wonderful as you. I know it is meant to be. I can't live without you. Everything is so perfect now in my life."

The message Daniel received was that he could do no wrong. Daniel couldn't believe how easy this relationship was. Susan accepted him unconditionally. She would listen to him, praise him, agree with him, satisfy him, and basically wait on him hand and foot.

Susan was seeing in Daniel her idealized perfect mate. She was immeasurably happy. In Daniel she saw a man who would love her the ways she had always dreamed of. He was kind, considerate, responsible, creative, spiritual, and would be very successful one day. He had tremendous potential. He was loved by everyone. But most of all, he needed her love.

The problem was that Susan did not love Daniel. She was in love with the perfect partner she thought Daniel would become if she was successful in loving him. The other half of the problem was that Daniel did not love her. He loved what he was getting; he needed love and he loved being loved.

Susan's vision of Daniel's potential was very accurate. He was potentially kind, considerate, responsible, etc., and given the right kind of loving support, those qualities would develop. What she didn't see was that he was not "right" for her. She only imagined that if she could be "the one" to love him and support him, he would reward her with his love and they would live happily ever after.

During their relationship, Susan was preoccupied with being a "perfect loving partner," while Daniel was absorbed in being loved. She had a picture of what a loving partner does and she did just that, determined to earn his love. Susan was so consumed by being loving that she never really saw who Daniel was.

On the other hand, Daniel did not really love Susan. Instead, he loved the way he was being treated. As long as she poured on all her love and devotion, he would love her. But when he felt mistreated, he would get upset and withhold his love until Susan apologized and promised to change.

Most of the time, Susan actually felt as though she was getting the love she needed. In truth she was not. For instance, Daniel would ignore her while she was talking. Deep inside she would be hurt. But on the surface she didn't mind, because she believed that if she loved him enough, he would change. Her strong expectation of one day receiving his love acted to suppress her pain.

Just like the person waiting to cash her million-dollar check, Susan faithfully waited with a devoted smile on her face. Her denied feelings of unhappiness and dissatisfaction were eventually expressed in momentary glares of disapproval and resentment. Over time, she unconsciously began trying to mold him into her ideal image.

This underlying tension gave rise to increasing conflict. Susan thought she was loving Daniel, but deep down he felt rejected. He received a very confusing double message. On the surface she was happy with him and said that they were perfect "soul mates." But at a more unconscious level, she was dissatisfied with him and sought to control, change, and rehabilitate him. In subtle ways she would tell him what to do, correcting, nagging, demanding, and complaining.

After two years of marriage, Daniel was no longer attracted to Susan, while Susan realized that she was in love with another man, her doctor. He was now the "perfect partner," the willing recipient of her devotion. Daniel was extremely intolerant of her feelings for another man and they got a divorce.

In counseling, Daniel learned the difference between real love and conditional love. He realized that he had not loved Susan, but instead had loved how he felt when she was adoring him. He later married a woman he truly loved and gradually learned to give love unconditionally.

Susan too went into counseling, where she recognized her pattern of falling in love with a man's potential and then trying to earn his love. She learned that by trying desperately to earn love she was not truly giving to a man, but was actually rejecting him. What she thought would ensure a successful relationship was actually counterproductive.

When a woman is living in the promise, she may appear to be happy and loving toward her man, but she is only loving his potential self, not the real man. What she doesn't realize is that he won't change as long as he is getting the message that she is happy with his behavior.

There is a paradox here. As I have mentioned before, men need to feel loved and accepted the way they are before they can change. Being accepted "as one is" does not mean being accepted "as one will be." Certainly men need appreciation and acceptance. But, on the other hand, they also need honest feedback to determine how they can become more supportive of their woman's changing needs. This is accomplished through loving but honest communication and persistence in asking for support. Then the love, acceptance, and appreciation he receives is real.

Love doesn't require you to be happy about everything your partner says and does. A woman can be loving and accepting and also express feelings of frustration, disappointment, concern, anger, hurt, sadness, and fear. She can be very happy some days and less happy on others. A part of her can be angry and yet another part is happy to be with him. When she is in touch with her true feelings and needs, then when she is happy and appreciative, those feelings will be real and will affect him in a positive way. Only then will he be able to truly respond to her needs.

No man can grow and realize his potential with a woman unless she is real. When a woman lives in the promise, she behaves to her partner as if she is getting her dreams fulfilled. She acts like a millionaire but each day her account diminishes. On an unconscious level, she is becoming increasingly dissatisfied, frustrated, and disappointed. Outwardly she is loving and happy, but her love becomes clingy and has a false ring to it.

He gets mixed messages. On one hand she seems so happy with him; and on the other he feels that nothing he does can truly satisfy her. She is always trying to improve him and mold him into her ideal image. He becomes increasingly turned off. He cannot truly respond to her because she is not communicating the truth. She is not communicating her needs, nor does she share how it feels to not get her needs fulfilled.

At some point, she wakes up and feels the void in her life. The pain becomes so great that she cannot deny it anymore. She goes from elation to depression.

It is not uncommon for a woman to feel she has a happy marriage, then, after ten years, wake up one day and realize how unhappy she has really been. She then rejects her partner for not fulfilling her. This blame is certainly her experience, but it is unfair. He is shocked when he finds that she is so unhappy. He says he is willing to change and she says she is tired of trying to make the relationship work.

Her fatigue arises from years of trying to make it work by pretending that it was working. She was trying to be loving and nice when deep inside she was furious and resentful.

Some women spend years living in the future, denying the pain in the present, while others go through much shorter cycles. She may flip from elation to depression in one week, twice a month, or once in ten or twenty years. The longer she denies her pain, the greater her depression when it comes up.

If a woman is to find more stability, she needs the opportunity to share her insecure feelings and be reassured by her husband or intimate friends. When an overly open person is happy, it may seem to them that they are always happy. When they feel bad, it seems as though *everything* is bad and it always will be that way.

To find greater stability she needs to remember how changeable her reality is. Keeping a journal of feelings, experiences, and impressions is very helpful, as are support groups and therapy.

In most cases, when a woman suddenly discovers that she is not getting what she needs, she feels like a victim. She blames her husband rather than taking responsibility for the mixed messages she was sending the whole time. It is important to note that when she does wake up, in order to find balance she has a valid need to feel like a victim for a while. Then she can work on taking responsibility.

This is not to say that living in the promise is all her fault. Just as women can live in the future, men can live in the past. A man may make his partner happy once and then expect her to stay fulfilled. Men do something nice and they imagine women will be happy forever. Men feel and say "I love you" and think that the loving part of the relationship is handled. They expect women to always know that those loving feelings are there.

Men also can live in denial. Tunnel vision causes them to deny themselves. They also may be unhappy in their relationship and not even know it. They will minimize the importance of problems in the relationship. Like an ostrich that buries its head in the sand, men bury themselves in work and don't acknowledge that there are problems in their love life. Some are so lost in work, they don't even know they need love and are not getting it. They don't realize that although their bank account may be getting bigger, they are emotionally empty.

Like women, men can also live in the future. When they are richer and more successful, they imagine, they and their mates will be happy and fulfilled. The hard truth is that in many cases success actually puts a greater strain on relationships. After "making it" these couples are confronted with the problems they ignored to become successful.

Just as women may wake up and realize that they are unhappy, so, too, men can experience a shift when their inner pain becomes too great. A man wakes and realizes that he wants more from a relationship. The problem is, he thinks he has to find it elsewhere. He doesn't realize that by learning to communicate better, he can heal the pain and fulfill his needs in the present relationship.

Too often the impulse to get a divorce is just burying one's head in the sand — denying that the problem is within and blaming it on the relationship. I have witnessed literally hundreds of couples on the verge of divorce who, through learning to communicate more successfully, were able to create a more loving marriage. When someone wants to get a divorce, I recommend they get help instead. If a couple feels they are tired of trying, they may simply have been trying ways that don't work.

SELF-BLAME VS. BLAMING OTHERS

Another common difference between men and women is that women tend to blame themselves first, while men first blame others.

Whenever there is a problem, conflict, or negative experience, women tend to feel too much responsibility. They first see themselves as responsible, and then they recognize how others share in the responsibility. They are especially hard on and judgmental of themselves, before they look to see how others contributed to the problem. This "blaming inward" is a symptom of open awareness.

Men are apt to accuse others before they look at their responsibility for problems. They tend to be immediately aware of the shortcomings of others, and then they become aware of their own. This "blaming outward" is a symptom of focused awareness.

Focused awareness sees problems as obstacles to achieving a particular outcome or goal. From this focused perspective, any obstruction is perceived first with blame.

On the other hand, open awareness sees problems in a larger context — as outcomes that need to be corrected. From this perspective, a woman is quick to see all the possible ways she could have done something differently in order to have produced a different outcome. Thus she easily feels responsible and accepts blame.

These basic differences give rise to much confusion in relationships. When a man reacts to a problem with blame, the woman mistakenly assumes that he has already considered his responsibility first, as a woman would do, and that his final conclusion is that she is at fault. This gives the impact of his blame much more weight than it really carries. If she can learn not to react defensively to his blame, it gives him a chance to cool down and explore his own responsibility.

When a man has poor self-esteem, his insecurity prevents him from becoming aware of his responsibility; he stays stuck in blame and self-righteousness. Women fail to recognize that a man's sanctimonious attitude is sometimes just a defense mechanism to hide his insecurity. The more insecure a man is, the more confident he may appear. Women don't see through this because when they are insecure, they tend to criticize themselves even more "blaming inward" rather than faulting others "blaming outward."

When a woman blames her partner, he may ignore her complaints because he assumes that she will later see her side of the problem, as a man would do. Many times, a man doesn't take a woman's valid grievances seriously because he assumes that she is totally blaming him without accepting any responsibility herself. He does not realize that she has already looked at her side of the problem and has tried her best to correct it.

In concluding this chapter's exploration of how men and women see the world in different ways, it is important to note again that no person is exclusively masculine or exclusively feminine. Within each person all sorts of combinations of focus and openness are possible.

A man or woman may be overly focused in one area of their life, have a balance of openness and focus in another, and be overly open in still another.

Recognizing these differences helps us to understand how and why relationships with the opposite sex can be so difficult. This increased understanding gives us greater compassion for each other's vulnerabilities, as well as greater clarity to work toward finding solutions to our problems as they arise.

In Chapter 5 we will continue to explore our differences and vulnerabilities by taking a look at the divergent ways that men and women react to stress.

CHAPTER FIVE

HOW MEN AND WOMEN
REACT DIFFERENTLY TO STRESS

The next major category of complementary differences between men and women is the way they react to stress. In a nutshell, masculine awareness reacts to stress in a more objective or analytical way while feminine awareness is more subjective or feeling in its reactions.

Masculine awareness is primarily concerned with what happens in the outer world: *by changing the outside objective world, the masculine nature attempts to reduce stress.* A man reacts to stress by withdrawing into his thoughts to determine what needs to be done in order to reduce the stress.

The feminine psyche is more concerned with the inner subjective world: *by changing herself, the feminine psyche attempts to reduce stress.* A woman primarily reacts to stress with an upsurge of feelings. These feelings allow her to center herself, explore her attitudes, and make changes within herself so that she can reduce her stress. For example, if something is upsetting her she can reduce her stress by becoming more flexible, tolerant, forgiving, patient, understanding, etc. By changing her attitude, she reduces stress and feels better.

BASIC DIFFERENCES IN HANDLING STRESS

Under stress a man will be motivated to affect or control his environment to fulfill his purposes. When undesirable things happen to him, to maintain his control he needs to analyze objectively how his actions are responsible for what happened and realize what he can do to change things.

To understand how he is responsible, he first needs to review the situation. He becomes very alert and attentive to what happened in his external environment. He is then able to determine what *he* did that led to the problem. His objectivity can then be put to determining what he can do to solve the problem. In this way, he can begin to understand and accept responsibility for his part in creating what happened.

Unlike a man, a woman under stress needs to center herself through exploring her feelings. She can then figure out what happened, why it happened, and what should be done about it. If a woman feels and understands her emotions, then her thinking will be open, flexible, and clear.

DESTRUCTIVE EMOTIONS

To react objectively is to detach, observe, and analyze what happened and why it happened. To react subjectively is to feel and explore one's emotional response to a problem or stress; it is to explore how one is affected by what happened and why.

When a man reacts to stress from his feminine, emotional side he tends to lose his positive attitudes. His negative emotions may make him destructive, moody, and self-centered. Negative emotions are not bad. They are a part of healing or de-stressing. But when a man experiences his negative emotions *and* has lost his objectivity, his emotions become mean, threatening, and unloving. When a man is angry it is easy for him to lose control and become violent, break things, or say cruel things. This is his dark side.

This is not to say that men should not be emotional. It is saying that when a man under stress gets into his feelings before he has established an objective perspective, then his emotions will tend to be unloving or destructive. When a man prematurely goes into his feelings there can be other symptoms besides meanness, coldness, cruelty, and violence — he may become moody, needy, wishy-washy, indecisive, apathetic, and apt to procrastinate. The main symptom is that he loses control of himself. He loses control because by indulging in his emotions he has disconnected from his primary source of power — his ability to be objective.

A woman, on the other hand, doesn't necessarily lose her positive feelings when she becomes angry. She has a greater ability to feel angry while maintaining a caring and respect for the other person. She can be angry and still be quite capable of hearing and understanding another's point of view. While anger may make men overly self-righteous and defiant, it can assist a woman in discovering what she deserves.

When a woman is under stress the most important thing she can do is look inside herself to her feelings. Being more subjective, women first need to react emotionally and then they are able to view a situation more objectively. Ideally, she will process her subjective feelings before drawing a conclusion about what is happening objectively. In processing her feelings, she explores and identifies her reactions, then questions their validity and corrects whatever feelings are not consistent with her true self. If she becomes too analytical or objective without considering her subjective feelings, she may experience rigid thinking and become controlling, opinionated, confused, demanding, petty, negative, and frustrated. This is the dark side of a woman.

A man who does not honor and support his objective reactions automatically experiences negative and destructive emotions. A woman who doesn't honor and support her subjective reactions becomes rigid and opinionated in her thinking.

As long as a woman is in touch with her positive feelings and attitudes, her thinking will be clear and flexible. As long as a man's thinking and attitudes are positive, his feelings will be loving and supportive.

BOTH ARE VULNERABLE TO ARGUMENTS

When a woman is emotionally upset but denies or suppresses her feelings in an attempt to be logical and rational, she is bound to experience many arguments with men. At such times, her statements will be rigid and opinionated. This is not only offensive to a man, but threatening. It tells him there is no room for his ideas to be true and that his differing point of view is not being appreciated. While she thinks she is making sense to him, he becomes angry and "dumps out" his negative emotions.

On the other hand, if a man just dumps out his negative feelings without considering his partner's point of view objectively, he can create in her serious defensiveness. Here again, she will tend to be opinionated and rigid. From this perspective, arguments are a "no win" situation and should be avoided.

In an argument, a man can sometimes just dump out all of his negative emotions and feel much better, but leave the woman feeling like a wreck. He can easily apologize for all the mean things he said, and expects her to forget it, just as he has. That is easier said than done. She will probably remember what was said and the pain it caused her for a long time.

In a similar way, if a woman becomes very opinionated, critical, and controlling, it can shut a man down for days. He generally does not know what happened, but he does know that he doesn't want to be open to her again. He decides to keep his thoughts to himself.

Both men and women are vulnerable to arguments, but they are unaware of the injurious effect they have on each other when they argue. The impact of arguments should not be taken lightly. Although the parties are not physically damaging each other, on a psychological level they are bruising each other and it takes time to heal. The closer we are to someone, the easier it is to bruise or to be bruised.

Because men derive their power from their objective analysis of a situation, they are naturally unaware of how delicate and vulnerable a woman's feelings are. He does not sustain his sense of self through his feelings. Hence, he will disregard her feelings as if they are not important, and stress what he experiences as important, namely, his ideas and beliefs. When a man is emotionally upset he is generally incapable of arguing in a way that would not hurt a woman's feelings. Furthermore, men commonly have no idea of how they hurt a woman's feelings. It is as though they are the proverbial bull in a china shop.

It is equally true, but less known, that women can hurt men with their rigid opinions. One disapproving comment like "you should have" from an upset or defensive woman can stop a man dead in his tracks. Men just instinctively shut down. One minute he is open and caring, and the next he is cold and offensive. The big difference between men being hurt and women being hurt is that men are much less *aware* that they are being hurt.

It is only by reading a book like this that a woman could even begin to understand how she is hurting him. He certainly can't tell her. He doesn't even know. This understanding is vital for men; at least when they are shutting down, they can become more objective by understanding what is happening to them. When men lose their objectivity, they move into their dark side; women move to their dark side when they lose their subjectivity.

STRESS MANAGEMENT FOR MEN AND WOMEN

These complementary viewpoints, objectivity and subjectivity, are two ways to decrease stress. The masculine way to reduce stress is to change or eliminate whatever object or situation is causing the stress. The feminine way is to adjust one's self or attitude so that one is not affected in a stressful way, i.e., change the belief or attitude that is causing the stress.

Changing one's behavior is the masculine way to reduce stress, that is, improving the situation by doing something differently. Our feminine side reduces stress by changing attitudes — to improve the situation through forgiveness, love, gratitude, or tolerance.

HOW WOMEN GO OUT OF BALANCE

What typically happens in a relationship is that a woman will tend to repeatedly compromise and adjust herself to preserve harmony and avoid confrontation. On a conscious level, she will try to change herself. After she has sacrificed or surrendered her position repeatedly, she will begin to feel resentful that he is not doing the same. Now, on a less conscious level, she will begin to try to change her partner. All communication at this point becomes somewhat manipulative and very distasteful to him. He will inevitably reject her or rebel.

A woman shifts into manipulating when her first means of getting what she needs fails. Her problem is that no one ever taught her what to change about herself to get what she needs. To change herself does not mean to give herself up; it does not mean to act a certain way. The emphasis is not on changing her behavior and speech, but on changing her negative attitudes, such as resentment and mistrust. It means to purify or release her negative feelings so she can be more of who she truly is. This self-discovery can be difficult if she has not been taught how to transform negative feelings. In childhood most girls only learn how to suppress, deny, and repress their feelings. They learn to be good, nice, and happy all the time, even when that is not how they are truly feeling. Suppression may appear to make her more loving and positive, but in truth it disconnects her from her true self, being, or "center." To effectively cope with stress, a woman needs to center herself. If she remains resentful or uncentered for long, she will inevitably become more manipulative or controlling.

HOW A WOMAN CHANGES

To cope with stress, a woman can change herself in a very natural way. In a sense, she is really not changing, but becoming more of who she already is. Being subjective in nature, she changes herself through sharing and expressing her feelings, thoughts, and wishes without being invalidated. To do this she needs to be heard with caring, understanding, and respect. These very important aspects of love nurture her and help to center her.

But, if she keeps her feelings to herself, she will gradually lose touch with who she is; her thinking will become shallow, superficial, and rigid. She will not be able to lovingly and gracefully adapt to the stresses of life, work, and relationships. She will be consumed by trying to adjust her behavior and speech to win the love of others. From this place of seeking to earn love, she will try to change others to get the love she needs. At this point she loses her ability to adapt and change in response to stress. She is unable to sustain a truly loving and positive attitude.

At times of stress, it is easy for a woman with low self-esteem to adjust her behavior and speech in relating to others. It is much more difficult to change or transform her feelings. She may give up the appearance of a loving and giving person, but deep inside she is hiding a storehouse of resentment, mistrust, and dissatisfaction. These negative feelings weaken her identity and her relationships.

HOW MEN GO OUT OF BALANCE

In a complementary way, men in relationships will at first be objective and then become subjective. This means that in the beginning of a relationship a man tries to improve things by making his partner happy when she appears unhappy. His instinctive strategy is to change the object: if she is unhappy, then he tries to make her happy by fulfilling her needs.

If, however, he begins to feel that he can't make a difference, he goes out of balance, becomes more subjective, and his attitude changes. He may feel self-righteous, defiant, resentful, spiteful, punitive, unforgiving, and judgmental. As a result, he becomes weak, moody, insecure, and passive. He loses his confidence and is no longer willing to take risks. He may even develop negative patterns for "getting his way" through emotional outbursts and tantrums. It is hard for him to shake off his negative mood when he has lost his objectivity.

HOW A MAN CHANGES

A man, being objective in nature, can best change himself through recognizing and solving problems outside himself. For example, a man becomes more loving and sensitive by recognizing how others are hurt or affected by certain things he does or does not do. Through a willingness to change his behavior he becomes a better person. By solving the problem, he automatically changes.

When he sees "himself" (as opposed to his behavior) as the problem, it is very difficult for him to change. This is hard for a woman to recognize because, being subjective in nature, if she identifies something about herself that needs to change, she can begin to change it by just choosing to *be* different. A man changes by deciding to *behave* differently. While self-awareness is the basic ingredient enabling women to change, objective awareness is necessary for a man to change: he needs to understand the problem outside himself.

A man feels compelled to change when he feels appreciated and accepted, but also recognizes that he is not creating the desired result and that he is responsible. A woman succeeds in changing the way she feels when she feels loved, understood, and safe, but recognizes that her feeling reactions are not true expressions of who she truly is, i.e., they do not reflect her loving and responsible self.

When a man repeatedly fails to satisfy his mate after trying everything he thinks should work, inevitably he gives up and becomes passively accepting. Instead of coping by changing his behavior, he defends his actions and blames her. This is weakening for a man. He needs to understand how he can make a difference; then he is inspired and remotivated.

HOW SHE UNKNOWINGLY TURNS HIM OFF

As a man continues to fail to satisfy and fulfill his female partner, he gradually changes his approach. He begins to deny his natural masculine impulses. He stops being responsible and decisive, feeling that whatever he decides is never good enough. He begins to turn off this part of him because it is too painful to make mistakes for which he might be corrected. He stops taking risks because it is most unpleasant for a man to think that he is not being appreciated, accepted, or trusted by the people he loves and who know him best.

When his plans fail and a woman corrects his decisions without being asked to, she unknowingly hurts him and lays a foundation for him to become less motivated and caring. He begins to feel unwilling to give of himself, because it is too painful to experience her correcting him. When she corrects him or is disappointed by him, deep inside he feels inadequate and powerless.

Women correct men because they think it will motivate or help them to change. The truth is, it just makes them more stubborn and unyielding. Women have no idea of how they affect a man when they try to improve him.

When a man fails, he needs time to mull things over and gradually assume responsibility for his mistake. Unfortunately, at such times a woman has a compulsion to make some offensive comment, like "I told you so," or some correction like "You should have . . . ," or one of those famous last words "You know that . . . ," or a rhetorical question like "Why didn't you . . . ," or a generalization like "You never . . . ," or a sympathetic gesture like "I know you must feel bad" (I feel so sorry for you).

She mistakenly assumes that these kinds of comments will get him to realize and remember his mistake. Their actual effect is to stimulate his self-righteousness and forgetfulness. Even if he acknowledges his mistake, he will forget the lesson he should have learned. A man remembers and learns from his mistakes when he is not corrected or rejected for them. He needs the support to correct himself.

What makes the above statements ineffective is that they are all attempts to help him feel or perform better *when he hasn't asked for help*. One of the most valuable things a person could say to a man under stress is "What happened?" This helps him to center himself by becoming more objective. Then, if and when he becomes talkative, ask him "why" he thinks it happened.

WHAT A MAN NEEDS

During a stressful situation, a man needs time to mull over his thoughts and feelings until he is able to understand what he did and how he could have done it differently. Then he will feel comfortable talking about what happened and why it happened. At this stage he becomes more accountable for his mistakes. Then he can change himself without repressing his masculine nature.

It is as though a man cannot admit he erred unless he can figure out a way he could have acted differently. He can recognize that he made a mistake when he realizes, "If I had known then what I now know, I could have and would have done things differently."

WHAT A WOMAN NEEDS

When a woman is upset she needs time to explore her feelings through sharing before she is able to be her loving, appreciative, accepting, and trusting self. When she is unable to explore her feelings she becomes overwhelmed, overreacts, and then feels exhausted. At that point, she requires even more time to come back to her center. What she needs most from a man is his caring and attention, respect for her needs, and understanding.

Men typically go into judgment and blame when a woman is upset. She needs, instead, for him to listen and support her without trying to fix her or correct her feelings. He must consciously resist trying to give advice or telling her how she should feel. When men truly realize how they unknowingly hurt women, they automatically become more considerate and respectful.

HOW MEN HURT WOMEN

Just as it is hard for a woman not to correct a man when he is irresponsible and fails her in some way, it is equally difficult for a man not to judge a woman's upset feelings as weak, crazy, foolish, bad, stupid, bitchy, and selfish. Little does he realize that when he casually makes his judgments he is hurting her in a much deeper way than he imagines.

A man's judgments cause a woman to go off center and lose herself. She begins to take on the negative qualities he judges her to have. For example, when he judges her to be selfish and unloving it can have the effect of making her more selfish and unloving. He judges her as crazy; she begins to actually feel crazy. Similarly, when a woman criticizes a man by telling him what he should do, he will become even more rigid in his way of doing things. Judgments that arise from resentment never serve to improve one's partner.

When a woman is upset or under stress, she needs the time and support to discover for herself how she can change to be more loving, accepting, appreciative, and trusting. This will naturally happen when she is able to share and explore her inner feelings.

Because men and women do not understand their respective stress reactions and the unique needs that they possess, they lose touch with their true or more mature selves and become possessed by the grip of their "dark sides." Their inherent positive characteristics become overshadowed by negative feelings, beliefs, perspectives, and attitudes.

OUR DARK SIDES

When a man is unable to support himself or get the support he needs as he is going through his stress reaction, inevitably his dark side will be provoked when he feels hurt, offended, or wounded. Similarly, when a woman doesn't get the support she needs her dark side emerges. Generally a man's dark side surfaces when he loses his objectivity. A woman's dark side emerges when she loses her centeredness.

When a man is unable to be objective, he starts to withdraw — and eventually shuts down his feelings — to assist him in becoming more objective. By being objective, a man is able to recognize his responsibility in creating what happened. *At this point it is now safe for him to be subjective*; he can safely explore how he has been affected (his emotions) and also explore ways he could change.

As we have discussed before, if a man is unable to maintain his objectivity when his subjective feelings emerge, then his feelings will tend to reflect his dark side. He may become moody, irritable, cruel, unfair, and violent. "Shutting down" prevents these feelings from coming forth. It is like a breaker switch that prevents a circuit from overloading.

Many times a woman will try to get a man to share his feelings when he needs to be silent and mull things over in his mind. She has no idea that she is fanning the fire of negative and dark reactions in this man by trying to draw out his feelings. She does this instinctively because being essentially feminine or subjective, she knows that she needs someone to draw her out when she is upset and she especially needs to explore her feelings.

MASCULINE VIOLENCE

When a man is hurt, if he indulges in feeling hurt emotions before he objectively analyzes what has happened, why it happened, and what he can do about it, he will tend to overreact with inferior emotions. This overreaction is not so terrible, except that men tend to act it out.

Probably the most negative form of acting out hurt is revenge. When a man is hurt he generally feels a compulsion to release his hurt by inflicting it on someone else. This is a very important element of the male psyche. Violence is generally the compulsion of the male psyche to release its pain and feel better. *Breaking something or someone is a backward or subconscious way of saying "this is what you have done to me."* As men learn to communicate more effectively this tendency gradually lessens.

In a primitive way, when a man is possessed by his pain, by inflicting it on others he can objectively experience his pain and release it. This means that he can see, hear, or feel the pain of another person, and it reflects his own.

Dick and Lynn were married for two years when he found out she was having a secret affair. Dick felt a compulsion to hurt Lynn back and make her suffer the pain he felt. To punish her, he became violent. He slapped her and called her abusive names. Eventually he felt better and all was forgiven. In this example, Dick began to feel better when Lynn appeared to suffer as much as he had suffered. In a primitive way he felt, "Now she understands my pain. She will not do that again."

In more extreme cases a man may even delight in another's pain and suffering. The most common example of this we can see in the movies. When the good guy, whose children were murdered, finally kills the really bad guy, everyone rejoices. They feel better. The pain of injustice is magically released when the "bad guy" suffers and is abused. This phenomenon is also true in women but it more strongly relates to men.

Ultimately, a person can only rejoice in the suffering of another if he or she is deeply wounded and unable to heal his or her wounds in a more civilized manner. This observation helps to explain the mysterious satisfaction the male psyche gets from hurting others or getting even.

WORLD PEACE

The inclination to release pain through hurting back is the basis of all violence and war. As men learn to communicate their pain they will become less violent. There is, however, a condition that must be met before men can communicate their pain. To communicate their pain, they must first be able to feel it. To feel his pain, a man needs to develop his feminine side.

Through listening to and feeling the pain of others, a man's feminine side (subjective awareness) is awakened, and he is able to feel and communicate his own pain. Then, through sharing his pain, he is able to heal his hurt and find relief without resorting to revenge.

In teaching my seminars on improving relationships, I witness men who have never cried opening up and feeling their pain and finding relief. Without this heartfelt experience of listening to others share their pain in a safe, supportive, and respectable situation, men cannot access and heal their own inner turmoil and pain. Their fathers were alienated from their own feelings, and so the next generation, too, is unable to feel. As a result, men remain trapped in a cycle of hurting back whenever they are hurt.

Taking seminars or being in a group that is safe and supportive atmosphere for sharing is the fastest and most effective way to develop this ability. Personal therapy and counseling can only be effective to the degree that the client is in touch with his feelings. It is a long process for a man to develop the ability to feel, especially if his therapy is limited to personal counseling. As he is able to feel more, the effectiveness of personal counseling increases dramatically.

Support groups are becoming increasingly popular. Men are becoming less dependent on getting even or hurting back to feel relief. This gradual transformation not only leads to more loving relationships, but is a basis for truly creating peace in our world. Our personal success in being free of violence will be mirrored in the world when we are able to maintain love and nonviolence in our relationships. From this perspective, peace in this world is a real possibility.

INFLICTING PAIN

When a man is hurt through some interaction, if he is unable to feel and communicate his pain (and thus heal it), then he is compulsively locked into hurting back. He can only react to meanness with meanness. He cannot express an appropriate firmness and justice from a compassionate place in his heart. The tendency to hurt back runs deep.

When Dick feels betrayed by Lynn's infidelity he is compelled to hurt her back. He wants her to suffer as he has suffered. This compulsion gives rise to violence, vindictiveness, revenge, and cruelty. Once she has suffered in reaction to his revenge, and he can see and feel her pain, he is able to feel relief. The cycle is complete.

To break out of this uncivilized cycle of revenge and payback, a man must be able to feel and communicate his pain. If Dick can communicate his pain to Lynn, the compulsion for revenge will be fulfilled without hurting back. Instead of acting out his hurt through revenge, he has communicated his hurt.

If Dick can communicate his sorrow, Lynn may naturally feel an empathetic and compassionate response. This compassionate response shows him that his pain has been acknowledged. When she feels his hurt — which she can do if she is not attacked with it — he will feel healed and be capable of forgiveness.

Most men, however, cannot communicate their upset feelings in a nonthreatening way, especially if they have been deeply wounded. To begin to develop an ability to communicate pain in a safe way, a man needs to listen to the pain of others who have suffered similar injustice. In hearing the pain of others, he is able to feel, share, and heal his own pain without taking revenge. As a result, he becomes more capable of hearing a woman's pain. He becomes more compassionate and understanding.

It is important to point out here that when a man is incapable of being compassionate, this does not mean that he does not care about his partner. When a man becomes detached, a woman often assumes that he doesn't care about her hurt. In truth, he does care, but becomes detached because he is getting in touch with his resistance to feeling his own pain. His apparent resistance to her is not a sign of his uncaring, but a symptom of his inability to feel his own emotions.

As men learn to listen and then feel and communicate their own hurt, they can be free of the unconscious compulsion to inflict pain. Men who cannot communicate and release their subjective pain will continue to inflict hurt on their partners in order to feel a relief within themselves.

PASSIVE AGGRESSION

Some men reading this description of masculine violence may feel they are exceptions to this. But if they look deeply into their behavior they may see the various ways they withhold themselves to secretly punish or get even with others. Revenge may even be disguised as helping a person by teaching him or her a lesson. Many times a person is completely unaware of his aggressive tendencies. This unconscious aggression becomes passive aggression. Rather than *acting* in a way that inflicts pain, their *inaction* causes pain.

Some common examples of passive aggression are being late, forgetfulness, loss of sexual appetite, fatigue, unwillingness to share thoughts and feelings, uncaring attitude, stubbornness, rebellion, secret judgments, having a holier-than-thou attitude, spiritual or self-righteous arrogance, and feeling satisfied when somebody "bad" suffers rather than feeling compassion for their pain.

RIGHTEOUS AGGRESSION

Another way men express their aggression is through being self-righteous. A man will justify his punishing behavior by blaming it on another. In a relationship he may withhold his love, sex, kindness, and attention, or he may directly punish through violence, meanness, and name calling. The deeper abuse, however, is that he makes his partner responsible for his negative and unloving behavior.

Certainly his negative behavior can be *understood* by hearing what was done to him, but this does not *justify* it. He feels he is right in hurting her because she has hurt him. He believes that she is responsible for his destructive and negative behavior, and deserves to be punished. This is never true. Two wrongs do not make a right.

At a global level, to justify their inner urge for violence, men imagine an enemy worthy of such treatment. In truth, no human being deserves to suffer. Men justify violence by defining it as a solution rather than a problem. As long as violence is seen this way, it will persist.

Until men are able to heal their pain, they will feel a compulsion to inflict their pain on others as a means to create change; they will continue to rationally justify their violence as a necessary evil. In reality, violence will only be a solution until men are capable of feeling and communicating their pain without inflicting it. The old way (violence) will be with us until we become adept in the new ways (healing and effective communication and negotiation).

Peace in our relationships and our world hinges on the development of our feminine side. In the future, compassion for the pain of others will motivate the decisions of the powerful, rather than this unconscious compulsion to punish.

FEMININE VIOLENCE

Woman can of course be violent, but this generally occurs when her feminine side has been hurt so much that she becomes more masculine to protect herself. Violence is not her first reaction. When women are violent, to whatever degree, the cause is their masculine side controlling them.

Essentially nonviolent, women may subject themselves to violence rather than becoming violent themselves. When they are abused, their inclination is to make others feel guilty or responsible for their hurt. Through this process, the female side feels relief. Just as the male side of us obtains relief through hurting back, the female side finds relief through making the abuser feel bad or look bad.

To truly assuage her hurt, a woman primarily needs her pain to be heard, shared, or felt by others. She needs compassion and understanding to release her pain. When she is unable to elicit enough compassion, she unconsciously seeks to compensate by trying to get sympathy. The strategy employed by the female psyche is to induce guilt in others, hoping that they will change their ways. Also, by making another feel guilty, a woman is able to prove to herself that she did not deserve such abuse. Instead of making matters better, this strategy hurts a man and he then seeks revenge.

As women are becoming more enlightened, they are beginning to become more aware of how they may be indirectly abusing men. The most powerful way to hurt a man is to take away your trust, acceptance, and appreciation of him through opinionated blame, doubt, criticism, resentment, and judgment. When women retaliate through negative feelings and attitudes, they generally don't realize how much they hurt men. They may not even be aware that they are doing it. In an equally abusive relationship, women generally feel the man is much more hurtful, because male abusiveness is so much more obvious. A woman can project guilt on her partner just by the tone of her voice, while a man tends to abuse more overtly.

As we explored earlier, when the female psyche is abused and a woman is unable to share her hurt and be heard, she falls into feeling guilty and unworthy. She is unconsciously driven to release her guilt by showing how others are guilty or responsible for her hurt. This relieves her of some of her pain, but only temporarily. Real healing has not occurred.

Women have felt compelled to be victims in order to warrant the sympathy of others. A woman may feel that she does not have the right to receive compassion unless she has been unjustly and unfairly treated or abused. *In a backward way, by being victimized she feels more worthy of love, compassion, and support.* Through learning to communicate her pain without making her partner a bad person, she can release this attitude and receive compassion without having to be an abused victim or martyr.

In some cases, a woman will begin to punish herself when her hurt goes unhealed and unheard. There are a variety of ways and degrees to which a woman hurts herself. She may deprive herself of fulfilling experiences or engage in self-destructive behavior. She may get sick or berate herself through criticism, doubt, and judgment. She may continue to give more in a relationship even though she is getting less.

One way of viewing illness is to recognize it as an expression of unhealed psychological pain. Disease is the "self" punishing the "self" through the body. From this perspective, illness and disease are manifestations of the dark side of our female self. Just as the male side punishes externally, the female side punishes itself.

In a positive sense, the male side of us is responsible to be of service to others, while the female side of us is responsible for self-healing and personal growth. Through hearing the pain of our female self, the tendency toward sickness and suffering is healed.

From this perspective, war and violence are the expressions of man's inability to heal his hurt; disease and weakness are the outcomes of woman's inability to heal her hurt. Of course these are very broad generalizations. Just as women can be violent, men get sick. But ultimately it is our male side that abuses outward through actions and our female side that inflicts abuse on itself.

NEGATIVE SELF-TALK

The main way a woman hurts herself, however, is subjectively. Through negative self-talk she abuses herself. As a result she may decide to outwardly and objectively punish or deprive herself. The major symptom of negative self-talk is a feeling of unworthiness, helplessness, and self-pity. Through self-pity she denies her power to create more in her life and indirectly blames others, thus affirming her powerlessness.

For example, feeling self-pity, she may say, "No one appreciates me; no one knows how hard I work and how much I sacrifice." In affirming "poor me" she is denying her inner potential to be happy and improve her life. In this way, self-pity is a form of inner violence. Just as outward violence restricts another's potential to be happy, through self-pity we restrict our own ability to be happy.

There are many ways we hurt ourselves through self-pity. Let's look at a few:

"Poor me, if only my partner were not so mean and uncaring I could be happy."

"Poor me, because he didn't call my whole day was ruined."

"Poor me, there is nothing I can do about it: I am completely powerless."

"Poor me, I didn't make that investment."

"Poor me, I have so much to do and I can't do it."

"Poor me, there is no one to love me; I am all alone and no one cares."

"Poor me, I give so much to my children and I get nothing back."

"Poor me, for years I gave and gave and gave and I got nothing back."

"Poor me, I am such a loving person but I'm the one without a relationship."

"Poor me, I have so much talent but no opportunity."

"Poor me, I didn't buy real estate in the 1970s."

"Poor me, they have money and I don't."

"Poor me, I gave the best years of my life and now I am alone, while he remarried in six months."

"Poor me, I am so good and noble and I have been betrayed."

"Poor me, I work twice as hard and I get less."

In each of these examples we limit ourselves to the experience of unhappiness by denying our potential to feel good about ourselves and our lives. Our ability to love and feel grateful is restricted. In addition, through feeling sorry for ourselves we indirectly send out a message of blame and induce guilt in others. The victim or martyr does not realize that when she feels sorry for herself, she may get more love, but she is reinforcing the pattern of being a victim.

As women learn to share their hurt without self-pity and resentment and consequently receive the compassion they need, they gradually can release the tendency to feel self-pity. As men learn to share their pain and listen to and understand the pain of others, they gradually release the tendency to be mean or violent. Given the needed understanding, love, and support, it seems almost miraculous how quickly a person can begin to release these deep and unconscious patterns. In teaching weekend seminars I have repeatedly witnessed such transformations.

The better we can learn to understand our different reactions and needs while under stress, the more hope we feel for our relationships as well as for the world. As men learn to listen to the feelings of women they become more aware of their own feelings; they become more compassionate, caring, understanding, and respectful of women. As women feel this compassion, they are able to share more of themselves and heal their hurts in a journey of increasing love, trust, acceptance, forgiveness, gratitude, appreciation, and empowerment.

Through learning to take care of ourselves at times of stress, rather than demanding that our partners fix us, we release the impulse to make others responsible for us. We then enjoy the beautiful experience of feeling responsible to be all we can be and skillfully supporting the ones we love, especially in times of stress.

In summary, under stress a man needs time and space to find objective solutions (positive behavior), and a woman needs time and attention to find her subjective solutions (positive attitudes). When they are unable to give themselves the support they need, they run the risk of being possessed by their dark sides. To avoid the negative tendencies of our dark sides, it is essential to recognize the distinct symptoms of increasing stress.

In the next chapter we will explore these different symptoms of stress in men and women. Understanding these differences can make it easier to support each other in times of stress. When you can recognize your own stress symptoms, you will be better equipped to come back to balance.

CHAPTER SIX

THE SYMPTOMS
OF STRESS

There are three major symptoms of stress in men. It is important to recognize these symptoms because women tend to take them personally and mistakenly assume matters are worse than they are. These three symptoms of stress are withdrawing, grumbling, and shutting down. When this happens, a woman generally feels unloved and afraid that things in the relationship are not good. A correct interpretation of these symptoms can help a woman relax and more skillfully support her partner in coping with stress and coming back into balance.

Likewise, there are three major indications of stress in women, which men tend to take personally and misinterpret. Her symptoms of stress are overwhelm, overreaction, and exhaustion. When a woman gets upset, instead of knowing how to support her, a man usually gets upset that she is upset, making matters worse. Through learning to recognize these stress reactions and interpret them correctly, men can also relax more and learn to better support their partners.

First we will explore the three common male stress reactions and then the three common female stress reactions.

MALE STRESS REACTION #1:
HE WITHDRAWS

A man's first reaction to stress is that he withdraws and detaches from the situation. While under stress a man tends to deny his feelings and emotional pain, and automatically withdraws. The overall symptom of withdrawal is that communication stops. He is unwilling to talk. Inevitably his female partner takes this personally, not recognizing that he is withdrawing because it is his way of coping with stress.

She mistakenly assumes the problem is much worse — she assumes he does not love her. This is understandable, because for her to withdraw would be a symptom of increased resentment in the relationship and a lack of caring and concern. She does not naturally relate to his feeling less concern for loved ones when under stress. Just the opposite, the more stressed she becomes, the more concern she feels for the welfare of those she cares about. His detachment at such times is, for her, very confusing and obviously very hard to understand.

Just as he is unaware of his pain, he becomes blind to the pain of others. He is unable to be compassionate. He minimizes the importance of problems that come up around him. When his empathy is needed, he automatically withdraws to avoid feeling his own pain.

He acts as though everything is fine; yet, because he is suppressing his feelings, he becomes distant and withdrawn. He will reject all forms of intimate communication or any attempts to assist him. A woman needs to understand that when a man is distant or withdrawn, he is struggling inside to resist his painful feelings. Any attempt on her part to help him will probably be resisted or rejected.

For example, when Bill is unable to solve a problem at work, he seems preoccupied and distant because he is in this first stress reaction. When he starts to withdraw, his wife Mary generally takes it personally and assumes that he no longer cares about her. In truth, he does care deep in his heart, but his caring is being overshadowed by his need to withdraw.

MALE STRESS REACTION #2:
HE GRUMBLES

Any attempt to make Bill change his mood may cause him to become irritable. If he does not release his stress and find balance, things just get worse. He becomes grouchy and grumpy, especially if his wife Mary tries to cheer him up or tries to create more intimacy. Any attempt to change him, or any request for him to do something will be met with resistance and grumbles.

In resisting Mary's attempts to change him or help him, Bill may become more testy. In this stress reaction, Bill seems dissatisfied with everything. Nothing excites him or turns him on. Much of the time when he is in this space he has no idea of how intimidating, threatening, unloving, and resistant he appears.

If he is asked to do something, he may moan, groan, scowl, growl, or mumble various expressions of resistance. Women generally misinterpret these grumbles as an unwillingness to support. They are not.

When a man is under stress he becomes increasingly focused. If he is focused on achieving a goal and he is interrupted by a request to do something not pertaining to his present focus, he will feel a resistance to shifting gears. The symptom of this resistance is grumbling.

For example, Bill is sitting on the couch relaxing and reading a magazine. His focus is reading the article. Seeing that he is not busy, his wife asks him to empty the trash. He acts as though his wife's request is a major interruption and an intrusion.

Mary cannot understand this reaction because women are much more capable of shifting from one thing to another. Men, however, tend to adhere rigidly to one task or concern at a time. Then, when that is finished, they go on to focus on something else. Thus, when a man is asked to do something that interrupts his present focus, he will tend to complain. The more stress he feels in shifting goals midstream, the more he will protest.

These grumbles are actually a symptom of his unfolding willingness to support. If he does not grumble at all but sits in silence, that is a sign that he is thinking about whether he is willing to do it. If he grumbles, that means he *is* willing to do it but is resisting. This resistance is natural and common in men under stress.

This increased male resistance is related to one very important physiological difference between men and women. Women have more corpus callosum in their brains. This is the connective tissue that joins the left and right hemispheres of the brain. Recent discoveries have revealed that because women have more corpus callosum, they are able to access more quickly and more readily different parts of the brain. This makes women more flexible in their ability to shift goals in midstream.

A woman only grumbles in response to a request if she feels that she is being unfairly used. Her grumbling has little to do with shifting goals. A man under stress grumbles because he is being asked for shift goals. He will grumble even if he feels the request is fair. He will even grumble if he is willing to do it. His grumbling is his way of *shifting gears*.

Women are generally intimidated by men in this stage. They are afraid to ask for support to help because they can sense a man's put-upon attitude. She assumes that he will think her request is unfair or invalid and feel resentful, because that is what would cause her to grumble. When a woman is asked for support and she grumbles, this indicates that she feels the request is unfair and she resents the requester. If she actually does what is asked of her, she will resent him even more. Women misinterpret a man's grumbles to have the same meaning they have for a woman.

As I was just writing this section, my wife entered my office and said in an almost playful way, "Interruptions, interruptions. I need your attention for just a moment. We can schedule your (medical) appointment on Monday at 6:00 or Wednesday at 11:00. What do you want me to do?" I observed myself feeling incredible resistance to her interruption. I put my hands up to my face with a sigh of frustration, and then shifted gears. I noticed she was very accepting of my frustration. She was able to correctly interpret my frustration without taking it personally. With this understanding she was able to be light and playful about her request, and even anticipate my cranky reaction. As quick as my grumbles came on, they went away.

There is another reason a woman misinterprets a male's grumbles. When he reacts peevishly to a request she assumes that he is saying the score in the relationship is uneven. Women assume this because they themselves are great scorekeepers. Just as they are good at giving and giving, they tend to be just as good at keeping track of how much they are getting back.

A woman has the amazing talent to continue to give with a smile on her face even when the score is 20 to 0. When the score becomes 30 to 0 (in her opinion), she will begin to grumble the way men do. What women don't realize is that when a man complains, it has little to do with them or the score in the relationship. Rather than risk his grumbles, she will avoid asking for help — and add another point to the score.

THE WOMANLY ART OF ASKING

To get support from a man, a woman must learn to ask. If she doesn't ask, she will not get. Women presume that if they just keep giving more and more, their male partners will surely feel more generous and give more in return. It certainly increases your chances of receiving if you give of yourself in a relationship, but more important is learning the art of asking without demanding, and asking directly rather than indirectly and subtly implying your needs.

Women are afraid to ask. Those grumbles are intimidating. She is not only afraid of not getting the support, but she is even more afraid of how much worse things will be if he does support her and then feels even more resentment. If she asks and he does help her with a grumble, what she doesn't know is that after a short time, he will recover and the grumble will not get worse.

As Bill begins to achieve his new goal (emptying the trash), he starts to feel better. If he comes in and she is appreciative, then his grumbles are long gone and he probably feels better than before.

This is an idea foreign to women, because if they were in a state where they felt like grumbling, and they responded to another request, they would generally feel even more fatigued and resentful after achieving the goal. Because this is a woman's reality, she projects it onto a man. She is afraid to ask for support because she imagines he will feel even worse and grumble more.

To overcome this intimidation, a woman needs to practice asking for help, and practice giving her partner the space to refuse. Giving someone the space to say no is an essential part of the art of asking.

Without this kind of acceptance and openness a request becomes a demand; it becomes an obligation or a "you should." To ask without being open is apt to make things worse.

If he says no and she doesn't make him wrong, that does not go unnoticed. He will feel a greater willingness to support her next request. Asking for support openly will at least let him know that the score is slowly becoming uneven. It will let him know that he is needed but not criticized or judged. It will let him know that she is gracefully deferring her needs for his, but continuing to want his support. It will give him more opportunities to help her and make her life easier.

This is the opposite of what many women do. They don't ask for help, but secretly resent a man for not being helpful. Then if the score is 20 to 0 they will ask, and if he resists, they react with resentment: "How dare he complain when I have done so much for him while he sits around." Even when they make a request, in anticipation of his grumble, they toughen up inside and demand, rather than ask. It is hard for a man to respond to a demand or a guilt trip. He wants to give freely, not because he is under an obligation.

This analysis helps women to understand why men appear lazy in relationships. Often a man assumes that the score is even because a woman continues to give when she is not getting. He can't imagine that the score is 20 to 0 when she continues to do things with a smile on her face. After all, if a man thinks he is giving more than he is getting, he tends to immediately stop giving until it is even again.

The other instruction for a woman to remember when dealing with a man's grumbles is to ask for support and then be quiet. Maintain silence. Don't defend the request with all the reasons why he "should" do it, or it is his turn to do it, or you have done it twenty more times. Just ask and be silent. This is the famous pregnant pause. It contains all possibilities.

Let him grumble as he gets dressed and bangs out the door. Then after he has gone, feel your appreciation for his love and support. When he returns let him be your knight in shining armor who saved you from having to go out into the night. Next time he will grumble a little less, until eventually he will look forward to doing supportive things for you because you are so appreciative. This loving acceptance of his grumpy side is what helps to cure him of it.

MALE STRESS REACTION #3:
HE SHUTS DOWN

If Bill is feeling even more stress, eventually he will completely "shut down." It is as though in an instant his feelings are completely gone. He becomes unfeeling and cold.

When a man shuts down it is an automatic reaction. Women do not understand this reaction correctly, because if a woman shuts down she does so by choice. She feels a man is unfairly punishing her when he shuts down. She imagines that he has some control over it. In truth, a man shuts down automatically when he feels painful emotions arising into his consciousness. It is a defense mechanism over which he has little control. When a man is shutting down, he is just asking for some space, but a woman interprets it as a declaration of complete rejection.

In Native American tradition when a brave was upset, he would withdraw into his cave and no one was to follow. They understood that men under stress need to be alone. The brave needed to go inside and mull over the problem that was disturbing him. His squaw was warned that if she ran after him, she would be burned by the dragon that lived in the cave. The brave would come out when he was ready.

When a man shuts down, that is a warning sign not to try to help him in any way. Just give him space and understand that he is silently dealing with his pain and frustration. Appreciate that he cares so much that he wants to solve his problem. Trust that he has the resources to handle what he needs to handle. Don't touch him. The Indians warned of the dragon, because when a man is shut down and he is provoked and drawn out, he will move into his dark side.

WHY MEN SHUT DOWN

Most men react to intense stress by shutting down their feelings and looking objectively at a situation. Even if a man's female side is overly developed in many areas of his life, when he is under stress he will most likely react by pulling back and trying to figure out what has happened. This is called mulling it over. His whole awareness contracts and becomes focused. He then tries to pull out of it by detaching himself from his emotional reactions. Becoming objective in this way, he can begin to recover.

Because a man's essential nature is masculine, to combat stress he needs to pull back and take some alone time. This pulling back intensifies his masculine strength. This is not a time for him to explore his emotional reactions. His imbalance during stress makes him inept at processing his subjective feeling reactions. For most men, if they are confronted with stress, their first reaction is to disconnect from their feelings in order to objectively review what has happened.

Women are greatly threatened by a man's withdrawal, because for a woman to shut down, she must be feeling so upset that she wants to reject a person. This is not the case for a man. Whereas men shut down automatically in reaction to stress, women shut down as the result of a conscious decision. A woman will only shut down after she has given up on a person. If she has been repeatedly hurt by someone and has lost all trust and acceptance, then she will make a conscious decision to shut down to her feelings. Women do not realize that a man becomes detached just to regain his balance and avoid the weakening onslaught of "negative emotions."

A man has the capacity to close down completely in an instant. A woman, on the other hand, gradually closes down over time. For her it is a gradual process of building a wall of accumulated resentment, brick by brick. Eventually, when the wall is built, she chooses to shut down to protect herself from further abuse.

Just as a man can close down in an instant, he can open up again in an instant. Women generally mistrust a man when he opens up that readily. They assume that he is just pretending to feel better. From a woman's perspective, she could never close down and open up so quickly. When a woman closes down she needs to do a lot of talking and healing to open up again. When a man closes down he generally just needs a lot of space, and then he can quickly open up again.

If a woman tries to pull a man out of his shutdown, it provokes his dark side. To ask him what he is feeling — at a time when his feelings are shut down — is asking for trouble. When a man is upset he will naturally tend to go to his "cave" to cool off and figure things out.

After a woman has been burned a few times she becomes even more afraid of a man when he shuts down. She does not realize that the dragon only comes out when he is pulled out of the cave before he is ready.

Men need to understand that because a woman doesn't readily shut down, she instinctively misinterprets when he does, and assumes she is in big trouble. She imagines the problem to be much bigger than it is. With this insight he can help matters by simply reassuring her that when he shuts down, he will be back and then he will talk about it.

I suggest that when men shut down, they say to their partners, "I need some time to think. I'll be back and then we can talk." In the early stages of practicing this, it may be that all he can say is, "I need some time to think and I'll be back." At such times, to say "and then we'll talk" is too big a commitment and too much against the male nature. As men become more balanced it becomes easier for them to talk about what was upsetting them.

When a man comes back from being shut down, he may have nothing to say because he has realized there was nothing to be upset about. He realizes that he was overreacting or viewing something the wrong way, and now everything is fine. In most cases, when a man says things are fine after he returns from shutting down, a woman needs to trust him and relax.

WOMEN AND STRESS

When a man experiences stress he will tend to draw back into his mind to reconnect with his true self and find balance. A woman, however, needs to feel her feelings to reconnect with her true self. If she is unable to process her feelings, she will tend to go further out of balance and will experience three common stress reactions: overwhelm, overreaction, and exhaustion. In a sense, they are the female equivalents of the male stress reactions.

It is essential that a man learn to correctly interpret a woman's stress reaction. Otherwise he tends to make her wrong and defend himself when that is not necessary. Having one's stress reactions misinterpreted throws a person even more out of balance.

FEMALE STRESS REACTION #1:
SHE BECOMES OVERWHELMED

In coping with stress, the female psyche becomes more emotional. If a woman is not used to being in touch with so much feeling, she is thrown out of balance and is unable to draw a clear line between her feelings and the feelings of others. She quite automatically feels an inner compulsion to respond not only to her feelings, but also to the feelings and needs of her partner and others.

She begins to feel overwhelmed, as though she has too much to do, and she can't rest until "everything" is done. She feels pulled in many directions.

As she denies her needs in favor of respecting her partner's wishes and the wishes of others, she becomes even more overwhelmed. She keeps giving and giving but doesn't take time to receive or to give to herself. She may even become compulsively submissive to the needs of others. She cannot say no until she is completely burned out.

In the state of overwhelm, a woman loses her ability to prioritize the various pressures and responsibilities she feels. It is increasingly difficult to separate her needs from those of others. It is as though everything is equally important: from paying the late bills . . . to cleaning under the bed . . . to watering the plants . . . to folding his T-shirts . . . to returning a few calls . . . to getting ready to go out that night . . . to getting the directions for a picnic next week . . . to walking a friend's dog.

Let's look at an example. When Mary goes into overwhelm, Bill might innocently ask her to make a call for him, a call that is not very important to him. (Bill is used to asking Mary to do little things that "aren't that important" because she usually says yes with a smile.) If she were to say, "Sorry, I'm running behind," that would generally be a fine response. Bill would make his call and make nothing of it. He might even see if he could help her in some way. Unfortunately, when Mary is in overwhelm that is not the response that pops out of her mouth.

As soon as he asks her, she reacts with a frustrated and helpless tone of voice. She says, "I can't right now, I have to cook dinner. I already have too much to do. I have to call Julie's teacher, I have to change the baby's diaper, I have to clean up this mess, balance the checkbook, finish the wash, and tonight we are going out to a movie. I have so much to do. I just can't do it all."

In an instant Bill reacts to her stress reaction with his stress reaction. He withdraws and detaches. It is hard for him to go back to sitting on the couch and watching TV without detaching from his inner feelings and connectedness to her.

Rather than wanting to support Mary's needs, he resents her neediness. Yet, he resents her for different reasons than she would imagine. He resents that she has not asked for help sooner. He resents her for making him feel like a failure (or in Martian language, he resents her for "bumming him out" or "bringing him down").

In truth she has not brought him down. He has brought himself down by misinterpreting her overwhelm. But being "bummed out" is nevertheless his experience. He is upset because he feels he has failed her in some way. When she is happy he feels as though he is responsible, but when she is unhappy he feels as though he has failed. In this way he takes her overwhelm personally, as if he caused it or should have been able to avert it. He does not realize that overwhelm has nothing to do with him.

To Bill, Mary's overwhelm sounds as though she is blaming him for not giving her more support. As she complains about all the demands being placed on her, he assumes that he is being reprimanded for not supporting her more and expecting too much from her. None of this is her intent.

When a man "withdraws," what a woman hears is that he doesn't care about her. In truth he is not saying anything — just taking care of himself. Similarly, when a woman becomes overwhelmed, she is not saying anything — just taking care of herself. She is trying to share her feelings in order to feel understood. Through being understood, she feels more centered and less overwhelmed.

WHAT HAPPENS TO A MAN WHEN A WOMAN IS OVERWHELMED

When a woman is overwhelmed, a man tends to withdraw and detach from her to be free of the feelings of guilt and inadequacy that he feels in response to her. He has taken her unhappiness, overwhelm, and helplessness personally. He feels that he has failed her in some way, but he does not know how to say this without losing face.

He does not tell her that he is frustrated because she is so unhappy, and that he wants her to be happy. He does not say he is disappointed that he has not done more to make her life easier. He does not say that he is worried for her and doesn't want her to feel so alone and unsupported. He doesn't say, "I understand how hard it can be around here." He doesn't give her a hug and say, "I love you, let's talk about it."

This is how he feels, but he doesn't say it because he doesn't know how, and he doesn't know that it is needed. What a shame. Because he does not understand what she needs at these times, and because he has not learned to communicate his feelings, he automatically withdraws. The irony is that she imagines that he is feeling the very opposite. She imagines that he doesn't even care. Inside he is unhappy that she is unhappy, but on the outside he acts as if everything is fine. And all along his resistance to her increases. As a result, she now feels even more abandoned, upset and helpless.

The fact that a woman in overwhelm pours out her problems as if they were all major crises helps to explain why men tend to misinterpret this state and feel blamed. A man holds his overwhelm inside and focuses his upset on one "big" problem. He will only list out a lot of problems if he is blaming someone for them. For this reason, he assumes a woman who does this is blaming him. As he withdraws, she does begin to blame him for being so cold and insensitive. This is another example of how our incorrect assumptions become self-fulfilling prophecies. Two people who love each other very much but don't understand how they are different, may in a short period of time, begin to resent, mistrust and fight each other.

When a woman is feeling overwhelmed she needs her partner to be a sounding board. He can help her find balance just by listening to and understanding her frustration. Unfortunately, he mistakenly thinks she is asking him to rectify the situation. He typically hears a few of her problems and then attempts to offer solutions, assuming that if his solutions are good, then she will feel better.

He expects this because when a man is upset and he discovers a good solution to his problem, he will generally feel better right away. When she continues to be upset and lists even more problems, he starts to feel rejected and helpless.

From his perspective it seems impossible to please her. She is rarely happy, and she appears to demand more than he can give her. Even though he may want to help her, he will resist because he feels blamed and accused of having not helped her already.

Bill generally becomes impatient with Mary when she is over-whelmed. To him it sounds like complaining and self-pity. He feels like saying, "Don't worry about everything. You are getting upset over nothing. Everything does not have to get done. It doesn't matter so much. Can't you be happy? Everything is not so difficult. You always have too much to do." Saying this, however, just makes matters worse. when Mary is in overwhelm she does not need a lecture. What she needs is an understanding and compassionate ear.

To get this kind of support she must realize that Bill easily mis-interprets her overwhelm as blame and rejection. She can ask for his support, but should warn him that right now she is rather over-whelmed and *it is not his fault.*

These five little words can make a huge differences to a man: *IT IS NOT YOUR FAULT.* She can simply say, *"If this sounds as though I am blaming you, I am sorry. It is definitely not your fault."*

After a man has listened for a little while, he needs to desist try-ing to fix her and understand that she doesn't need to be fixed. She is already in the process of healing, even though it sounds to him like she is complaining. Through being heard, her attitude will shift auto-matically. One phrase from him can be particularly helpful: after lis-tening for some time he can say, *"I just don't know how you do it."* This backfires, of course, if it is not done with sincerity.

GETTING WHAT SHE NEEDS

What an overwhelmed woman needs — to have someone understand and validate her pain and discomfort, to explore and share her fears without being made wrong for them — is almost impossible to receive from a man unless she reminds him that it is not his fault and she appreciates his help. It is hard for a woman to get support in over-whelm because when she shares what she is feeling, it comes out sounding like blame.

Generally speaking, however, another woman listening to such feel-ings can and will immediately understand. For this reason it is impor-tant that women look to each other for support, and not expect it solely from their male partner. It is a worthy goal for men to learn to fully understand overwhelm. But until that skill is developed, a woman should look mainly to her female friends for support at such times.

FEMALE STRESS REACTION #2:
SHE OVERREACTS

As a result of being overwhelmed, a woman naturally moves into the second stress reaction. She begins to accumulate emotional upset and thus overreacts to situations. Easily mistaken about why she is upset, she may confuse cause with effect. If she is upset from a long day filled with stressful calamities and her husband walks in, she can forget that the day is bothering her and react as if he is the cause of her upset. In a sense, the weight of the day gets focused on the man.

Eventually, by talking about all the other things that are upsetting her, she can and will start to lighten up. But until that happens it will sound as though whatever she is talking about is solely responsible for how she feels. She will appear to be blaming him and punishing him.

In this state, an overreacting woman will tend to say things that are irrational, unfair, inconsistent and illogical — things that she will later on forget or say she did not mean. A few minutes later she may laugh about it. This is similar to the way a man responds under stress. He will become irritable and grumble, but if you don't resist him or make him wrong, it will quickly pass. Just as a woman must learn to ask for support and ignore the grumbles, a man needs to ask how she is feeling and listen without taking it personally, without defending, without fixing her, and without interrupting her with corrections, explanations, and lectures.

Even though she appears to hold him responsible for her upset feelings, that is not her meaning. She is in the process of sorting out what is upsetting her. She truly doesn't know what is bothering her and how much of it is her partner's fault, or how much of her upset stems from other sources.

Denise is 38 years old and the mother of three children. She is also a bookkeeper. Her husband Randy is an architect. One day he came home from work fifteen minutes late. When he walked in his wife was cold and silent. He said, "Is dinner ready? I'm starved."

She then dumped his food on the table saying, "Here, it's burned."

His inner response was to become furious and indignant. He felt, "How dare she be this upset with me, when I was only fifteen minutes late. I could understand her being a little upset but not this much" He scraped his chair back and stood up, said a few profanities, and stalked out to eat elsewhere.

Randy's response to Denise's overreaction was equally confusing to Denise. When women overreact, men feel punished. In return, men feel, "If I am going to be punished for a crime, then 'let the crime fit the punishment.'" A man then commits a crime to fit the punishment she has dished out. He treats her in a way that deserves her intense reaction.

This inner compulsion to punish her, by treating her in a way that would rationally warrant a negative reaction from her, is the source of major problems in relationships. As a man comes to understand that she is not deliberately dumping all her upset feelings on him and that *there is always a long list of other things bothering her when she overreacts*, then he doesn't take it personally. He can graciously realize that she is not as upset about his being late as it appears. In truth, she must have really had a long and upsetting day, and he has arrived home at the end of it. She finally has someone she can talk to and it all comes out on him.

Let's look at what really happened to Denise on that day. As Denise was balancing the checkbook, she realized that a couple of check entries were missing and thus, she couldn't balance it. She assumed that the culprit was her absent-minded husband, who would occasionally do this. At this point in the day, she was more upset that she didn't have the information than she was about Randy's absent-mindedness. This was her first upset. Let's call it a 20-degree upset.

One half hour later she made some tea in the kitchen and saw that her daughter Katherine had forgotten her lunch. Now Denise faced a new stress. Should she bring the lunch to school, or should she let her 12-year-old go hungry. Let's call this a 10-degree upset. Because Denise is already 20 degrees upset, this new problem is experienced as a 30-degree upset.

This is called accumulating emotional charge. It does not just occur in women who are bookkeepers, but in all women when they are experiencing overreaction to stress. This is the rational explanation for a reaction that to men appears extremely irrational and unfair.

Let's continue reviewing what happened to Denise that day. After pondering over her decision, she decided to bring Katherine's lunch to school. She got into her car and it wouldn't start. The battery was dead. Someone had left the car door open all night. Now she had a new stress. Let's call this a 30-degree stress. But because of what preceded this upset, it becomes a 60-degree upset.

Imagine for a moment that Katherine called home just then and asked Denise to bring the lunch. What kind of reaction would she get? Instead of a 10-degree upset, which is what Denise originally felt about the forgotten lunch, she would now be the target of a 60-degree upset reaction. Fortunately for Katherine, she didn't call home.

Denise headed back toward the kitchen to call the motor club to come out and recharge the battery. On her way into the house she picked up her mail. As she was making the call she noticed a letter from the bank. She opened it and found an overdrawn statement. Normally an overdrawn statement would be a 30-degree upset. But on this day it automatically accumulated with what preceded it, becoming a 90-degree upset. As Denise called the motor club, which would normally cause her to feel 30 degrees of frustration and embarrassment, she now felt 90 degrees of upset

Now imagine what would happen if Randy called home just then to tell her he had forgotten to enter a particular check. Instead of being 20 degrees upset, which is how she originally felt, she would now feel 90 degrees upset. Instead of being mildly frustrated by his absent-mindedness, she would now resent him for being such an irresponsible, inconsiderate, and immature idiot. Fortunately, Randy didn't call home.

After Denise finished her humiliating call, she went to her cupboard to find relief. As she looked for her hidden stash of cookies, she found a trail of mouse droppings on her kitchen shelf. "Mouse turds" she screamed as she hit the ceiling with frustration and rage. Keep in mind that for the past three weeks, Randy had been trying to trap the little culprit. On another day, when Denise was not so upset, this discovery of a mouse in the kitchen would rate about a 15-degree upset. But today it registers 15 plus 90, or 105 degrees.

Certainly if one was to observe Denise's reaction to mouse droppings, one could think she was quite irrational. But considering what has preceded her experience of the mouse droppings, her overreaction is very understandable. This very understanding is what she needs when she is in overreaction.

At such a moment it is not within her power to rationally discriminate that she is only 15 degrees upset about the mouse, and 10 degrees upset about Katherine's lunch, and 20 degrees upset about the missing checkbook entries, and 30 degrees upset about the car battery, and 30 degrees upset about the overdrawn account. It all flows into one feeling reaction of 105 degrees.

When men are able to understand this process they are less inclined to take a woman's overreaction so personally. Let's continue to review what happened that ill-fated day in Denise's life when she dumped Randy's food on the table.

After the motor club man recharged her battery, she got in her car. As she drove off she realized that she had forgotten Katherine's lunch. She pulled up the driveway, parked her car, and ran into the house. When she returned to the car, she couldn't start it. Another dead battery. Well, earlier in the day a dead battery rated 30 degrees. This time it made her feel 105 plus 30 = 135 degrees. Denise felt completely humiliated in calling the motor club back. She painfully endured the man on the phone saying, "Didn't you just call 45 minutes ago?" On a different day she might have felt a little embarrassed and made a joke of it. But because she had already accumulated 105 degrees of upset, this was a major setback for her.

Becoming exhausted from so much inner turmoil, Denise headed for the bedroom to lie down and wait for the second tow truck to arrive. As she closed her eyes she felt a moment of peace. But when she got up for a drink of water, she saw on the floor another little trail of mouse droppings. Never before had she seen them outside the kitchen. "Mouse turds," which was previously a 15-degree upset, was now a 150-degree calamity.

In that moment Denise panicked. Her mind raced with fears and concerns: How many more mice could there now be? How were they getting in? What kinds of diseases were they carrying? Were they in her children's rooms? Did they crawl over her children in their sleep? Were there other creatures in the attic? Instead of being a little afraid of a mouse invasion, she was now 150 degrees upset about it. Needless to say, she was now unable to relax and enjoy her rest.

After the battery was recharged, Denise was more determined than ever to bring Katherine's lunch to school. She had only ten minutes to get there before her daughter's lunch period would start. On the way she got stuck in road repair traffic for an extra five minutes. Such a minor delay would generally rate a 10-degree upset or perhaps a 30-degree upset if she was in a hurry. On this day, however, it rated 30 degrees plus 150 degrees, which made it 180 degrees upsetting to Denise.

By the time she reached the school, Katherine had already left to eat lunch off campus with a friend. A wasted 10-minute trip to school would certainly warrant a 20-degree upset. That brought the total up to 200 degrees.

It was now time for Denise to pick up her three-year-old. Susie whined the whole way home that she wanted to go swimming, but Denise explained repeatedly that it was too cold. Susie picked this day of all days to throw a big tantrum. Children seem to do that. They can sense the buildup of explosive feelings and they act it out. All day Susie was especially whiny and needy. This kind of treatment from their child would make most mothers react with at least 20 degrees upset. For Denise it was now a 220-degree upset. She regretted the day she had wanted children.

She was determined to do something right, so she decided to fix a very special meal for her husband Randy. Making the meal was particularly frustrating because little Susie kept pulling her and needing so much of her attention. When Randy didn't come home on time, she left the salmon in the oven to keep it warm. Then she was distracted again by Susie. When Randy walked in she remembered the salmon. She rushed to the oven and found that it was burned.

Randy noticed his wife was cold and silent. He said, "Is dinner ready? I'm starved."

On a normal day when Denise had not accumulated so much upset, Randy's being 15 minutes late would have been a small matter — generally about 10 degrees of upset. But today it was 15 plus 220 — 235 degrees. She was fuming mad at him. If Katherine had walked in the room, Denise would have been 235 degrees upset with her. If she had seen a picture of a mouse, she would be 235 degrees upset about the mouse invasion.

When Randy asked if dinner was ready, Denise's inner reaction was, "Is that all you have to say to me? After all I have done for you. You walk in here late. You don't even call. You don't even greet me or ask me how my day went. You're so selfish, all you care about is yourself. I hate you. I could care less if you are starved. I hope you do starve." There was so much upset feeling inside that she didn't know what to say. She remained cold and silent and just dumped his food on the table saying, "Here, it's burned." The look she gave him communicated her 235 degrees of upset. That and the tone of her voice said it all.

Randy's response was to become 235 degrees mean and furious. Indignantly he thought, "How dare she be this upset with me, when I was only 15 minutes late. I could understand her being a little upset but not this much." He then got up, said a few profanities, and silently went out to eat. He fumed, "She will pay for that overreaction."

What a man in this situation doesn't realize is that a woman has already paid for it. She has lived it all day. What she needs is some compassion for what she has gone through. Instead of assuming that she is punishing him, and instead of becoming defensive, he needs to back up a little bit, take a few breaths and try to relax. Then he should proceed with caution, carefully attempting to empathize with her but not attempting to fix her, correct her, or defend himself.

THE "WHAT ELSE" TECHNIQUE

What he can say, perhaps while holding her, is "How are you feeling?" or "I can see you are upset. What's the matter?" After he listens for a while, and when she stops talking, instead of responding to what she has said with a list of explanations as to why she shouldn't be so upset, he must remember the magic phrase, "*What else* is bothering you?" Or he can simply keep asking "What else?" or "Go on" or "Tell me more." Then he should listen some more.

These questions tell her that he cares and that he is interested in understanding. "What else" also helps to keep her from getting lost while focusing on only one source of her upset. These questions help to validate her pain, which is what she needs the most. As she talks, it allows the listener to truly understand what she is going through with more empathy and compassion. As she feels heard and understood, the intensity of her upset will decrease. She may even start laughing about the awful day she had.

When a man uses this technique he must be responsible to ask only if he truly can hear. He should respect his tolerance for hearing complaints. If he can only listen for two minutes before he becomes defensive, frustrated, and angry, then he should *not* continue to ask, "What else is bothering you." He should back off and take some space. He should try to be civil and say something like, "I know you're upset, but I need some time to think about what you've said. Then we'll talk some more." In the quiet time that follows, he can help himself by remembering that he is unnecessarily taking her upset personally. He can remind himself that this is not her intention.

If he has not reached a point of complete frustration, he could try two other approaches. He can ask, "Is my listening to you helpful?" If she can say, "Yes, I do appreciate it," then he can continue to listen longer. Just a little appreciation can help a man dramatically.

He might also say, "I know you are upset and I want to support you. After a while, though it starts to sound as if you are saying it is all my fault. Is that what you are saying?"

Generally she will say, quite surprised, "No, I'm not saying that." Then he can say, "Thanks. Tell me more."

When a man has this understanding, he can listen and truly understand and feel a growing compassion. When he practices listening, the last thing he should try to do is explain why he is not responsible for her hurt. If he does, then her mind will begin to look for all the reasons he could be the cause of her upset. Then they will argue about that. He must consciously choose a non-explaining but investigative or explorative posture when he listens. His job is not to defend himself but to give her a chance to unwind. When she feels heard without blame or judgment, quite automatically her attitude shifts and becomes more loving, positive, centered, and accepting.

In a similar way, when a woman learns not to blame or judge a man's grumbles (the male equivalent to overreacting), quite automatically his grumbles go away as he succeeds in doing something to please her. If a woman makes a man wrong for grumbling he will justify why he should complain, then grumble some more. When a woman overreacts and a man defends himself — thus making her feelings wrong — she will overreact even more to his immediate lack of support. If his invalidating her is normally a 30-degree upset, on Denise's terrible day it would cause her to feel 265 degrees of upset.

AVOIDING THE BUTS

When a woman is experiencing the stress reactions of overwhelm or overreaction she will often become confused. In this confusion she will tend to ask questions. If this doesn't sound like blame, then it generally sounds to a man as though she is asking for a solution. The man assumes she is expecting him to make her feel better by answering her questions. She could be upset and begin talking about what is bothering her; he will listen for about two minutes maximum and think he now understands her problem and has a solution.

In reality she is in the process of figuring things out. Regardless of how good his solution is, she will say "but" and continue talking about things that are bothering her. This is frustrating to a man because he assumes that once he gives her a good solution to her problem, she should feel better. This, of course, works for men but not for women.

He must remember that when she is upset she will not feel better until she has talked things out for a while. She does not want, nor is she capable of appreciating solutions. This is hard for a man to remember, because when *he* talks about problems it is generally to ask for help in finding a solution. If someone gives him a good solution he feels great. When she doesn't feel great he takes it personally. He gets upset because she doesn't appreciate his brilliance.

Another male/female difference helps to explain why many men have the mistaken idea that women are incompetent. Most of the time, when a man talks about a problem, it will be something that he has thought about for a long time before he utters it out loud. To speak what is bothering him is to acknowledge that he is somewhat stumped by this problem. He is loathe to admit this, because if someone were to come along with a simple solution, he could be quite embarrassed. He might feel very foolish and inadequate.

When a woman starts talking about what is bothering her, she may need to talk for about 10 to 15 difficulties before she has a clear grasp of what is really upsetting her. Then she feels better. From a more centered place she looks at how she can solve it. For this reason a woman shamelessly shares her list of problems without feeling threatened that she has not figured out solutions to them. After listening to a women unwind this way, a man commonly begins to form two very incorrect judgments or conclusions.

HOW HE MISINTERPRETS HER UNWINDING

The first mistaken assumption a man makes when a woman shares a long list of things bothering her is that she must really be incompetent not to see the solution to these "petty problems." A man assumes that the degree of upset expressed indicates one's frustration in trying to solve a particular problem. But the extent of a woman's upset as she mentions a problem has little to do with her ability to solve it. Rather, it has to do with the accumulation of stress. It points to her need to sort things out.

The second false assumption a man makes is that a woman can't be happy unless all of her problems are solved. Because he cares about her he wants to make her happy, and believes that the way to make her happy is to solve her problems. He mistakenly believes that in talking about her problems she is asking him to solve them. To him, her long list of woes and difficulties sounds like a series of demands, complaints, and criticisms. He feels attacked, as if she is saying he is responsible.

As he listens to her roster of problems, he becomes frustrated because he knows that he cannot solve them all. He then concludes that she has too many problems. He makes her wrong for having too many problems, when all she really needs to be happier is to be heard and understood. He takes it all too personally.

As a woman's stress increases, her awareness opens and she sees more possible problems. This is why women tend to worry so much about many things.

Men worry just as much, as we have seen, but they tend to focus on one particular problem. Just as a woman associates her accumulated degree of upset with an increasing number of external problems, a man will take the accumulated degree of upset in his life and place it on one problem, minimizing the importance of other things in his life. When focused on one problem he will seem indifferent to other problems. If, however, he is distracted from this overly focused state, he will appear indignant; he will grumble, complain, resist, or throw a tantrum.

A woman makes two mistaken assumptions about his stress reaction. She concludes that he doesn't care about her or her needs, or that he doesn't love her. She also errs in concluding that he resists responding to her needs because he sees her needs as invalid. After grumbling for a while, he will remember that she does deserve more of his support and he wants to give it to her. Likewise, after overreacting a woman will realize that her partner is not to blame.

HOW BOTH SEXES CAN HANDLE OVERREACTION

When a woman overreacts, if her partner would give her some understanding and a sign of empathy for her stress and struggle rather than make her wrong for it, she would quickly recover. The most powerful way to do this is with a hug. Women need to be touched and hugged. It is one of the most powerful ways for a man to communicate his support. Many times a man doesn't know what to do or say. That is either his cue to take a deep breath, relax, and feel his love, or it is the time to quietly hold his partner and give her a hug. Correspondingly, if a woman can give a man "space" to grumble he will recover more quickly.

When a woman gives a man the space to grumble she should also give him the opportunity to be her hero. So many times women think of asking their partners for support, but because they are afraid of his resistance, they don't. By not making the request, they keep him in a box as the uncaring, selfish, bad guy.

Likewise, when a man gives a woman understanding, he must also give her the opportunity to feel special, worthy, and loved. He can, from time to time, do and say things to make her feel loved and special. When she is actually talking about her upset he can use reassuring phrases like "you deserve that" or "you have a right to feel that way" or "You deserve to feel . . ." or "you have a right to do that," etc. In addition to understanding, she needs validation, empathy, attention, and compassion. One useful way to think of validation is "to understand with respect."

A woman needs to share outside herself to the same degree a man needs to go into his "cave" and mull things over alone. In the process of "mulling" a man quickly identifies the problem and then looks to find a solution. Finding a solution makes him feel better. A woman, on the other hand, needs to discover what she is feeling and then what she is feeling upset about. Instead of looking for a solution, she explores the possible relationships between what she is feeling and what is happening to her.

Just as a man tries many possible solutions to his problem, a woman will explore many possible relationships between her feelings and what is happening around her until she finds one (or more) that fits. Her awareness expands and reviews all the possible external happenings in relation to her upset feelings. When she can clearly see her relationship to her environment, then she is able to take responsibility for her feelings. At this point she is able to realize that no one is responsible for her feelings. She can now change her negative feelings to positive feelings.

While a woman is sharing in order to discover what she is feeling, if a man tries to solve her problems not only will he feel as though nothing can please her, but he will prevent her from finding balance.

HOW MEN ARE MISLED

What men find so misleading when trying to support an overreacting woman is that when a woman is upset she will ask many questions as she talks. She will say things like:

"Why do you think my boss does that?"
"How am I supposed to know . . . ?"
"Why doesn't she realize that I am trying to help?"
"What am I going to do?"
"I just don't know why I am so upset?"
"What am I supposed to do when that happens?"

Hearing this, a man naturally thinks she is asking for an explanation or solution. On the contrary, she needs his silent understanding or empathy to support her in exploring and discovering what is going on inside of her. Men typically respond to this idea by saying in frustration, "Well, if I am not supposed to solve her problems, then what am I supposed to do?" The answer to this question is generally obvious to women, but not to men.

It can be a very difficult task for a man to listen without "doing" something — especially when he is being asked questions. The following are some ways a man can make listening into something he can "do":

1. He can make a decision to give his full attention.

2. He can practice not saying anything that might sound like a solution.

3. He can nod his head.

4. He can make reassuring responses like "hmm," "uh-huh," or "tell me more."

5. He can use the phrase "I understand." A word of warning: don't use this too often or she will get the idea that she is being patronized. She may feel, "How can *he* understand when I know that I haven't gotten to the heart of the matter."

6. He can avoid answering questions. He should assume that she is
    asking rhetorical questions, which make a point rather than
    require an answer. If she insists on an answer, be indefinite. Say
    things like "I'm not sure" or "I need some time to think about that"
    or "I don't have a ready answer." Certainly it is appropriate to ask
    and answer questions, but when a woman is upset it is best to stay
    in the posture of listening and understanding rather than explain-
    ing and fixing.

If he tries to solve her upset he is not helping; he is only resisting
her natural process of exploration. When he gives solutions he will
expect her to feel better; when she doesn't, he will start grumbling
and blaming her for being upset. When she says "but" in response to
his solutions, he feels rejected.

She is not really rejecting his ideas or solutions. She is merely
saying, "I still need to be upset; I haven't gotten to the real issue. I
need you to continue supporting me and not expect me to feel better right away."

He can't hear this message because he already thinks he knows
the real issue. He becomes frustrated when she does not agree. What
really disconcerts him is that even if he is right about what is bothering her, his telling her will not help. This is something she must discover for herself.

The reality is that when she is upset, confused, and out of balance,
she needs to come back to balance. No one can do it for her. She can,
however, be assisted by a loving and attentive listener who serves as a
sounding board. In the literal sense, a sounding board is a thin plate
of wood built into a musical instrument to increase its resonance.
When a person serves as a sounding board they increase the speaker's
self awareness, which allows them to find their most loving and accepting self when they have gone off-balance.

It greatly aids a woman to share in her journey back to center. This
is very difficult to do unless a man understands that she is not asking
for solutions, and that she is not even capable of appreciating them
at this point.

When a woman has become overwhelmed and her upset increases
to the point where she overreacts, if she doesn't get the support she
needs, she will move into her third stress reaction, exhaustion.

FEMALE STRESS REACTION #3:
SHE BECOMES EXHAUSTED

As a result of being upset and overwhelmed, Denise may instantly break down, feeling completely exhausted. She feels hopeless, like giving up. In this reaction, she is truly reaching out for support. Unfortunately, the message others get — especially men — is that they have failed to support her and nothing they could do would please her.

The major symptom of this third stress reaction is that she begins to feel exhausted and drained. Up to this point she may have appeared to have things "together," then almost instantly she appears completely drained, powerless, miserable, and bitchy.

A man feels very threatened by an exhausted woman, because it is extremely painful to think he has been negligent in fulfilling her. He doesn't realize that exhaustion is an inevitable consequence of her being out of balance. He needs to realize that it is not his fault. He must also realize that because she is human, she will go out of balance again and again, no matter how successful he is in providing for her.

Just as men "shut down" from time to time in response to stress, a woman becomes exhausted. Just as women misinterpret and are threatened by a man's shutting down, men misread and are threatened by a woman's exhaustion. Similar to the way a man can open up instantly after he has shut down, a woman can be energized and positive immediately after she has been exhausted.

One way a man can understand a woman in exhaustion is to realize that metaphorically speaking, his male physiology is equipped with a pressure gauge that warns him when he is giving out more than he is getting back. It tells him to rest and take care of himself to avoid burnout. But women do not have these pressure gauges. The more stressed they feel, the more they forget themselves. Her solution to burnout is to center herself through feeling heard and supported. In a practical sense, she needs a little help!

At such a time she needs to feel she is not alone. She needs the assistance of others. Most men are greatly threatened by this. A man sees the burden she is carrying and assumes that to make her feel better, he has to carry the whole load. He presumes that she has no more energy to fulfill her responsibilities. This is a huge mistake. In truth she has just reached her limit. Actually, he can make her feel much better by taking on just a few of her responsibilities and then later handing them back.

When a woman reaches her limit, she appears to be completely empty and powerless. The truth is, she still has energy — she is just disconnected from it because what she feels she "has" to do, she knows she cannot do alone. She needs help. Until she feels supported, she is disconnected from her energy resources.

THE STRAW THAT BROKE THE CAMEL'S BACK

Women break down when they go beyond their limit. The actual factor that causes the breakdown can be likened to the straw that broke the camel's back. It is not the weight of the load that causes her to break down, merely one or two straws. If a man can listen to her tell of all the pressures and responsibilities that are weighing her down, and then offer to lighten her load by carrying a few straws, he will help her tremendously. She may not feel better right away, but she will appreciate it greatly and recover much more quickly than he could imagine.

A man is generally reluctant to help a woman in her exhausted state, because he assumes the way to help is to identify and then do the most difficult tasks. This is not necessary. Moreover, he will resent doing her most difficult tasks. What he can do is pick those chores on her list that would be easiest for him to do. All she needs is two or three straws lifted from her back and her strength will return.

This works because when she is exhausted, every straw seems to be equally heavy. What she needs is for someone to carry a part of her load. What she doesn't need is his resentment toward her neediness. If he realizes that he doesn't have to fix *everything* to assist her, then it is much easier for him to offer his support without feeling resentful.

When men are confronted with an exhausted woman, they are notorious for giving lectures on how a woman shouldn't do so much. They say things like:

"You take on too much."
"Relax, you worry too much."
"All this is not that important."

"It's no big deal if we are late."
"That's not your responsibility."
"Well you don't have to do that."
"Life is not this difficult."
"Lighten up will you."

Not only is this kind of advice not helpful, it makes matters worse. She will be hurt in the same way that he may be offended when she tells him "I told you so" or expresses some truism like "Well, that's what happens when you don't plan" after he has made a mistake.

Sometimes it is next to impossible for a man to listen and respond lovingly to an exhausted woman. After all, he assumes she is blaming him and/or is expecting him to solve all her problems. If he too is under a lot of stress, he is apt to immediately shut down.

This is why it is essential for women to have many areas of support in their lives. It is unrealistic to expect a man to give her all the support she needs, especially when she is experiencing her stress reactions. He would have to be in balance all the time, which is quite unlikely.

People are generally drawn together because their degree of inner pain is similar. To the extent she goes into her reactions, he will generally follow suit. When he goes into shutdown she becomes exhausted; when she becomes overwhelmed he withdraws and detaches.

At such times, Denise should be responsible to come back to balance on her own or through the support of others. After she is in balance she can successfully support Randy if he is still in need. In a similar way, Randy may be the first to come back to balance, and then he can have the strength to support her if she is still in need.

A HEALTHY RELATIONSHIP

The reason for pointing out our different stress reactions in so much detail is not to excuse our partners, but to free ourselves of taking their reactions personally. As we have repeatedly observed, without this knowledge of how we are different, even with the best intentions we can easily make matters much worse.

We sometimes need to be reminded that when we relate with real love we see ourselves in our partners. With this feeling of connectedness and oneness, when we support their needs we automatically receive back. It is through giving with an open heart (or with real love) that we experience joy in our lives.

When loving is not joyful, then we are confused about love. When love is difficult or a strain, then we are demanding that our partner fix us. So many of us confuse love with needing. We get things backward. We assume that being loved means having one's needs fulfilled. In reality, a healthy relationship supports both members healing themselves.

The real joy of a special, intimate, and committed relationship is the opportunity to share and celebrate the good times, and give to your partner when he or she is in need. When you are in need and your partner is not giving to you, you can safely assume that he or she is also in need and thus unable to actively support you.

It is unrealistic to look for our intimate partners to heal us when we are out of balance. They are sometimes capable of this, but it can't be depended on. When we start to depend on others to heal us, fix us, or change us, then we make it even more difficult for them to support us.

Understanding our differing stress reactions gives us a constructive approach for healing ourselves or for reaching out to others to assist us in healing ourselves. The bonus is that when we succeed in finding balance, we know the correct strategies for supporting our partner. In Chapter 7 we will explore how we can move toward balance and the expression of our full potential by developing both our male and female sides.

CHAPTER SEVEN

FINDING BALANCE

So far we have explored how our male and female sides determine how we experience others and ourselves, and even influence how we react under stress. When we can identify our different sides it becomes easier to find balance. Simply recognizing that we are out of balance helps us to move in the direction of greater equilibrium. Regardless of whether you are a man or women, to find greater love and effectiveness in all your life's pursuits you need to balance your male and female sides.

When both sexes are able to balance focused awareness and open awareness, their creativity is enriched. When they are able to balance their work activities with relationships, greater fulfillment and success is assured. When they can react from their minds as well as their hearts, then they can respond to others with love and other positive attitudes.

How can balance be achieved? To find balance, a person needs to understand, accept, appreciate, and respect both sides of himself or herself, masculine and feminine. Ideally, it would happen this way:

As a boy naturally developed his masculine energy, his feminine energy would be allowed to simultaneously and spontaneously unfold. He would swing back and forth naturally between his male and female sides. As he grew in his manhood, he would have the freedom to express both his feminine and masculine sides. His feminine energy would support in harmony with his masculine energy what he does and who he is.

For example, as Billy grew up in an ideal environment, he would witness, thousands of times, his father successfully supporting his mother. Through his father's example he would learn to honor and respect femininity. When his mother was stressed, overreactive, overwhelmed, or exhausted, he would see his father respond with compassionate understanding and respect, rather than with indifference or judgment. His father would hug her, hold her, and listen to her. In this way Billy would learn how to listen to his own feminine feelings.

As he grew up he would feel secure in simultaneously developing and expressing his masculine and his feminine sides. For example, he would not be judged for crying or showing his feelings. Not only would his mother hold him and hug him, but his father would hold and hug him and understand his feelings as well. His father would feel proud of him for both his masculine qualities of competence and efficiency and his feminine qualities of goodness and love. In addition, his father would know that to support his son, they would need to do things together. Billy's dad would make the time to teach him sports and other hobbies, take him on outings, and enjoy his son's activities. He would not demand success, but would rejoice in his accomplishments and empathize with his losses.

In an ideal environment, a boy is appreciated for his male qualities and respected for his feminine qualities. If he is respectful of his environment and nurturing to others, he is appreciated for that. If, however, he is more masculine and self-centered, he is not judged to be defective by his mother. He is not seen as bad, and when he does bad things he is forgiven. Boys with a lot of masculinity will tend to be mischievous and need a lot of acceptance and forgiveness.

His ideal mother will learn how much trust and space to give Billy and where to take control. She respects that he has a need to feel independent and in control of his life. She trusts that he has to learn his own lessons, knowing that overprotection can weaken him and undermine his self-confidence. She accepts his differences and is appreciative of him. She does not take anything he does for granted. She allows him to be decisive and feel important. She respectfully asks him for support, rather than demanding it through guilt and disapproval. She believes in him and trusts his process of development.

Most important, Billy gets to experience his mother loving his father. As a result, the masculine qualities within him have a chance to come forth and be developed. He does not need to apologize for being the way he is, or deny himself to win his mother's love. He feels safe to explore his aggressive tendencies by asserting himself and taking risks. He is not made to feel bad for being selfish, withdrawn, grumpy, or irritable. Above all, he does not have to be different from Dad in order to be loved by Mom. He feels secure in his masculinity because he sees his mother repeatedly loving and appreciating his father, who represents his male side.

In a similar way, a girl would ideally develop her feminine energy, and as she grew into womanhood, she would discover and allow for the full expression of her masculine energy as well. Her masculine energy could then support who she is and what she does.

For example, as Sharron grew up in an ideal environment, she would repeatedly observe her mother successfully supporting her father. Through her mother's example she would learn to trust and appreciate her own masculine side. She would feel safe being feminine in ways that she would see her mother being feminine. When her father was stressed, withdrawn, grumpy, or shut down, Sharron would experience her mother continuing to love herself, accepting Sharron's father with trust and appreciation.

Free of resentment, her mother would be assertive yet forgiving. In this way Sharron would learn how to get her wants and needs fulfilled in a relationship without resorting to manipulation. She would see her mother acknowledging and appreciating her father for all the ways he contributed to the family. By this example she would feel secure in her own masculine power to contribute to others and make a difference.

As she grew up she would feel safe in concurrently exploring and developing her feminine and masculine sides. She would not be judged as unladylike if she wanted to achieve great things and make a difference. If she was good in math, she would be appreciated for that. If she was assertive, precocious, or demanding she would be admired for her strength and will. And yet when Sharron felt emotional, tender, or vulnerable, she would be nurtured and reassured. Her mother would spend the needed time sharing with her, listening to her, and comforting her.

Sharron's mother would not expect her to be "grown up" while still a child, but would allow her to develop in her own time. She would also teach Sharron to respect her boundaries by respecting her own: Her mother would not be a martyr and resent giving to others. She would teach Sharron how to ask for what she wanted and how to share feelings when she was upset. Sharron would grow up staying in touch with and trusting her feelings.

In an ideal environment a girl is both respected for her feminine goodness and admired for her masculine strength. When she is assertive, creative, and aggressive she is admired and acknowledged. When she is loving, good, sweet, cute, and pretty she is adored and praised. When she is not good, however, she is still loved. She does not feel pressured to be good or happy all the time. If she is tender and vulnerable, she is not made wrong and told to grow up. She feels safe to express anger as well as to be afraid or to cry. She can be selfless or selfish and still be acceptable to her parents.

Sharron's ideal father is careful to respect her feelings, vulnerabilities, and needs. He knows that she is supposed to be different from him and he respects those differences. And yet when her masculine qualities emerge, he is right there to play games with her, teach her, and do things with her. He thinks about her day and asks questions that let her know he is interested. Just as he has learned to support her mother with little presents, he also surprises Sharron with little gifts from time to time. This makes her feel special. As a result she will feel secure in her worthiness. She will grow up without feeling a need to control, but with a trusting willingness to empower others with her love.

He understands that little girls have a strong tendency to blame themselves, and so he is extra careful to show concern or apologize when he makes mistakes or upsets her in any way. In this way he helps her to respect herself. In the presence of her daddy she feels safe to express her feelings, opinions, and wishes. When she speaks, he gives her his attention. When she gets overwhelmed and overreacts he does not put her down; he knows how to listen and comfort her without trying to fix her. She feels safe being pretty and attractive. She feels comfortable asking for support. He is able to set limits, yet make her feel deserving.

Most important, Sharron gets to experience her father loving her mother. She learns that being feminine is lovable. This makes it safe for her feminine self to emerge and develop. She does not need to hide herself, deny herself, or pretend to be someone she is not. She also does not need to change herself to win her father's love. She sees her mother being herself and being loved by a man. This is a very important experience. She does not have to be different from her mother to be loved by Dad. She feels secure in her femininity because she sees her father repeatedly loving and respecting her mother, who represents her female side.

Children brought up in such a loving and respectful environment have an opportunity to develop their male and female sides simultaneously. This balanced interaction of male and female energies is later reflected in every aspect of their lives. Thus they are able to actualize more of their human potential. In particular, this internal equilibrium is reflected in their ability to have harmonious and mutually supportive relationships.

THE INFLUENCE OF REPRESSION

Of course, few if any of us grew up in this ideal way. Every time little Billy experienced Mom rejecting Dad, he had a choice: "Do I reject Dad and thus reject the part of me that is like him, or do I reject Mom and reject the part of me that is like her?"

Every time Billy himself is rejected or opposed, he has another choice: "Do I choose to deny myself or do I choose to lose love?"

When Dad gets angry and yells at his daughter Sharron, does she realize Dad is dysfunctional, or does she assume that something is wrong with her and that she should be more like him to protect herself?

Does Billy reject his masculine side because Dad hurt Mom?

Does Sharron reject her female side because she sees how weak and helpless her mother is?

These are just a few examples that reveal how our childhood shapes us. No one escapes childhood without repressing or denying some part of themselves in order to survive, be secure, be free, and be loved.

Consequently, we have repressed the natural development of different aspects of our male and female sides. If, while he grows, Billy's male side is not loved, appreciated, accepted, and trusted, he may begin to repress his masculinity to get his mother's love. In this case his female qualities have a greater chance to develop. But if schoolmates make fun of him or he starts to feel rejected by his father, he may then deny aspects of his female side. Boys generally grow up fluctuating from normal and balanced to overly sensitive (or nice), and then over to macho (or unfeeling).

As little girls develop, some parts may mature in balance while others are rejected. By repressing her female side she becomes more masculine or overly responsible. This can give her a lot of power, but at the price of feeling disconnected from her true self. She feels as though she does not know herself and experiences an emptiness or lack of fulfillment. If she then rejects her masculine side, she becomes not only disconnected but also weak, needy, and hopeless. She becomes overly vulnerable to others and overly dependent. She may feel unable to take care of herself. In many ways she feels like a little girl, unable to assert herself.

When a boy represses his masculinity, his masculine qualities remain undeveloped. When, as an adult, he chooses to awaken these qualities, he must recognize that they will need time to develop into appropriate behavior. For instance, by being aggressive and breaking things, a little boy gradually learns to be more respectful. If this aggression is pent up for years and then comes out in adulthood, one must be careful to channel it appropriately.

Similarly, if a little girl grows up too quickly and takes on the role of Mommy because her mother is dysfunctional or not available, then that little girl and her neediness may suddenly engulf her as an adult. This is the price she pays to heal her past and become whole and complete. Fortunately, this is a temporary phenomenon that may recur but gradually goes away. If she can love and accept this "disowned" needy part of her, it can be integrated into her awareness and make her more whole and complete.

It is important to note that it is possible and very common to selectively repress different aspects of masculinity or femininity. Thus, in reading the examples throughout this book of male and female tendencies, a man might relate to many of the male examples but sometimes relate to the feminine examples, and vice versa for women.

SEXIST ASSUMPTIONS

Unfortunately, because we haven't had clear role modeling for being fully male or female, we often get confused about who we are. Consequently, since we haven't been taught how to balance and express our male and female energies, we fall into sexist assumptions about ourselves and others. These assumptions limit the expression of our inherent potential. In our effort to conform, we must suppress parts of ourselves.

Listed below are seven common (faulty) sexist assumptions:

1. Women are loving and men are heartless.
2. Women are irrational and men are intelligent.
3. Women are supportive and men are destructive.
4. Women are weak and men are powerful.
5. Women are submissive and men are dominant.
6. Women are dependent and men are independent.
7. A person's role is predetermined by his or her gender.

These general sexist beliefs give rise to thousands of other, more specific, unfair assumptions such as "a man should work in the world while a woman stays home" or "women make better nurses and men make better doctors."

The above seven categories of sexual discrimination are significant because they directly inhibit and restrict our potential, which ultimately transcends our manifest sexual differences. Certainly, gender influences the expression of our potential, but it in no way determines what we can do.

Our true, inner potential to give transcends our sexual differences. Each one of us is meant to be:

1. purposeful
2. intelligent
3. creative
4. loving
5. powerful
6. decisive
7. self-reliant

Each and every one of us has our own, unique blend of these essential human qualities. Naturally, every person has his own limitations, but those limitations are not determined by sex. To assume that gender determines our ability to love, or to express power, or to understand is a great mistake. Such attitudes box people into imaginary categories and inhibit the full expression of who we are and what we can do.

THE TRUE MEANING OF EQUALITY

Men and women are created equal; ultimately, the essence or spirit of men and women is the same. All men and women have intelligence and loving hearts. But the way we develop and express our individual potential is different for each person.

Our greatest power is to love and support each other. Every person is unique and has a special gift to offer. It is unfortunate that we assume that in order to find equality, we must be the same as others. Through respecting and appreciating our singular differences, we give ourselves a chance to fully blossom and discover our true gifts. In reality, we're all different and interdependent. It's through the recognition of this interdependency that we can come to express our full power.

As human beings, we are all purposeful. The more we understand and accept our male and female energies, the more able we are to discover the sacred treasure of knowing who we are and what we are able to do. We can unlock this treasure chest by exploring the male and female energies within us. This exploration leads to greater understanding, which opens the door to greater self-esteem, self-worth, confidence, happiness, and peace.

Without this knowledge, trying to love ourselves and others can be very confusing. Sometimes, even when we are trying to support ourselves and others, we unknowingly sabotage our success.

CHAPTER EIGHT

WHY WOMEN FEEL UNLOVED

Women often complain that they feel unloved, whereas their partners have no idea what they are talking about or how to change things. Typically, the man will ask, "How could she possibly feel unloved? Look at all I do for her!" He then proceeds to list everything he does to support his family, such as earning a regular paycheck, concentrating on making his business grow, taking her out to the movies, etc. He truly doesn't understand why she feels unloved.

Let's look at an example that reveals the differences between men and women could create this confusion.

MASCULINE AND FEMININE AWARENESS

John, a football coach, tends to focus on one goal at a time. He is aware of all the factors relevant to his goal, but in the process of focusing exclusively on one point, in masculine fashion, he becomes unaware of the people and circumstances in his life that are not directly relevant to his purpose. His awareness is restricted to the distance or path between himself and his point of focus. For the most part, nothing matters but the goal.

When his focus changes from one goal to another, his awareness shifts dramatically, bringing in the information he needs for the new goal. His awareness is redirected, but still focused on a single point.

Since John has not balanced his male and female sides (focused and open awareness), each change in focus means he becomes unaware of anything other than his new goal. He can even forget what he was doing just a moment ago, if it doesn't have some relevance to his new point of focus.

· John's view of his own worth is determined by how well he thinks he's moving toward whatever goal he has in mind. In fact, his very sense of himself comes from the way he affects his environment. He identifies with his actions, his "doing." You could almost say that as long as he's doing something, he stays in touch with himself.

On the other hand, John's wife Pam, with her feminine awareness, takes in the whole picture. If she's aware of John's goal, she'll not only see his goal, but see how it relates to her and to other people in their lives. She'll automatically be concerned with how his goal may affect their relationship with each other and their children. She will tend to be even more aware of how his focus on this goal affects his health. She'll also have some sense of what will happen if he is successful and if he isn't. John's focused awareness doesn't readily envision all these consequences. He is first concerned with the possibility of getting to the goal; she sees all the possible consequences of going after the goal.

Pam's open awareness allows her to see a multitude of possibilities in any situation. But because she doesn't understand John's focused awareness, she jumps to the conclusion that he doesn't care about her or the family when he makes a decision without first considering how it would affect them. She knows that she would consider her family because she loves them. And so she wrongly assumes that he doesn't love the family.

WHEN HIS WORK IS HER LIFE

Each year in mid-August, John begins drilling his football team for the fall season. During the first part of the school year, he spends extra hours at team practice, extra time at home watching videos of the team's performance, and even extra time tutoring the star place kicker who is close to failing algebra.

When football season is over, he spends after-school time watching other high school and junior high sports events in hopes of spotting a potential football star for the next year. At the beginning of summer vacation, John is finally able to relax. But within a couple of weeks, the new season will become his primary focus again.

Chances are, with all the attention John is paying to his job, he'll have a winning team. His high school will be happy with him and he'll eventually receive tenure, securing his income for many years ahead.

Meanwhile Pam is home, raising the kids and trying to support John and his goal of a winning football team. She fixes a hot breakfast every morning so he'll have plenty of energy; he bolts it down and rushes off to school. She spends time shopping carefully for his favorite foods and prepares dinner every night. (Often John is late for dinner when practice runs longer than expected.) She makes sure the kids behave when he gets home so he can enjoy some peace and quiet, and she's always careful to hold discussions about the family when John's work is going well.

Pam makes sure John has clean, pressed clothes, taking care to remove as many of the grass stains as possible. She listens as he describes the problems he has with various players, and often helps him understand how to approach a recalcitrant team member. She goes to all the games. As a matter of fact, that is the only time they go out together.

HOW BOTH CONTRIBUTE TO THE PROBLEM

As you might expect, eventually trouble erupts between John and Pam. At first glance, it looks as though John is the "wrong" party in this situation, but in truth, both are just doing what their respective energies direct them to do. John has no understanding of the problem, and Pam has no idea that her way of coping with the problem is only making matters worse.

Pam has gradually lost track of herself and her own needs, and resents that John does not respond to or consider them. John is so totally focused on his goal of winning football games that at first he doesn't even know there's a problem, and when he finds out, he doesn't understand it. He has no idea that Pam's needs aren't being met — in part because she has not communicated what those needs are. She thinks she has expressed her needs, unfortunately, she did so in a way that John could not hear.

As John gets involved in the new season, Pam tries to be loving and accepting. After some time, when he doesn't seem to notice or appreciate the sacrifices she is making, she feels resentful. Pam begins to complain about all the things John isn't doing around the house. Sometimes he tells her she shouldn't worry about it; sometimes he promises to get something done and then forgets about it. Occasionally she suggests ways he might spend some more time with his kids. He nods distractedly or comments that everything will be OK.

Pam feels unloved when John doesn't respond to her needs. At first she reacts by working even harder to understand and fulfill his needs. But he hardly notices, because it's just not in his nature to notice anything that isn't part of his goal.

Eventually, Pam can't take this anymore and she explodes, telling John she feels totally unloved. He becomes defensive and points out how hard he works to support the family. If she pushes, he negates her feelings entirely, saying that she is overreacting and being irrational.

SHARING NEGATIVE FEELINGS WITH LOVE

Pam doesn't understand that in an attempt to be loving, accepting, and supportive, she has merely withheld her negative feelings of anger, frustration, sadness, disappointment, fear, and worry. These feelings build up inside until she finally shares them with an attitude of rejection, which says "I have done all this and you have done nothing in return. I love you, but you don't love me back."

No one has ever taught Pam how to share her negative feelings with a loving attitude. She oscillates back and forth between two extremes: either she suppresses her negative feelings to be loving, or she becomes unloving (resentful) and expresses her negative feelings.

Neither of these formulas work. If John is to respond to her needs and problems, he needs to hear the truth of how she feels. If she has an unloving, resentful, unaccepting, unappreciative, or untrusting attitude, he will not be able to take in what she is saying. But if she pretends to be loving, happy, and accepting, that won't work either because he will assume that everything is fine and remain focused on his work.

Pam needs to practice sharing her negative feelings before they have built up, and John needs to practice listening to her feelings. When verbal communication is not working, the next step is to try writing. The best way to learn to communicate upset feelings with love is to write them out and later read them to your partner.

In Chapter 13 of this book I will describe a technique for writing feelings in a way that both centers a person in loving feelings and communicates her experiences and needs. If writing fails, then another workable option is getting the help of a counselor.

Unless John makes time to listen to and support Pam, and unless she learns to share her feelings and needs without resentment, it is inevitable that Pam will continue to meet John's resistance.

HOW PAM CAN CHANGE

Pam will feel unloved as long as she doesn't understand her responsibility to communicate her feelings, wishes, and needs. But it is almost impossible for her to accept this responsibility unless she first realizes that a man's focused awareness causes him to behave very differently from a woman.

Because her open awareness naturally motivates her to keep track of the needs of those she loves, Pam can't fathom how John could forget her if he truly loves her. *Her* experience of loving someone is to become absorbed in caring for their needs. When he doesn't reciprocate, she mistakenly concludes that he doesn't love her.

When Pam feels unloved, she initially focuses on becoming more worthy of love, rather than on sharing her feelings, wishes, and needs. She tries to become more deserving of love by giving more to her husband and suppressing her negative feelings. There is nothing wrong with giving more to John. Giving is always good. Pam's problem is that she is not good at receiving. The more she gives without receiving, the more unreceptive she becomes.

Pam thinks she is being strong and self-reliant. But as she becomes less receptive, John experiences less attraction to or interest in her. When Pam gives without also being receptive (feminine) she gradually becomes hard and loses the soft feminine qualities that originally motivated John's interest in her. When she suppresses her emotions, she gradually disconnects from her natural feelings of love, joy, gratitude, and trust. John, being focused on his work, is not even aware of the change.

SYMPTOMS WOMEN CAN LOOK FOR,
ACTIONS THEY CAN TAKE

To help women recognize that a relationship problem is growing, here are a few warning signs:

1. Your partner consistently forgets to do things for you.

2. You don't feel comfortable asking for support.

3. Your partner does something for you, but you feel it is not enough.

4. You don't feel safe to be upset, and find yourself hiding your feelings.

5. You find yourself getting upset over very little things and avoiding the real issues.

6. Your partner doesn't seem to be passionately attracted to you, and you don't care.

7. You feel resentful that you are giving more than he is.

8. You feel that if he would change, you would be happy.

9. You feel guilty or petty being unhappy.

Most women have experienced each of the above symptoms at some time in a relationship with a man. It is natural to feel these things, especially if you don't understand how men and women are different.

Some suggestions for women to counter these symptoms follow:

1. Accept that he is different from you and practice asking for support.

2. When you are upset, practice sharing your upset, but try sandwiching it between positive feelings of trust, acceptance, and appreciation.

3. As you are sharing, periodically reassure him that he is not being blamed and that his listening is helpful and appreciated.

4. When you feel resentful, talk with female friends or practice the feeling letter technique (Chapter 13) to find forgiveness. From a more forgiving attitude, share your feelings.

5. Practice asking for support and making it OK that he doesn't always say yes. Give him the opportunity to support you in his own ways.

6. Acknowledge whatever he does for you. Don't take anything for granted.

7. Take care of yourself before you take care of him. If you are tired or under a lot of stress, don't martyr yourself by giving more. Give less so that he knows you need more support.

8. When he makes suggestions to support the relationship — "Let's go out to dinner" or "Let's go on a vacation together," for example — be especially careful not to correct, criticize, or improve his ideas.

9. Join or start a support group of women. Meeting weekly if possible, read sections of this book together and share your experiences of using this new information.

10. Make friends with someone who has a good relationship, and share with them. If you can't find a friend, then find a mentor or therapist to assist you.

11. Read and discuss sections of this book with your partner. Find out his ideas and reactions and work on accepting him. Share with him your feelings so that he will have a greater understanding of you.

HOW JOHN CAN CHANGE

John can change only by understanding Pam's needs. First, he must realize that she needs his assistance to explore how she feels inside.

He has to respect that she has needs but isn't aware of them. His job is to help her discover what she needs. Then he will naturally be motivated to participate more in the relationship.

The problem men have is that they generally are unaware that they are losing interest. They are just aware that they are interested more in their work or play than in their relationship.

Here are a few warning signs to help men recognize that a relationship problem is brewing:

1. You have become so focused on your job that you consistently forget to pick up items that you promised your partner you'd bring home from the store.

2. You have promised your partner you'd fix things around the house, and then become distracted with other projects of your own.

3. You don't understand your partner's feelings and find yourself telling her how she should and shouldn't feel.

4. You wonder why your partner gets so upset about little things.

5. You often find yourself half-listening to your partner or children because you are preoccupied with a problem from work or you are distracted by the TV.

6. You turn off or become impatient when your partner begins to talk.

7. You are no longer passionately attracted to your partner when you have sex.

There probably isn't a man on the planet who hasn't experienced each one of these, probably a number of times. Each is an example of focused awareness, which, by the way, isn't bad. Without focus, nothing would get done, but each of the above situations is an example of too much focus — focus that keeps a man from being aware of others' needs. Focus becomes a negative when it is not balanced by openness.

By recognizing the signs of being overly focused, he can begin to open his awareness by listening to his partner. Some men, if they are too focused, find it unbearable to even consider taking time to listen to feelings. This stress of "having to listen" can be avoided if a man encourages his partner to write out her feelings and then schedules time to listen.

PLANNED INTIMACY

This scheduled time is called "planned intimacy." Its purpose is for a man to listen to his partner's feelings and understand her needs. The best way for John to do this is to read Pam's feelings as written in her letter out loud. This activity is most effective when she learns to express her negative feelings in a loving and nonresentful way. Not only does Pam write out her feelings, but she also writes a short response letter that she would like to hear in return. This helps Pam to get in touch with her feelings, and insures that John will have the words and awareness of what Pam needs. In this way, John will be able to respond to her feelings in a loving, caring, respectful, attentive, and considerate way.

As John learns to listen and Pam learns to share, both become more balanced. In time, they communicate without having to depend solely on writing letters and scheduling time to read them. John steadily gains the ability to turn off work when he is relaxing and spending time with his wife. Pam learns to freely share her feelings, needs, wishes, and preferences without sounding critical or demanding.

One of the most essential ways a woman reading this book can receive more support is to become conscious of the things that she truly needs. If she is in a relationship, she could underline the points that relate to her, and then ask her partner to read the book and do the same, so that each can better understand the other's needs. Listening to my "Secrets of Successful Relationships Tape Series" (see the listings in the back of the book) is another way to absorb this material and be inspired by a new understanding of how the sexes differ.

In the next chapter we will explore a number of approaches to make a woman feel loved and supported.

CHAPTER NINE

THE ART OF
FULFILLING RELATIONSHIPS

Men generally assume that once a woman is fulfilled, she should stay that way. Once he has proven his love, she should know it forever, and never need to be reassured or reminded. From the male point of view, this attitude makes perfect sense.

Women find this attitude hard to accept. It is just plain inconsistent with their internal reality. A woman needs to be reassured that she is special, worthy, understandable, and lovable. Men also need to be reassured, but they get that encouragement mainly through their work. Women, however, primarily need reassurance through their relationships.

When a man's work fails, he begins to doubt his worthiness. In a complementary way, when a woman is ignored by her husband, she begins to doubt her worthiness. She needs ongoing signs, symbols, and verbal reassurance that she is loved. Men too have this need for reassurance through relationship, but as long as a man is in a relationship, he will tend to be unconscious of this need. The mere fact that he has a relationship reassures him of his competence. The happiness of his wife will tend to bolster him, while a woman needs direct, caring attention to reassure her.

If a man is in a relationship, he isn't apt to worry about rejection unless it happens. He doesn't consciously feel a need to be reassured,

175

because his successes in the world gives him that reassurance. As a result, he doesn't readily respect a woman's ongoing need to be reassured.

His focused reasoning goes something like this: "Even though I am preoccupied with work these days, she should know that I love her today, tomorrow and forever, unless I tell her differently." To a woman this is just as absurd as the following comments would be to a man: "Even though he is broke and out of work, he should know that he will be rich again, because he was rich at one time before the business went bankrupt" or "Although he came in last today, he should know he's a winner because at one time he did win a tennis tournament."

Certainly a man's failures challenge him to realize his worth independent of his successes, but it is equally true that as he follows his failures with increasing success, his sense of self-worth is strengthened. After his business has failed he must regroup himself and try again. As he begins to succeed, his confidence becomes more solid. This can be likened to the process of building muscles: by breaking down one's muscles, they grow back stronger. In a similar way, through a series of setbacks, the man who is able to try again strengthens his self-esteem.

A woman's self-worth is challenged when her partner withdraws or temporarily ignores her. This painful experience is a time to center herself and realize her worth independent of his love. However, it is equally important that her feelings of insecurity are followed by reassurance and support from her partner. This reassurance is necessary to strengthen and deepen her confidence, trust, and self-esteem.

If she approaches her partner with blame, however, it is predictable that he will resist and she will go uncomforted. In Chapter 13 you will be introduced to the Love Letter technique, a way to reach out and ask for support without offending your partner.

VERBAL REASSURANCE

Every day, a woman needs to receive some form of verbal reassurance that she is loved. This means saying things like "I love you, I love you, I love you, I love you, I love you, I love you, I love you, I love you. . . ." There is basically one way to say it and it needs to be said over and over.

Men sometimes stop saying "I love you" because they want to be new and original. They imagine that a woman would grow tired of it or become bored by it. But saying "I love you" is never redundant. Saying it is actually a process of allowing her to "feel" his love. He may love her, but if he doesn't say it she won't feel it. One way a man can relate to this is by comparing the simple statement "I love you" to a phrase that he never tires of hearing. That phrase is "Thank you." Rarely does a man weary of being told "thank you" after he has done something for someone.

Another phrase that is very validating for a woman is "I understand." If (and only if) a man does understand, then it is very helpful to say this out loud. When a man says "I understand," a woman is assured that she has been heard. A complementary phrase that men appreciate is "That makes sense." When a man hears "That makes sense," he feels equally supported.

SYMBOLS OF LOVE

A woman needs symbols of love. When a man brings a woman flowers, for example, they validate her beauty and femininity as being of great value. Women need to be given flowers on an ongoing basis. To her, flowers are symbols of a man's love. They make his love concrete. It is unfortunate, then, when a man assumes that she will tire of them and therefore stops giving them to her.

Big presents or very little presents, all serve a very important romantic function. They help a woman know that she is special. She feels special when he treats her in a special way. Giving presents is a way of honoring a woman's need to be reassured.

Little notes are also effective symbols of love. They are affectionate reminders that simply reassure. It is not necessary to be original or even creative. Just say the basics, over and over again. As long as your notes express what you feel, they will be effective. Some of the basic reminders are: "I love you, I miss you, you are the delight of my life, just a reminder to say I care."

A nice addition is to occasionally purchase a loving, funny, or beautiful card. These little reminders can be written on cards that accompany a small present or a flower, or they may stand alone. When giving a card, try hiding it in a place where the recipient will be surprised. This works wonders. These reminders can also be expressed by surprise phone calls whose simple purpose is to say "I love you."

Many men instinctively know and do this in the beginning of a relationship, but stop after a while because they mistakenly assume that the gesture will get old or is no longer necessary.

WHEN SIGNS OF LOVE DISAPPEAR

Often in relationships, a woman ends up feeling unloved because her man stops giving her the same quality of attention he did in the beginning of the relationship. When the quality of attention changes, she, not understanding men very well, assumes he's unhappy with her and doesn't care for her. *The quality of attention is the most important sign of love.*

Let me give you an example:

When Phil and Ann came for a counseling session, she complained that he didn't love her anymore. Phil couldn't understand what she was talking about. He knew he loved her; it didn't make any sense to him that she didn't know it. He was terribly frustrated.

After some discussion, Phil began to realize that when Ann said "You don't love me," what she really meant was "You don't treat me the same, special way you used to." He wanted to know more, so I asked Ann to close her eyes and remember how Phil's love used to make her feel.

She explored her feelings, then she slowly said, "It made me feel warm, it made me feel loved, it made me feel special, it made me feel happy, it made me feel calm, it made me feel peaceful, it made me feel playful, it made me feel free, it made me feel accepted, it made me feel noticed, it made me feel desired, it made me feel secure, and it made me feel fulfilled."

I asked her to go deeper and she added, "soft, delicate, loving, appreciative, deserving, trusting, and vulnerable."

Next I asked her, "When you feel this way, what are you most grateful for?"

Ann listed the following:

"I feel grateful to be loved and cherished. I feel grateful to be a special part of Phil's life. I feel grateful when he treats me with respect. I feel grateful when he goes out of his way to comfort me. I feel grateful when he listens to me and makes me feel heard. I feel grateful when he initiates new activities and adventures for us to share.

"I feel grateful when he notices that I need to talk and asks me how I feel, and takes extra time to listen. I feel grateful when I can share my sadness and he holds me—that makes me feel so comforted. I feel grateful when he notices a new outfit or haircut and appreciates it. I feel grateful when he wants to be with me. I feel grateful when he surprises me with little gifts or notes. I feel grateful when he calls me when he's on a trip, and gives me his number. I feel grateful whenever he anticipates my needs. Then I trust that he really cares and is there for me and not just for himself."

As Phil listened, tears ran down his face. When she finished, he said, "As you spoke, I remembered some of our happiest moments, and I realized how things have changed over the years. Somehow, until now, I just hadn't noticed." Giving his wife a hug, he said, "I've missed you too."

Until then, Phil had been so focused on other things, he'd forgotten how important and wonderful being needed by Ann made him feel. He realized how important her love was to him, and remembered how special and precious his wife really was.

That day he learned that when his wife doesn't feel loved, she isn't being irrational; it's an important signal that she is not getting what she needs. He now knows that when her needs are overlooked, they run the risk of losing track of their special love.

If a man doesn't stay in touch with his partner's feelings, not only does he forget what's important, but she does too. She probably won't know exactly what she needs, but she'll begin to resent him. She may not know what she is missing, but she will know she is missing something.

When a man is willing to hear a woman's needs, they both win. Ann learned the power of letting Phil know how important he was to her. By letting him hear how positive his love made her feel, he became more motivated to support her. Expressing her gratitude helped him feel appreciated, accepted, and empowered.

LITTLE THINGS MEAN A LOT

Before I came to understand how a woman's awareness was different from mine, I couldn't understand why my wife would get upset when I forgot to do what seemed to me like little things — little things like bringing home a newspaper, picking up the dry cleaning, fixing a window, painting kitchen cabinets, or telling her that someone had invited us to a party. In this context, big things would be earning money, telling the truth, being monogamous, "being there" in times of emergency, paying the mortgage, etc.

From time to time, when I'd forget something, she'd come unglued, often telling me she didn't feel that I loved her. How, I wondered, could she interpret my forgetting to pick up a newspaper as a signal that I didn't love her?

Finally I came to realize that from her point of view, remembering the little things was an expression of my love. Those "little things," being her needs, were related directly to her. When I'd forget them, it was hard for her not to interpret my action as a lack of concern and caring for her. When I'd treat them as unimportant, I was actually making her feel as if *she* was unimportant.

When a man ignores something a woman considers important, she feels he's ignoring her. I found that being responsive and responsible about the little things was a significant way I could express my love for my wife and give her reassurance. Since she really is the most important person in my life, once I understood the importance of "little things," it became more automatic to pay attention to her wishes. In fact, once I understood that this was a legitimate need of hers, I could bring my masculine focus to bear on solving the problem.

Now that I understood how my wife was affected by my absentminded professor routine, I was able to understand her feelings when I would forget things. I no longer felt compelled to tell her she shouldn't get so upset. She, on the other hand, has grown to understand my masculine tendency to focus, and doesn't take my forgetfulness as personally.

If men only knew how important these "little things" are to women, there would be more happy women. Some women are embarrassed to let a man know how important they are. If, however, you make the effort to remember the "little things" a woman needs, you will see what a difference it makes.

INCREASING A MAN'S CREATIVITY

Reassuring a woman isn't the only reason to honor little things. As I started following through on more of my wife's wishes and preferences, I found that doing the little things often helps me gain momentum for doing other things that I might be putting off. Such changes in focus can actually help to release me from concentrating too much on tasks that may be wearing me down.

Shifting focus is also a very powerful problem-solving technique. After you have focused for a long time on solving a problem, if you can let go and temporarily redirect your focus to something else less demanding — one of the "little things" your female partner needs, for example — this gives the unconscious mind an opportunity to solve your problem. The solution will probably emerge in your awareness when you are not even thinking about the problem.

WOMEN LOVE SPECIAL TREATMENT

Women love to be singled out and treated specially by the men in their lives. I learned this the hard way, when my wife and I had our first big family party. I'd gone to my office while Bonnie had gotten the house ready. When I returned home, I was so proud of myself because I'd actually remembered to bring home the video camera. Although taking videos of a family party was something that I valued, I could have easily become absorbed by work problems and forgotten.

When I got home, everyone had already arrived. I went straight to the living room to set up the recorder, lights, and camera. As I moved equipment around, the kids ran to greet me. Gradually each family member found their way into the living room and we exchanged hugs and small talk as I continued to work on preparing the video equipment exactly right.

When I was finished, I went to the kitchen to say hello to my wife. I, of course, was expecting Bonnie to be delighted that not only had I remembered the camera, but I had gotten it all set up. Instead, she was distant and aloof. It turned out she'd expected me to greet her first, and then go about setting up the camera. Instead, she was the last person I spoke to. I was surprised, because from my male point of view, if she wanted to see me, she could have come into the living room at any time.

When we finally had a chance to talk, she told me she was hurt because it seemed to her that I was ignoring her. She wished I had come home, gone directly to her and given her a big hug, greeted the others, and then set up the camera. By setting up the camera first, I hadn't made her feel special. From her point of view, my focusing on the camera meant the camera was more important than either her or our guests.

ROMANTIC LOGIC

Certainly, if I was defensive I could have judged my wife as being un-reasonable and demanding. But from a romantic point of view, what she said made sense. I certainly love it when either Bonnie or the kids get excited to see me. That always makes me feel special and good. Why shouldn't she enjoy that feeling?

I realized how important it is to women that we men single them out. Women actually don't know how special they are to us unless we tell them and demonstrate it. Since a woman can see so many possi-bilities, she can easily imagine that a camera, or something else, might be more important to a man than to her. It never occurs to a man that his wife might feel like that. After all, he knows he loves her, so he assumes she knows it too. But she doesn't, not automatically; she has to be told, over and over again.

As I came to understand this difference, I also realized it would be easy to give my wife the special treatment she needs. To this day, when-ever I arrive home, the very first thing I do is find her, give her a kiss and a hug, and ask her about her day.

When she visits my relationship seminars I go to her first and give her a hug, even if there are people waiting to talk with me. I used to give preference to the people waiting to talk — after all, this was their time, and I could talk to my wife any time. This attitude is definitely not romantic, and makes a woman feel unimportant and mundane. The simple formula to make a woman feel special is: treat her differ-ently and first. Don't save the best for last. A woman never tires of hearing and seeing the ways her man loves her.

ONE SECRET TO MAKING A WOMAN FEEL LOVED

Possibly the most important way a man can make a woman feel loved is completely the opposite of what most men think. Most men uncon-sciously think that if they don't complain about the relationship, their partners will feel loved and valued. After all, if a woman doesn't complain about him, he will feel appreciated. Men don't understand that when he acts as though everything is fine in the relationship, his partner infers that the relationship is not important to him, which makes her feel as though she is not important to him.

Generally a man tends to get upset and worry most about problems at work. When he comes home, his mind is still on his job. His partner gets the message that work is more important to him than she is. If this man can learn to identify his frustrations, disappointments, and worries in the relationship, he will communicate to the woman that she is important, appreciated, and needed. Herein lies one secret to making a woman feel loved: A woman gains in self-worth when her emotional support is acknowledged, desired, and appreciated.

Jean, 36, constantly complained about not being appreciated by her husband Paul, 43, who is a very successful doctor. Although Paul was the traditional breadwinner, Jean took exception to being the traditional homemaker. Paul resented that he made all the money and his wife wasn't willing to be responsible for the domestic duties.

When I asked her why, Jean said, "I resent being his maid. All he does when he comes home is complain about what a lousy job I do caring for him and the house. He says he works hard and he wants equal effort from me. I don't mind giving more, but no matter how much I give he doesn't appreciate me. He just criticizes me or points out what I haven't done. It hurts when I feel that he considers me his maid."

Paul went on to explain that he just wanted her to have the house clean and dinner cooking when he came home. In a frustrated tone he said, "It only takes two hours of her day to make me happy. All she has to do is keep the house clean and make a nice dinner. Then she is free to do anything else she wants. All I ask is two hours of housework."

To Paul's remark, Jean responded, "It makes me furious, when I feel as if I am just a maid to him." Paul had no idea that he was sounding so condescending to his wife. Jean was hearing that all he needed from her was housework. On the other hand, he thought he was saying, I value you so much that I only expect you to do a couple of hours of work.

I then asked Paul why it was so important to him that the house be cleaned and that his dinner be prepared. Becoming emotional, he answered, "It means that she really appreciates how hard I work for us. So much of the time she says money is not important to her. That makes it seem as though I am doing all this for nothing. I am trying to secure our future, and she thinks I just care about myself.

"It is painful when I think that she doesn't appreciate me. If I could come home and feel her love for me and her appreciation for what I do for her, it would make my life worth living. Otherwise I become resentful of her. I need her appreciation for all that I do for her. Without that I do become overly critical."

As Jean listened, her face began to glow and tears ran down her cheeks. For the first time, she could feel how important her loving support was to Paul. She saw that in fixing his meals she was not just being his cook. Instead, it was a way she could make him feel appreciated for his efforts to support the family financially. By hearing his frustrated need for her loving appreciation, Jean was able to feel like an important part of his life.

From this heartfelt interaction Jean was able to wholeheartedly release her resentment and enjoy being a homemaker as well as pursue her other interests. Paul realized that by showing her he needed more from her emotionally, rather than just needing more in terms of her labor, he was able to make her feel more valued, loved, and special.

This is difficult for most men, because they are generally unaware of what *they* really need in a relationship. To help a woman feel loved and valued, a man needs to share his frustration and disappointment when he is not getting the appreciation and emotional support that he needs. Not only does this support a woman in feeling her importance, but it also lets her know how to give more support effectively. As a man learns to communicate his emotional needs, this not only increases a woman's self-worth, but also inspires her to give more.

As we have seen, one of the major reasons why women don't feel loved is that men have no reference point to instinctively give women what they need, nor are men able to articulate what they need themselves. In the next chapter we will explore in greater depth our primary emotional needs.

CHAPTER TEN

HOW TO GIVE AND RECEIVE EMOTIONAL SUPPORT

The rules governing successful relationships change as society changes. Political, technological, and scientific advances have shifted most of humanity above the immediate worries of survival and security. No longer are men and women primarily in need of each other to ensure their physical survival and security. Today, men and women are drawn together in relationships not only to support each other's physical needs, but also to fulfill their higher psychological or emotional needs.

When the physical needs for survival and security are generally fulfilled, relationships take on a new orientation; the emotional needs take precedence and, consequently, new problems and conflicts emerge. These conflicts arise because a whole new set of needs begins to surface into consciousness. In a sense, it is as though the emotional needs become more demanding. They have been there all along but were in the background. As they rise to the fore, our psychological needs play a key role in the success of our relationships.

For example, during a period of financial hardship, a couple may get along great. It is the two of them against the world. Finally they achieve a higher degree of financial security. Rather than enjoying greater peace and fulfillment, they experience increased conflict or dissatisfaction. When the battle is over in the outside world, they find it at home.

Mike was 22 when he married Ellen, who was 26. For eight years Mike and Ellen were quite satisfied in their marriage. When they started out, they were both poor. Ellen worked as a flight attendant to support Mike through law school. They remembered those times as hard but filled with loving, fun, and tender moments together. The couple seemingly had no problems in their relationship. It was as though they were a team fighting to ensure survival and security. They could easily ignore their problems because they imagined that one day things would be different.

Eight years later, Mike was a highly paid and successful lawyer and Ellen was the mother of two children. Although everything seemed to be working in the relationship, it was not. As soon as their material needs were taken care of on the outside, they began to notice how dissatisfied they were with each other. Mike was no longer interested in or excited by his wife. Ellen pretended that everything was fine. Three months after they moved into their beautiful new four-bedroom house, Mike fell in love with his secretary.

When Ellen found out, they came for counseling. She realized that she had been equally dissatisfied. After some hard work on their relationship, they were able to patch it up. Mike and Ellen were lucky. Many couples don't seek out help, but just get divorced.

When a relationship undergoes the shift from being physically based to being emotionally oriented, a couple needs to know it is inevitable that new problems will come up. The old ways of relating to each other will not be satisfactory or fulfilling.

Because women are generally more conscious of their emotional needs, the woman is first to experience a lack of fulfillment. Her male partner, in turn, begins to feel a lack of fulfillment in response to the woman's dissatisfaction. As they become more successful, he grows more intolerant of her dissatisfaction, because there are fewer physical reasons to account for it. He reasons that because they are more materially abundant, she should be happier.

The reality is that because they are more financially secure, emotional needs emerge that require his continued support and attention. He tends to resist because he thinks that having achieved financial prosperity, he has completed his job. Neither is happy and each tend to blame the other. One of the biggest problems is that they both resent having these difficulties in the first place.

These new problems cannot be avoided. If the two *understand* and *accept* that this is inevitable, then they will not be as resentful of each other. *They will not question the relationship; instead they will question their old styles of relating and communicating.* Rather than changing partners, they can focus their energies on improving their abilities to give and receive emotional support.

CREATING EMOTIONAL SUPPORT

It is significantly easier to offer true emotional support when one has received that support in childhood. It is also easier to correct a situation in which one is not getting one's needs fulfilled, if one is already familiar with the kind of support one needs. People have chronic difficulties in their relationships because they do not have concrete experiences of what is possible, an image of how a loving and supportive relationship looks and feels. If their parents were dysfunctional, how can they even conceive of what real emotional support is like?

For example, if a person was ignored or disrespected as a child, it is hard for him or her to gracefully draw in attention and respect as an adult. Because they haven't had the experience of drawing in respect by being themselves, they may end up resentfully demanding it — which pushes others away. Or, they may resort to denying their true selves in order to earn it. The problem with being demanding or denying one's self to receive emotional support is that even if one does succeed, the support is hard to let in. It never seems to be enough.

Gail, a travel agent, was 42 years old when she woke up one morning on a vacation and realized that she was "completely unhappy," dissatisfied with her life and her relationship. She felt empty and alone. She felt that no one had ever "really" loved, respected, or appreciated her.

With the help of some counseling, her husband Glen tried everything to support her and convince her that she was important and loved. In assisting them, I could see that he loved her deeply but she was unable to accept his love. I also discovered the ways he unknowingly made heartfelt communication almost impossible.

She said, "I can see he is trying hard to please me. I even feel guilty for not appreciating everything he does do. I don't know why nothing he does is enough. But when I speak he really doesn't hear me. He doesn't see who I am. I don't think he really loves me."

As deep emotion began to well up within her, she took a deep breath and she began to cry, "Nobody loves me. Nobody has ever loved me. The only person who loved me was my father, and he died when I was seven."

For the first time in a long while, Gail began to soften and share her inner pain with Glen. She was amazed that he didn't reject her. As she became able to share and not merely complain, he was able to hear her and respond with profound compassion and understanding. With some assistance, Gail started to open up and reveal her insecure, sad, and even angry feelings. This was completely new to her; she was used to holding everything in and trying to appear loving and nice.

As she exposed this "not so together" side of her, Glen responded with greater love. This confused Gail. She asked, "How can you love this part of me. You've always said how much you loved how strong, good-natured, and independent I was."

"I do love that part of you," Glen said. "But I also love this soft and warm part of you. It makes me feel needed and important to you. I wouldn't want you to be this way all the time, though. I also like the other, strong side of you."

Gail said, "This is confusing . . . how am I supposed to know how much you can take? How am I supposed to know how to be, in order to be lovable?"

Taking her hands gently in his, Glen leaned closer and with tears of love in his eyes said, "I love you just the way you are. I love you when you are happy and I love you when you are sad. I love you most when you are just being you. Whenever you are *trying* to appear happy when you are not feeling it, then it is not you. It is hard for me to deeply feel my love for you when you are not being or sharing the real you. I love this soft, warm, vulnerable part of you."

She smiled and responded by saying, "I love this warm, caring, understanding part of *you*. For the first time I feel I am really being loved. I feel safe. I can say that I like who I am."

Gail was able to truly feel Glen's love because, for the first time, she really opened up to him. As long as she pretended to be what she was not, when Glen would love her, her false persona was getting the love.

The more her strong side had been appreciated, the more she had felt that her vulnerable and needing side was weak and unacceptable.

As Gail shared the complete truth of who she was, she was able to let in the love she truly deserved. Through taking responsibility to be herself and to truthfully share her feelings in a nonresentful way, she was able to draw Glen's emotional support to the deeper and more hidden parts of her that needed his love the most. As she received his support, she began to love both sides of her. Increasingly able to respect herself, Gail began to appreciate and trust Glen's love.

Gail learned to share her emotional needs with her husband and reach out for his assistance. As he learned to give her what she needed, she was able to learn what he needed. This process is greatly facilitated if we have a clear picture of how we need to be supported, as well as how our partner's needs might be different.

THE SEVEN POSITIVE ATTITUDES

There are seven basic emotional needs or attitudes that are essential to creating a truly loving and emotionally supportive relationship: love, caring, understanding, respect, appreciation, acceptance, and trust.

All of these attitudes are present to various degrees when a person feels emotionally supported. Positive sentiments like fulfillment, peace, happiness, gratitude, satisfaction, excitement, and confidence are automatically generated when we are able to fulfill our primary emotional needs.

Love. Love is a connecting, uniting, sharing, or joining attitude. Without judgment or evaluation it says, "We may be different but we are also alike. I see myself in you and I see you in myself." On a mental level, love is expressed through understanding. Acknowledging a sense of relatedness, it says, "I relate to you in this similar way." On an emotional level, love is expressed through empathy. It acknowledges a relatedness of feeling. It says, "I relate to your feelings; I have had similar feelings." On a physical level, love is expressed through touch.

Caring. A caring attitude acknowledges one's felt responsibility to respond to the needs of another. To care is to show deep interest or heartfelt concern for another's well-being. When we care about some-one, it is a sign that we are affected by their well-being or lack of it. The more one cares, the more one is naturally motivated to fulfill or support others. Caring is also an acknowledgment of that which is important to a person. Caring for a person validates that he or she is special.

Understanding. An understanding attitude validates the meaning of a statement, feeling, or situation. It does not presume to know all the answers already. An understanding attitude starts from not knowing, gathers meaning from what is heard, and moves toward validating what is being communicated. Through understanding we are able to see the world through another person's eyes. An understanding atti-tude says, "Before I judge you, I will take off my shoes and walk in yours for a while."

Respect. A respectful attitude acknowledges another person's rights, wishes, and needs. It yields to another's wishes and needs, not out of fear, but through acknowledging their validity. Respect acknowledges the value and importance of who a person is, as well as their needs. Respect is the attitude that motivates one to truly serve another because he or she deserves it.

Appreciation. An appreciative attitude acknowledges the value of another's efforts or behavior. It recognizes that the expression of another person's being or behavior has enriched the well-being of the appreciator. Appreciation is the natural reaction to being supported. Appreciation inspires us to give back to others with a feeling of full-ness and joy. Appreciation acknowledges that we have benefited from the gift offered to us.

Acceptance. An accepting attitude acknowledges that another's being or behavior is received willingly. It does not reject, but rather affirms that the other person is being favorably received. Indeed, acceptance is accompanied by a sense of gratitude for what we have received. It is not a passive, overlooking, or slightly disapproving attitude. To accept a person means to validate that they are enough for you. It does not mean that you think they could not improve; it indicates that you are not trying to improve them. Acceptance is the attitude that forgives another's mistakes.

Trust. A trusting attitude acknowledges the positive qualities of another's character, such as honesty, integrity, reliability, justice, and sincerity. When trust is absent, people commonly jump to negative and wrong conclusions regarding a person's intent. Trust gives every offense the benefit of the doubt, positing that there must be some good explanation for why it happened. Trust grows in a relationship when each partner recognizes that the other never intends to hurt. To approach one's partner with trust is to believe that they are able and willing to support.

MALE AND FEMALE NEEDS

What is most interesting and significant regarding primary emotional needs is that *some are more significant than others according to one's sex.* Love, the first of the seven needs, is equally important to both men and women. The importance of the other six emotional needs varies. The male side of a person primarily has the need to be trusted, accepted, and appreciated, while the female side of a person primarily needs to be cared for, understood, and respected.

Because men and women don't understand that their primary needs are different, they make a very common mistake: they give to their partner what they themselves would want, assuming that this is what their partner also wants. They are shocked when their partner does not return the favor.

For example, many times a woman will act toward a man with so much caring and understanding that he feels she doesn't trust him. She gives caring and understanding because that is what she primarily needs from a partner. She mistakenly assumes that he will rejoice in her caring attitude and respond to her in the same way. Instead, he may respond by being neutral, or may even interpret her support as smothering and annoying! When he resents her caring behavior, she is perplexed and confused.

On the other hand, a man may be so accepting and trusting that a woman assumes he doesn't care at all about her, and resents him. A man will give his partner trust and acceptance because that is what he needs the most from her. If she gets upset, for example, he may give her some space to work things out and completely ignore her. From his perspective, he is offering acceptance and trust. He is trusting her to handle her problem alone, and accepting her by not trying to change things. She, however, interprets this as abandonment and rejection. She feels greatly uncared for.

In both of these examples, because the couple did not fully understand each other's different needs, they were unsuccessful in supporting each other — when not only were they trying to support, but they thought they were doing a good job of it!

This is exciting information. When it is properly understood, it gives a person an awareness of why he or she may not be receiving the support he or she deserves in relationships. So many people in intimate relationships report that they give so much and yet their partner does not give back. Yes, they are giving, but not necessarily what their partner really needs. If one truly succeeds in giving, the result is that the receiver rejoices in supporting back. It is very natural; what we give out comes back to us. Give and you will get back is the promise of every relationship.

The main reason this golden rule doesn't always work in our relationships is that what we give is not always what our partner needs. Both sides think they are giving, but no one is getting. This statement and perception only reinforces that they are both victims.

To realize our power to create what we need, we must accept that *when we are not getting, then we are not giving. Or more precisely, we are not giving what our partner needs.* To receive more in our relationships we must learn how to give not what we would need, but what our partner needs. When we succeed in truly fulfilling their needs, they will spontaneously begin to respond to our support by supporting us in return.

The success of our giving, then, is determined by our partner's willingness to support back. If our partners are unaffected by our gifts, rather than blaming them as unappreciative, we must be accountable and explore ways we can give more successfully.

Giving, for most people, is like putting money in a parking meter. They resent the parking meter for not accepting dollar bills when it only accepts coins. If we are to successfully give to our partners, we must be accountable to give in the currency they cherish. When we don't give what our partner can use, we are like the businessman who complains that his customers are not buying his product, rather than finding out what his customers truly need and then supplying that.

To sum all this up, one of the major causes of frustration and resentment in relationships is that men tend to automatically give to women what men need, while women give men what a woman would most appreciate. I hope this will be one of the insights that you will remember most from this book. Applying this knowledge has dramatically improved thousands of relationships literally overnight. In the next chapter we will explore more deeply how men and women differ in their primary emotional needs.

CHAPTER ELEVEN

OUR PRIMARY EMOTIONAL NEEDS

All men and women have an equal need for love. But regarding the six other basic emotional needs, three are primarily needed by men and the other three are primarily needed by women. Most conflict and dissatisfaction in relationships stems from our inability to fulfill these primary needs. When these needs are not fulfilled it is easy to have our feelings hurt, for which we blame our partner.

A man is most often hurt, offended, or drained when a woman does not *trust, appreciate, or accept* his motives, abilities, thinking, decisions, and behavior. Because a man tends to identify with his actions, when he feels his actions are not being trusted, appreciated, or accepted, he will exhibit all the symptoms of being wounded, offended, or resentful. Deep inside he begins to doubt his adequacy and competence.

A woman primarily needs to be cared for, understood, and respected. She is most vulnerable to feeling hurt when her feelings are not *respected, understood, or cared for.* When she is not respected by someone she loves, she commonly begins to doubt her worthiness and her rights.

THE UNIVERSAL NEED TO BE LOVED

The most important of the seven primary emotional needs is the need for love. To love someone is to acknowledge the goodness of who they are. Through loving a person we awaken their awareness of their own innate goodness. It is as though they cannot know how worthy they are until they look into the mirror of our love and see themselves.

When we are "seen" with love, we become aware of our goodness. Then we are able to know and love ourselves more.

As we mature in that positive self-awareness, we become less dependent on others to see ourselves. However, as long as we are growing in self-awareness we will always need to be loved, just as we always have the need for physical survival. Over time this need to be loved is overshadowed by the need to be of service to others, just as in an earlier stage the need for physical survival and security takes a back seat to the need to be loved.

Love is also a connective feeling. Love relates you to another. It says you are like a part of me. When a man loves a woman, he is able to feel and connect with the goodness of his own female side. When he is loved by her in return, he awakens to experiencing the worthiness of his male side. Likewise, when she is loving him, she is recognizing and experiencing the goodness of her masculine side. As he loves her she is able to also experience the merit of her female side.

Through giving and receiving love, men and women can more fully love themselves and experience their inner goodness. In this way they feel whole and complete.

Love is an attitude that embraces another as one would embrace oneself. It upholds, nurtures, and supports. Whenever we are truly feeling love, there will also emerge a selfless desire to serve the well-being of the loved one.

We feel our connectedness to ourselves and others through love. When we are loved, we experience the truth of who we are. When we are loved, we feel that we are worthy and "enough." When we are loved, it is easier to be our true selves.

GIVING THE GIFT OF LOVE

As little children we all come into this world giving the gift of love to our parents and all those we meet. We look upon them with wonder, seeing only the beauty and goodness of their souls. We see them as great beings, certainly worthy of all we can give. If that love is returned to us, then we are able to love ourselves. It is as though God gives us the ability to love outwardly, but we need our parents to reflect that love so that we can love ourselves.

Unfortunately, if that love is not returned to us, we begin to reject or "disown" parts of who we are. Generally we reject, deny, and then change ourselves to win our parents' love and acceptance; we become someone else in order to be loved. To the extent that we disown parts of who we are, it is hard for us to love similar aspects of other people. Once we have disowned parts of ourselves it is also hard to receive love.

To let in the love we deserve, we must risk being ourselves again in the context of a loving relationship. As we grow in our ability to receive love, it becomes easier to truly give of ourselves and realize our deepest potential.

THE FEMALE NEED TO BE CARED FOR

Relationships are an ongoing process of giving, receiving, and sharing. The success of a relationship is based on our ability to give of ourselves. Our ability to give, however, is directly related to our ability to receive. One cannot continue to give unless one is also receiving support. To receive support we must first feel worthy of being supported. To feel worthy of being cared for, we need to have someone care for us.

It is essential that those with whom we are in relationships are responsive to and care about our needs. The need to be cared for is the need to have someone respond to our needs to the best of their ability. A caring attitude allows us to open up and trust that we are special and entitled to receive support.

Women are especially vulnerable to caring or lack of caring from a male partner. He can make her feel heavenly and then drop her into hell. When a man is caring towards a woman, she trusts that her needs are valid and not selfish. But when a woman is in an uncaring relationship or environment, it is very hard for her to assert her needs without feeling guilty for being too needy or selfish. She easily judges herself as weak and unworthy of sharing her feelings and needs.

Men are vulnerable to caring in a different way. When a man is in a relationship with an overly caring woman, he may become weak and dependent. She gradually takes on the role of a mother to him, and he regresses to behaving like a spoiled and demanding child. He may swing back and forth from being dependent to being resentful of her smothering, overly caring love.

Because women are so aware of their need to be nurtured and cared for, it is easier and more automatic for them to nurture and be caretakers. Men must work much harder to develop this attitude. As we explore the seven primary emotional needs, we will see consistently that what women need, they can give easily, but men must work to develop, and what men need, men can give easily, but women must work to develop. The better we understand this concept, the more we can be understanding, tolerant, and forgiving of our partners when they don't fulfill our emotional needs. We can begin to appreciate that what is easy for us to give, may not be so easy for them to give.

THE FEMALE NEED TO BE UNDERSTOOD

Understanding from others is crucial if we are to fully understand ourselves. The more we share ourselves the more we are able to know ourselves. In order to know one's own needs, thoughts, and feelings, they must be communicated to and fully understood by another. To understand means to share or take on the thoughts and feelings of another, even if they are very different from your own.

Understanding is sharing and validating a person's point of view, rather than judging it as invalid. It is being willing to discover why they see and experience the world the way they do, instead of explaining to them why they shouldn't see it that way.

Again, this need to be understood is essential and primary to being female. When a man doesn't devote the time and attention necessary to understand a woman's feelings and needs, she can easily become confused and will have a greater tendency to overreact. While a woman shares herself, if her man only waits passively, hoping that soon she will finish, he affects her in a way that actually adds to her confusion or upset.

When a woman is upset and confused and a man begins to judge her as nuts or crazy, it is very easy for this woman to begin doubting her sanity. It may well be that many women have been committed to mental hospitals simply because men were incapable of understanding and validating their upset feelings.

It is interesting to note that even the dictionary defines insanity as "behavior not based on rational, logical thought." If this were a valid definition, almost every woman would be diagnosed as insane. It is a woman's normal and quite sane nature to act on her instinctive and intuitive feelings, rather than always relying on her logical and rational thought processes.

For example, a woman does not decide to have a child just because she has weighed the pros and cons and concluded that it is a good idea. Even if she does think it is a good idea, her decision is supported by the intuitive *feeling* that it is time to be a mother. Relying on her intuition, she may do things just because she feels like it, and then later discover that there was also a good reason for her actions.

Conversely, men tend to make decisions based on logic and reasoning. Later on they may substantiate their decisions by making sure they feel good. Just as a man's logic is fallible, so is a woman's intuition. Yet both are valid ways of knowing and deciding.

When women try to think like men and make logic more important than their feelings, they tend to become frustrated and confused, especially when they are upset and under pressure to make decisions. Generally when a woman is confused she is trying to make a decision. She needs instead to relax her mind and explore her feelings. Going within herself to her intuition, she can then be decisive.

In a similar but complementary way, a man needs to mull over or think a problem through before he decides. Men who make their feelings more primary than their thoughts become indecisive and procrastinate. These immobilized men need to get out of their feelings and into their minds. One way a man benefits from listening to a woman (once he becomes competent at this art) is that he automatically gets to put his own feelings aside and use his thinking to understand what she is feeling and why she is feeling it.

For a man or a woman, the ideal place to make decisions is balanced in mind and feelings. When a man "listens to understand" he automatically becomes more balanced; a woman becomes more balanced when she shares and is understood. This can only come about when men learn the language women speak and women learn to speak in a way that men can hear. Practicing the Feeling Letter technique (see Chapter 13) trains women to share their feelings in ways that men can understand. Writing also helps one to understand what one is feeling without the assistance of a listener.

Ultimately, understanding is essential to our female side. It aids us to discover the truth that lies within us and frees us to release negative feelings and discover our positive feelings. Through learning to communicate with positive, loving attitudes, we can cultivate the understanding we need in order to resolve or, better yet, avoid conflict in a relationship.

THE FEMALE NEED TO BE RESPECTED

As one shares in a relationship, it is essential to maintain one's sense of self. Respecting one's partner means not trying to change or manipulate her, but rather, supporting her in being herself and upholding her rights. Respect honors another's needs, wishes, values, and rights. To respect is to keep agreements and honor commitments. It is to give equal importance and sometimes greater importance to another.

The need to be respected is the need to be yourself in a relationship without giving up who you are. When a person feels respected they don't feel that they have to earn their rights; they don't feel unworthy. The need for respect is the need for fairness as well as the acknowledgment that you are entitled. Respect recognizes that a person deserves support without having to earn it.

Because of their expansive nature, women are especially vulnerable to the need for respect. It is difficult for a woman to maintain her sense of self when she is expanding out to love a man. She needs him to constantly remind her of her rights and worthiness. When a man doesn't esteem who she is or respect her rights, she becomes unsure of her rights and self-worth. The more emotionally attached she is, the more susceptible she is to his level of respect. If a man is not respectful of a woman's needs, feelings, and rights, eventually she will have to close her loving feelings to him so that she can find herself again. Loss of sexual interest is common at this stage. Having sex with a man makes her vulnerable to his level of respect for her.

Men are usually quite unaware of how much women need to be respected, because when men are not respected they react very differently. When women are not respected they tend to give more to prove their worthiness. Men, however, are apt to become self-righteous and indignant about their needs, and to demand more than their share. They may even give less until they get what they deserve.

Unfortunately, as children we were all overly vulnerable to our parents' ability to respect us. If they did not respect our needs, it was hard for us even to know what we deserved. Girls are especially affected by the way their father respects their mother and how much their mother respects herself.

As stated before, it is a common reaction for a man to feel even more worthy of respect when others don't respect him. Under certain circumstances he may become aggressive to earn respect. For example, most fights start when a man is not feeling respected. It is also interesting to compare this concept with military basic training (which, although times are changing, is still designed primarily for the training of male soldiers). In boot camp, a trainee is systematically demeaned as worthless. This stimulates his aggression to prove he is worthy of respect. He sets out to earn respect through increasing achievement. Gradually he feels that he is truly worthy of respect and appreciation.

While a man's first reaction to being disrespected is commonly aggression and dominance, a woman's is submission. A woman is most vulnerable to this submissive reaction when she is in a relationship with a man whom she loves. When, as a result of not feeling respected, she comes to resent her partner, their roles may begin to switch. To compensate for her submissiveness she may become more dominant and demanding, while he becomes passive and dependent.

THE MALE NEED TO BE APPRECIATED

The primary need for appreciation is generally confused with the need for respect. To appreciate a person is to acknowledge that what they do or how they express themselves is of value to you personally, and that it is of some benefit. We need respect, on the other hand, to experience the validity of our needs, feelings, values, and rights. Appreciation is an act of evaluating, while respect validates.

Appreciation acknowledges that the value of our actions, intentions, results, and decisions — ultimately, our personal value, usefulness, and importance — has been received. It is the feedback that tells a man his behavior has served a purpose. If he can feel appreciated, then he is much more willing to explore and understand why his actions have failed.

Without appreciation, a person begins to feel inadequate and incapable of giving support. Without respect, a person may feel unworthy of receiving support.

Appreciation allows us to experience our intentions, decisions, and actions as valuable. It is the necessary support that inspires us to repeat an action that works or motivates us to change what doesn't work. Even when we fail to achieve our desired results, there is always something in what we did that can be appreciated.

Without enough appreciation we lose our will to give. When a man fails to reach his goal, if he is unable to feel that there was some value in his actions, he may give up. Or he may have the opposite reaction, and stubbornly repeat the action until he is appreciated.

Men are especially vulnerable to this need to be appreciated. If a man is not appreciated, he loses his motivation and becomes passive, lazy, weak, dependent, insecure and apt to procrastinate.

When a woman doesn't get appreciated her reaction is quite different. She tends to be even *more* motivated to earn appreciation. When her partner ignores her, her first impulse is to try harder to please him. Expecting men to do the same, she is confused when a man doesn't try harder to earn appreciation. She mistakenly assumes that he doesn't love her. When she is not getting enough from a man, she may begin to unconsciously or consciously manipulate him into giving more through withdrawing her appreciation. She is then confused and resentful when he reacts by giving even less.

When women are critical of a man's behavior they have no idea how damaging this is to his personal power. A man's response to not being appreciated is equivalent to what a woman experiences when a man judges or invalidates her feelings, needs, wishes, and rights. So when a woman begins to pick his behavior apart — criticizing the way he does things, correcting his thinking, challenging his decisions, and being dissatisfied with what he provides for her — a man loses his power. He retaliates with negative, demeaning judgments and disrespect, and withdraws from her. He is drained of the magical power that her loving appreciation gives him.

Conversely, when a man is appreciated by a woman, nothing can get him down for long. Being appreciated is a male's primary need. It lets him know he can make a difference; he measures his worth through his ability to make a positive difference in the lives of others. Appreciation becomes a fuel that motivates his every action. Even when he is unable to resolve his problems at work, if he can come home to a grateful and happy wife, his stress from work can be more easily released.

The strongest drive in a man is the desire to please a woman. This willful desire gives him power. It first manifests as the sex drive. Later, as he is able to blend it with the desire to love, respect, understand, and care for a woman, it becomes even more powerful. When a man can be appreciated physically, mentally, emotionally, and spiritually, then his power is maximum.

WHEN WOMEN SEEK APPRECIATION

A woman is misguided if she seeks appreciation to realize her worthiness to receive support. Regardless of how much she has given, she deserves to be respected and honored for who she is. When a woman finds herself seeking to earn appreciation, many times she is overlooking her own needs.

For example, she makes too many sacrifices for her job, and then says she resents not being appreciated. What she really resents is giving so much and then not being supported or respected. When she is not being respected, even if people appreciate her it will never be enough. Certainly a woman in the work world needs and deserves appreciation for her hard work in the same way a man does, but to support her feminine side, she has a greater need for respect.

Especially in her personal relationships, a woman needs her values, needs, intuition, feelings, and wishes respected. Many times a woman will be strong at work and feel entitled to respect there, but when she falls in love with a man who ignores her, she begins feeling unworthy of asking for more support. This is a sign that her feminine side is deprived of love. She must fulfill her primary needs for understanding, validation, and respect. By learning to be feminine and having her feminine needs fulfilled, she will find that she can be even more successful at work.

By her nature, a woman is able to discover her true dignity and worthiness by "being" rather than by "doing." Through *being* loving, appreciative, accepting, trusting, respectful, understanding, and caring, she earns respect and becomes more graceful. In cultivating positive attitudes a woman manifests her feminine power, the power to attract the support she desires. This power can make her more successful in the workplace when combined with her masculine power to create results.

When a woman has developed more of her masculine than her feminine side, this evokes in most men a resistance. Men don't readily want to support her. Deep inside a man, his strongest desire is to fulfill a woman. He feels secure when he knows he can make a difference. When she appears too independent, a man feels as though there is nothing he can do to help her or fulfill her. He may be offended that she mistrusts his willingness to support her, and threatened because he cannot make a difference and be her hero. If she can slay her own dragon, then this knight in shining armor is out of a job.

When a woman is able to balance her feminine with her masculine energy, men are much more willing to support her, assist her, and work with her. Some women have a special grace that allows them a power to enlist others in their service. Men who have a balance of male and female are also able to evoke this kind of support.

The easiest place for a woman to develop her feminine side is in relationships that are personal rather than work oriented. When she then brings her feminine qualities into the work world, where she is competing with men to be appreciated, she is less threatening to men.

Developing her feminine side also enables a woman to sustain her self-respect and avoid becoming a martyr. When a woman tries to prove her worthiness through *doing* (in an attempt to be appreciated) she finds herself burning out and never truly feels entitled to respect or support. Even if she does express her entitlement, she tends to do so in a resentful, bitter, and demanding tone. But through the qualities of her *being*, expressed through heartfelt loving attitudes, her presence can draw out from her man warmth, respect, and the desire to serve.

Her wish is truly his command. Yet she does not need to command, because he wants to serve and please her. It is the ungraceful woman who feels the need to command her man and all that results are power struggles and strife. In later chapters, we will explore further how a woman can develop her powers of "being."

When a woman actively seeks appreciation in a relationship, she unknowingly competes with her man for the opportunity to be of service. When he feels her competing he generally pulls out of the race, because he is not getting his fuel, which is her appreciation. He begins to feel drained in the relationship when she demands his appreciation. In most cases he may be very grateful for her services, but her quest to earn his appreciation has the effect of making him lazy. When she is trying to earn merit badges, he is content to sit back and go into "idle."

This does not mean that a woman should never serve her man through her actions. But when she gives through actions, it must be without the demand for appreciation. *When she serves her partner it should be with the desire to express her appreciation, rather than earn his.*

Women unconsciously give with strings attached when they do not feel cared for, understood, and respected. These women do not understand that a woman's ability to truly appreciate a man's actions earns her the right to have her wishes fulfilled.

THE MALE NEED TO BE ACCEPTED

When a man is "accepted," he is received willingly. This attitude cultures a man's belief in his abilities. When a man's actions are unconditionally accepted then he feels free to explore ways he can improve those actions. For this reason, acceptance is the basis of behavioral changes in a relationship.

The need for acceptance is especially important for men. Sometimes women appear to accept a man based upon his potential, however, this is not true acceptance. They are waiting for the day when he will change, and then they will be able to accept him. But men need to be accepted for who they are today, not who they will be tomorrow. A man will tend to become stubborn and resistant to change when he senses that he is not being accepted.

When a woman does not accept a man, she will feel compelled to change him. She will tend to offer suggestions that will assist him in changing, even when he has not asked. Some men are open to suggestions as long as they have requested them, but a man typically feels unaccepted when a woman is preoccupied with changing him or "improving" him. She imagines that she is respecting his needs by wanting to help; he feels disrespected, manipulated, and unaccepted. When a man does not feel accepted, he will unconsciously or consciously resist change.

A man is motivated to change by hearing and understanding a woman's feelings and needs. When he senses that his attempts to support her will be welcomed and appreciated, then he is easily inspired to fulfill her wishes. Her acceptance ensures that if he fails he will not be disapproved of, but will be willingly received with some gratitude for his efforts.

Acceptance allows him to feel that who he is today is enough to please and satisfy his mate. With this kind of confidence he is more willing and able to give his partner the respect and understanding she deserves. Most women do not know this secret about men. They mistakenly believe that the way to motivate a man to change is to complain, nag, or disapprove.

When a man feels his imperfections are unaccepted, it may take days before he can come back to his true, giving self. One of the ways he unconsciously or consciously gets revenge for his partner's nonacceptance is to repeat the very behavior that she resists.

A woman does not understand this, because when a man is unaccepting of her behavior, one of her first reactions is to change or improve her behavior. In this respect women are much more secure than men; they can listen to feedback about ways they can improve their behavior without as much resistance, sensitivity, or defensiveness. Certainly a man can take feedback, but he needs to be feeling good about himself and be willing to hear it. Rarely is it effective to give unrequested criticism or advice to a man.

A man is sensitive to correction when he is feeling his need to be accepted; if he already feels accepted, he can easily take the feedback.

THE MALE NEED TO BE TRUSTED

Trust is a firm belief in the ability, honesty, integrity, reliability and sincerity of another person. The need to be trusted is the need for an acknowledgment from your partner that you are a "good" person — upstanding you might say. When trust is absent, people consistently jump to the wrong, negative conclusion regarding a person's intent, whereas trust gives every offense the benefit of the doubt. Trust says, "There must be some good explanation why this happened." Trust grows in a relationship when each partner recognizes that the other does not intend to hurt, but seeks only to support.

Trust is the third primary need for a man. To approach a man for support feeling trusting is to approach him with the feeling that he can and will help. On the other hand, to ask for help without trust is to reject him before he has a chance. When he is not trusted, he will automatically begin to withdraw. Not only does lack of trust make it very difficult for him to respond, but it offends and hurts him.

It is a woman's trust in a man that draws him to her. When a woman is trusting of a man, she is able to draw out the best in him. Of course, if she trusts him to be perfect, he will let her down. But if she trusts that he can and will help, then he gets the message that he is of value and that his best is enough for her to accept and appreciate. Her trust will draw out of him increasing greatness. Through a woman's loving trust, a man is supported in realizing his powers, abilities, skills, and talents.

When her partner is not supporting her, trust allows a woman to assume that there must be some logical reason, and that when she lets him know her needs, he will respond to the best of his ability.

When a woman trusts a man, she feels safe to share her vulnerable feelings. If this man is indeed worthy of her trust, he will be greatly empowered by her trusting him to support her at such a delicate time. A trusting woman also intuits how much a man can support her, and doesn't demand or expect more. She is able to appreciate and accept what she gets. She does not naively go around sharing her vulnerabilities with just anyone. At the same time she does not withhold her vulnerable feelings from the people who are truly trustworthy.

The issue of trust can make communication very difficult. Say a woman doesn't trust a man with her delicate feelings. If she decides to test the waters by sharing a more diluted version of her feelings, a man will sense he is not being trusted and begin to withdraw. She then concludes, "Since these diluted feelings turned him off, I'm sure glad I didn't share them all." If she had been more honest, he would have been more receptive.

There is a time when a man is not put off by her lack of trust, especially at the beginning of a relationship, but a man will generally withdraw when a woman takes back a trust that she had previously bestowed. When at first a woman doesn't fully trust a man, it serves as a challenge for him to prove himself. If he has never tasted the nectar of her trust, he will patiently seek to prove his worthiness. But once she has opened herself to him and trusted him fully, and then due to some disappointment she begins to mistrust, he feels as though something has been taken away. In an indirect way he is wounded emotionally.

Many times a woman will withhold her feelings because she is afraid her partner is not really interested. She rationalizes her uncommunicativeness by making some excuse for him, but inside she doubts that he would respond caringly to her feelings. She may end up denying her needs, thinking she has avoided rejection. In reality, she has built a wall between them.

When a woman doesn't trust a man's loving intent and does not give him a chance to be her knight in shining armor again, she prevents him from being attracted to her. It is the trusting glimmer in a woman's eye that enchants a man out of his self-absorption and inspires him to respond to her needs.

It is a woman's responsibility to find, again and again, that trusting part of her. But men have to share in this responsibility by earning a woman's trust. If a man hurts a woman without apologizing, he is unknowingly building walls. Most of the time a man doesn't realize the importance of compassion or an apology. It is a woman's responsibility to let a man know what she needs to hear.

Although a man's primary needs are to be loved, appreciated, accepted, and trusted, he also has the other primary needs — but to him they are secondary. In the same way, a woman's primarily needs are to be loved, respected, understood, and cared for, but she also has secondary needs to be appreciated, accepted, and trusted.

In review, these male and female needs are listed below:

Male Primary Needs	Female Primary Needs
1. To be loved	1. To be loved
2. To be accepted	2. To be cared for
3. To be appreciated	3. To be understood
4. To be trusted	4. To be respected

Not only do we all have primary needs, but we also have primary and secondary natures. A man's primary nature is to complement a woman's primary needs. A woman's primary nature is to complement a man's primary needs.

When a man cultivates his caring, understanding, and respectful attitudes, he is best able to support a woman. When a woman cultivates her feminine nature, she is best able to support a man.

CHAPTER TWELVE

THE SECRET OF COMPLEMENTARY NATURES

As men and women mature, they develop and express themselves differently. As a man matures and grows in personal power he primarily develops his caring, understanding, and respectful nature. He moves from being cold, calculating, self-centered, and distant to being fully present, warm, and human. As a woman matures and discovers her personal power she expresses more of her accepting, appreciative and trusting nature. She moves from being manipulative to being empowering, from being chaotic or frantic to being graceful and fluid.

When men and women learn to develop their complementary natures in balance, the potential for peace and love in a relationship as well as for dynamic growth is insured. When a man develops his caring, understanding, and respectful nature he automatically supports a woman's primary needs, which are to be cared for, understood, and respected. When a woman develops her nature to accept, appreciate, and trust she automatically supports a man's primary emotional needs. In learning to most effectively support each other, they are required to nurture those attitudes that increase their personal power and maturity. Let's look at the three sets of complementary natures.

CARING AND TRUSTING

As a man becomes more caring he supports his partner by becoming more trusting. As a woman becomes more trusting she supports a man in becoming more caring. Many times a man is willing to support a woman much more than she could imagine. But when her reactions imply that he is unworthy of her trust or when she reacts to him as if he were the enemy, he automatically stops caring for her welfare. Her image of him is reinforced because he appears so uncaring.

Sometimes it may seem to a man that he is just too tired to care about or respond to another's needs. This, however, is a misconception. It is not that he is too tired, but rather that he is too uncaring to have the energy. Energy, creativity, and power stem from caring. As a man begins to care more, he discovers new resources of energy and vitality within himself. When he is uncaring, he is easily exhausted and unmotivated. For example, if a man is not trusted in his relationship, he is depleted of energy and has little stamina. He may come alive at work, where his talents are trusted and relied upon, but when he returns home he is exhausted.

Look to a man as a "hero," and he is energized; view him with mistrust as "the villain" or "the problem," and he stops caring. When a man is considered to be the problem, he cannot become the solution, nor is he motivated to be supportive. As women learn to trust, giving their men the benefit of the doubt rather than jumping to the wrong or worst conclusions, they will find men becoming more caring and supportive.

One of the reasons a man can be so caring, considerate, and concerned in the beginning of a relationship is that a woman looks to him with greater trust, adoration, and admiration during this time. In a sense, her trust gives him the power to be more caring. She draws it out of him. She can trust in the beginning because she has not yet been disappointed by him.

This trust empowers him but cannot make him perfect. Because he is human he will inevitably let her down, and she will begin to doubt and mistrust. As she becomes more mistrustful, he becomes more uncaring. An uncaring man has a greatly reduced capacity to give and tends to be self-centered. This person may have great energy reserves to serve himself, but in trying to have a relationship, he can be easily drained and exhausted. He must learn to be less self-centered and more caring. A trusting woman who loves him can do wonders for his power.

To become more caring is, for a man, no easy task. It takes time and support. Unfortunately, women are easily impatient and intolerant of a man's tendency to be uncaring, because a woman's primary nature is quite different. For her, to be caring is very easy; it is not her big lesson to learn as a person.

A woman's challenge in relationships is to trust and then, when she is disappointed, to be able to appreciate and accept and trust again. Since childhood, little girls have been nurturers and caretakers, while little boys are risk-takers. Just as it is difficult for men to learn to care for others, it is difficult for women to learn to trust.

When a woman has been let down repeatedly in a relationship, she will tend to deny her trusting nature. Moreover, she soon begins to mistrust a man's love for her when he appears unmoved or detached in response to her upsets. In a similar way, all it takes for a man to stop caring is to be mistrusted or unappreciated for his efforts in a relationship. If he feels his ability to please his partner is doubted, he stops caring about her happiness very quickly.

These two primary natures, caring and trust, are in themselves complementary. This explains the common scenario of the mother who is always worried about ten things at once and the father who stays glued to the couch, acting as though everything is fine. She is overly caring and thus worried; he is overly trusting and accepting, becoming passive.

Being overly caring, this mother can easily become too cautious or untrusting. In caring for a child she is apt to be overprotective. On the other hand, in the name of being trusting, a father can easily be uncaring. He may be too trusting and mistakenly assume everything is fine when it is not. In this case he is not caring enough; his daughters especially get the message that Dad doesn't care.

The fact that it is difficult for a man to care and a woman to trust can create many problems unless these natural tendencies are fully accepted and understood. What commonly happens in a relationship is that he acts in an uncaring fashion and she immediately assumes that he is falling out of love with her. As she mistrusts his love he reacts by beginning to care less about giving to her. This in turn causes her to trust less, and he then cares less. In this way their love begins to wilt over time.

With an awareness of these differences, rather than move in a negative spiral, relationships can progress. Rather than restrict us, they can assist us in developing our creative powers.

By expressing himself in a responsible and caring way, a man fulfills a woman's need to be responded to in a caring way. Because this is her primary need, she is capable of deeply appreciating him. As she begins to rely on his support, her trust increases. He then feels fulfilled in his needs for appreciation and trust, and is inspired to be of even greater service. Her deep trust and need for him increases his capacity to care and give, encouraging him to be even more caring. As she receives more and more support she grows in her ability to relax and trust, which in turn enriches her creative powers.

To create this kind of relationship, a woman must be aware of how difficult it is for a man to respond in a caring way when her reactions say to him that he is not being trusted. Likewise, with knowledge of male and female differences it is easier for her to correctly interpret his detached behavior. She can be more accepting and forgiving of him when he forgets things or doesn't think of things that would come automatically to her.

Men with this understanding are better able to accept a woman's ongoing need to be reassured. Rather than make her wrong for it, he can realize that this is a very important way he can support her in her personal development and happiness.

With this knowledge it becomes easier to take responsibility for getting what you need. First of all, if a woman's partner doesn't seem caring, she doesn't have to take it so personally. Likewise, if a woman needs to be reassured, her partner doesn't have to let this frustrate him.

Also one can see clearly how they can receive more in a relationship. Rather than complain about what they are not *getting,* they can begin to focus on what they are not *giving* their partner. For in giving more they are much more likely to receive.

UNDERSTANDING AND ACCEPTANCE

Through expressing himself in an understanding way, a man can consciously give more support to a woman. This support comes directly back to him, because the more understood she feels, the more she is able to accept and feel grateful for him. Through being understanding he helps her to be more centered and capable of accepting him just the way he is.

When she can cultivate a presence of acceptance, quite miraculously he will begin making changes in his behavior based on his increasing understanding of her needs. The secret truth is that men would be highly motivated to change to support their women if they really understood a woman's reality. Over time, as he is able to truly understand her feelings and needs, he can and will make solid changes to build a mutually supportive and empowering relationship.

As a man learns to "communicate to understand" rather than to correct or fix, he gradually masters the art of listening. In the beginning he will have to consciously resist the temptation to find fault with his partner's feelings. To do this he must realize that she is not asking for solutions, nor is she asking him to make her feel better. She is asking for him to understand what she is going through. She is asking for some validation for being upset.

When a woman knows that her partner has not heard her, she is compelled to try to change or manipulate him. But when a woman feels heard, then she can relax and trust that things are not as bad as they seem. She can also appreciate all that there is to enjoy, rather than worry about what isn't working. When she feels understood, she can better accept things as they are, knowing that she is not alone.

Many times men become so focused that they do not see all the day-to-day problems that gradually need to be solved. To the extent a man ignores them, a woman will feel overwhelmed by them. Simply because she sees them, she feels a responsibility to handle them; she will feel the pressure of solving them herself if she sees her partner is oblivious to them. She feels alone with all this work and needs to share the burden of this awareness. Sometimes a man will make a woman feel immensely better just by listening and understanding the pressures she is feeling.

When a woman is upset, she does not demand that her partner solve all her problems before she can accept and appreciate him. Seeing her upset, though, he may think she is demanding solutions to her problems before she will feel better. After all, when a man is upset over a problem he generally can't feel better until it is solved or a concrete solution is at least planned. He mistakenly assumes she thinks the same way.

Women don't demand immediate solutions if they can feel heard. The female gender has an incredible capacity to accept imperfection and incompleteness if their feelings can be fully expressed, heard, and validated. A woman's acceptance of imperfection can be one of man's most refreshing experiences. Most men have no idea that they have the power to draw this kind of support from a woman.

I will always remember the telling experience of driving my mother around Los Angeles. I wasn't familiar with the freeways and at some point I became completely lost. My mother didn't mind being lost and hardly noticed it; she was just enjoying the scenery. In a flash I noticed that something very special had happened. I felt as though I had been liberated from a jail sentence. I experienced the freedom and inner ease of being fully accepted.

In my intimate relationship at that time, I had been used to getting a disapproving look whenever I seemed absent-minded. In contrast, the drive with my mother was such a profound experience of feeling accepted, that in that moment I humorously decided to test any woman I ever considered marrying to see how she would react if I got lost.

Through learning to cultivate her inner acceptance, a woman insures that her man will be more motivated and capable of hearing and understanding her. As women learn to accept their men without trying to change them, slowly but surely men will become more understanding of a woman's unique needs and want to give more. And as men learn to understand women, they will begin to experience the incredible capacity that women have to forgive mistakes and accept a man just as he is.

RESPECT AND APPRECIATION

In a similar fashion, as a man learns to respect a woman's rights by acknowledging her equality in the relationship, he will experience increased appreciation from her for what he gives to her. To respect a woman's rights, a man needs to honor her differences. She deserves the right to be imperfect and overreact at times without it being a major offense to him. Respecting her means knowing that she will have her times when she is overwhelmed or confused, and that she deserves his support when that happens.

Respecting her rights calls for including her in all decisions that will affect her in some significant way. When he makes a decision, he should then ask for input. His request can be as simple as "Is that OK with you" or "I would like to _____, how do you feel about that?" or "I think we should _____, what would you like?"

Whenever there is a disagreement, he will, out of respect for his partner, acknowledge a need to continue their discussion until a win/win solution can be discovered.

Respecting a woman involves taking the time to learn her special needs and, to the best of his ability, attempting to anticipate them without always depending on her asking.

Respecting a woman also means to support her in fulfilling her dreams and aspirations. Out of respect, a man acknowledges and supports a woman in feeling worthy, special, and entitled to assert herself and her feelings.

Feeling special is one of a woman's most important needs. Making a woman feel special is the essence of romance. For example, by bringing home a surprise flower for his wife, a man is respecting and honoring her femininity.

Commitment and sexual monogamy are probably the most powerful and basic ways a man respects femininity. Commitment demonstrates to a woman that she is most special to him. Sexual monogamy insures that they continue to share something very special and precious to both of them.

In return for this respect a woman will be able to relax. She will not feel a compulsion to prove herself as an equal, but will automatically feel his equal. She will not be preoccupied with receiving appreciation for what she does, but will be able to focus on appreciating and valuing her man and all that he does to make her life easier. As she serves her man, it will not be with strings attached — her every gift to him will be an expression of her appreciation and gratitude.

Appreciating a man means doing all she can to make his life easier in return. She creates a peaceful and beautiful environment in which he can feel important, valued, special, and competent to make her happy.

When a woman appreciates a man, she desires him sexually and takes time to make herself attractive to him. In a sense she treats him like a royal guest in her palace.

Out of her appreciation, a woman processes her feelings so that she can be in a good mood for him whenever possible. She makes an effort to communicate her feelings and needs before resentment can build up. Appreciation prompts her to let him know that when she is upset or overwhelmed, it is not his fault.

Appreciating a man means feeling genuine joy that this man is in her life. An appreciative woman refrains from expressing critical opinions unless her partner asks for this. Appreciating a man calls for actually receiving his support so that she doesn't become overly tired.

THE BENEFITS OF LOVING

Through learning to cultivate our primary natures, we insure that we are able to give and receive more support in our relationships. Although we have been focusing on romantic relationships, these principles apply to all relationships — professional, family, and friends. Understanding the complementary nature of emotional support gives us a new power to create more support in our lives. If we want more trust, then we need to be more caring. If we are needing to be cared for, we must work on trusting enough to reach out and ask for support.

When a man is not getting the support he wants, the first question he must ask is how can he be more caring, empathetic, understanding, validating, respectful, considerate, and compassionate. These seven qualities, the rainbow of his primary nature, spring from the three primary qualities of caring, understanding, and respect.

It is important to recognize that by developing these traits he is not just being supportive of his female partner; he directly benefits as well. Through expressing and developing these loving qualities, combined with his basic masculine programming, he will become balanced and powerful. A man's most effective tool to de-stress and find his power is to act, think, or decide with a caring, understanding, and respectful attitude.

Sometimes all a man needs to do to feel better is to do something that is respectful of the needs of another. When he does something in support of another, he can make a difference. But if he is not respectful, then when he acts he will not make a positive difference. As a result, he will feel less inspired to give and only willing to serve himself. In serving himself, he can never be fully satisfied.

A man must have a purpose to serve, a cause or direction. When he stops caring he begins to burn out. Prisoners of war have reported that it was thinking about people they cared about that gave them the strength to survive. When a man does not care he becomes lifeless, empty, and devoid of purpose.

When a man stops caring his life also becomes boring. To temporarily break free from his boredom he may begin taking big risks such as car racing, mountain climbing, breaking societal taboos, breaking laws, gambling, high-risk investing, etc. When a man is about to lose his life climbing a mountain, or about to lose all his money or his freedom, all of a sudden he begins to care about his life, his money, or his freedom. At such times he gets a huge adrenaline rush similar to a drug high. Unfortunately, this feeling of happiness is only a temporary illusion that leaves him even more bored, depressed, and dissatisfied. To create a more lasting happiness, he needs to cultivate relationships and develop his ability to care for other beings.

Through culturing loving relationships, a man doesn't have to take dangerous risks or create emergencies and drama to feel that he cares. As he listens to and understands the feelings of others, he becomes more aware of their differing needs and feels a greater desire to be of service. By respecting their needs, through service, he is able to feel he is enough, without competing to be better than, to have more than, and to do more than others.

When a man is married he has the opportunity to be even more empowered. In a special relationship, he cares more for his mate and family than anyone else. This special caring empowers him to be more giving and motivated in his life. If his marriage is not loving, it may equally disempower him.

In a similar way, when a woman practices loving her man with increasing appreciation, acceptance, and trust, not only does he benefit but she directly benefits. Trusting allows her to contact her inner source of power and self-esteem. Accepting lets her relax and culture her positive attitudes. Through appreciation she is able to open up and receive the abundance she deserves. In trusting, accepting, and appreciating, a woman gains the power to fully enjoy and delight in her life.

As a woman works to release her negative feelings in order to nurture her positive, loving attitudes, she is not only earning and evoking the support of others, she is also connecting with herself.

As she gives love in this most important and difficult way, she begins to express the full spectrum of positive feelings that most fully support a man. They are trust, approval, acceptance, recognition, appreciation, acknowledgment, and admiration. When a woman can feel these attitudes, a man feels graced by her love. She likewise blossoms and is able to fully actualize who she truly is at the core of her being.

CHAPTER THIRTEEN

THE FEELING LETTER TECHNIQUE

The feeling letter technique is probably the most important skill a person can learn in order to have a successful and lasting loving relationship. This technique will help you learn to release resentment and other negative feelings in order to become centered in the positive attitudes of love, understanding and forgiveness again. It has saved thousands of marriages. and has helped others experience divorce in a more loving and peaceful way.

Since it was first published in 1984 in my book, *What You Feel, You Can Heal,* the feeling letter technique has been rewritten in three other best-selling books by other authors, and is used by numerous therapists, self-help groups, twelve-step programs, church groups, college counseling courses, and hundreds of other support groups. The feeling letter technique is the ultimate method for processing and transforming negative feelings into positive feelings.

In brief, the feeling letter has two parts. The first part consists of writing out the complete truth about how you feel, while imagining that you are being heard and understood. The second part is then to write a loving response to your letter. In this response letter, imagine the person to whom you have written the letter responding with an open heart. Write a response expressing the feelings and acknowledgments that you need to hear.

THE PURPOSE OF A FEELING LETTER

The purpose of writing a feeling letter when you are upset is to expand your awareness, to incorporate positive, loving feelings without having to repress your negative emotions. It allows you to open your heart.

Writing feeling letters helps you to incorporate all of the new and loving strategies in this book. No matter how much you know about having a good relationship, if your feelings are hurt it is difficult to be loving and supportive.

The feeling letter helps you give yourself the support you need when your partner can't. When you are writing a feeling letter, you are taking the time to listen to yourself with love, caring and understanding. If you are not willing to take the time to love yourself by listening to your feelings, you cannot realistically expect others to do this for you. When you feel the need for emotional support but you are not getting it, this is a sign that you need to give to yourself by writing a feeling letter.

The purpose of a feeling letter is not to dump resentment, judgment, and criticism on your partner. It is not written to try to change them or correct them, nor to point out their inadequacies. If used in this way it will not work. The feeling letter works only when it is written *for you to feel more loving*.

WHAT A FEELING LETTER ACCOMPLISHES

When your feelings are not being heard by your partner, it is essential that at least you hear them. Then, once they have been expressed, it is essential that you imagine the response you need in order to feel supported and heard. Writing a feeling letter assists you in removing the obstacles that are in the way of giving and receiving love. When you experience and explore the full range of your feelings, negativity is released quite automatically.

In writing out the response letter, your subconscious mind gets to feel and hear the support it deserves. Through being responsible to express what we need to hear, we open our hearts to feel and accept the support that does exist. The response letter also helps the recipient of your feeling letter know what you need from them in response to your letter.

The precise structure of the feeling letter format assists you in experiencing and feeling deep levels of emotion. As you write, your awareness spontaneously expands until you discover the positive feelings that are always already there, but are generally hidden.

Whenever you are upset or disturbed, it is because your awareness is focusing on the negative side of things. But through exploring your negative feelings, your awareness begins to expand and see the good side of things. Instantly, you are free from the gripping influence of negative emotions. You are suddenly aware of a wealth of positive feeling and emotion.

To bring about this catharsis and transformation, there are four levels of negative emotions you need to consciously experience or feel. Then, as a result, you can feel the loving emotions that were blocked by the negativity. Thus, after writing out the four levels of upset, you always finish the letter by writing out the fifth level, the level of love. When you write out these emotions, you experience them more consciously and are therefore able to release them fully. These levels are:

Level 1: Anger
Level 2: Sadness
Level 3: Fear
Level 4: Remorse
Level 5: Love and other positive attitudes

Following this emotional map you are able to explore the depths of negative emotions, and rediscover the loving feelings that are so quickly forgotten during times of stress. When your feeling letter is complete, write a letter in response. Write out expressions of apology, understanding, agreement, acknowledgment, love, and gratitude. In response to your feeling letter, write out what you need to hear, what would make you feel good, and what you feel the other person's response would be if they were able to hear you and respond with an open heart.

HOW TO WRITE A FEELING LETTER

In writing a feeling letter, you write out the feelings of one level and quite naturally your awareness moves to the feelings of the next level.

Begin by writing out any feelings of anger. As long as you are feeling anger, continue writing at level one. At some point you will notice a softening of your awareness. Then you are ready to explore the feelings of level two.

Write down your feelings of sadness. As you fully explore level two, your awareness will shift automatically to experience the deepest and most vulnerable feelings of level three. Write out your feelings of fear. As you write out the feelings of the first three levels, you may notice the emotions becoming more intense. This is a sign that you are letting go of these feelings, and a catharsis is taking place.

Spontaneously you will begin to feel a sense of responsibility. At this point, move to level four. Write out your feelings of remorse and apology. This shift will most effectively release you from holding on to any negative feelings. A surge of positive and loving feelings will emerge.

At this point you will probably feel much better. However, it is still vitally important to write out your positive feelings. Express love, appreciation, respect, understanding, acceptance, caring and trust. Setting down your positive feelings will make them last longer. Each time you write a feeling letter you will be strengthening your ability to sustain a positive and loving attitude, especially during stressful, upsetting times.

When writing a feeling letter, imagine that you are sharing your feelings with someone who is really listening to you and willing to support you. If you are upset with someone, you may address the feeling letter to that person. But keep in mind that you are just sharing your feelings with them; you are not trying to tell that person about himself or herself. You are not giving a critique of that person. Rather, you are sharing feelings with them so that they will better understand how to support you.

You can benefit from writing a feeling letter to someone even if you don't give it to them. If someone can't support your feelings, by all means write the letter to them, but do not give it to them. By writing the letter you will feel better. It is much more powerful to be able to share your feelings with the person you are writing to, but if they cannot hear your feelings with love and understanding, sharing them will only upset both of you.

To help you discover the full range of your feelings, the feeling letter format includes lead-in phrases for each level. Write out the lead-in phrase and then complete the sentence. This sentence completion technique helps to draw out your feelings. Lead-in phrases are especially helpful when you are not sure how to express what you are feeling.

These lead-in phrases not only help to bring up feelings, but they also lead you to deeper and deeper levels of emotion. You may choose to use just one, over and over at each level, or you might use them all. It is up to you to use the phrases that best assist you to express your feelings. Most of the lead-in phrases are "I sentences," which will help you stay in your feelings.

Whenever you feel upset, find a pen and a couple of pieces of paper and just start writing. Writing out what you are feeling will always help you to become more centered. Following the feeling letter format ensures that you will quickly find your loving center again.

THE FEELING LETTER FORMAT

Dear _____,

I am writing you this letter to release my resentment and negative emotions, and to discover and express the positive feelings that you deserve. I am also writing this letter to ask for your support without demanding it.

Level 1: Anger
I don't like . . .
I resent . . .
I feel frustrated . . .
I feel angry . . .
I feel furious . . .
I want . . .

Level 2: Sadness
It hurts . . .
I feel disappointed . . .
I feel sad . . .
I feel unhappy . . .
I wish . . .

Level 3: Fear

It is painful . . .
I feel worried . . .
I feel afraid . . .
I feel scared . . .
I need . . .

Level 4: Remorse and Apologies

I apologize . . .
I feel embarrassed . . .
I am sorry . . .
I feel ashamed . . .
I am willing . . .

Level 5: Love, Understanding, Gratitude, and Forgiveness

I love . . .
I appreciate . . .
I realize . . .
I forgive . . .
I would like . . .
I trust . . .

Love,

———————————

Remember, whenever it is hard to be loving, that is the time to write a feeling letter. Following the feeling letter format will help you fully process your negative feelings and bring out the true and loving feelings within you.

Give yourself the time to explore each level. Even if the feelings don't seem to be there, take a deep breath, relax, and search for them. Take whatever comes up and write that out. Try to spend equal time at each level. When one level is missing, sometimes that level needs most to be explored.

Feelings letters generally take about twenty minutes to write. Take about four minutes to explore each of the five levels. Don't worry about spelling or punctuation. Just continue to feel the emotion as you write it out. Whenever you get stuck, just start writing the lead-in phrase. Then write out whatever feeling or thought comes up, even if that feeling is unrelated to the lead-in phrase or even unrelated to the person to whom you are writing this letter. Writing a feeling letter is a tool to assist you in opening your heart. Using this tool, you will gradually develop the ability to keep your heart open all the time.

THE RESPONSE LETTER

After writing a feeling letter, take a few extra minutes to write a response. For many people this is what allows the feeling letter to be most healing. In formulating a response you are giving yourself the love you deserve. We generally get upset because we are telling our feeling self that we are being abused in some way. To write a response letter is to tell our feeling self what we deserve to hear in response.

After writing a feeling letter, your feeling self is wide open to receive positive input. A response letter allows you to take responsibility to affirm the love and support that you deserve. The response letter should include:

1. Apologies expressed in a way that makes you feel heard and supported

2. Understanding and validating statements that express warmth and compassion for your feelings

3. Loving statements that praise, appreciate, and acknowledge what you deserve

4. Whatever else you need to hear to feel good

In addition to being a good way to take responsibility for your own emotional well-being, response letters train the people in your life to know how you need to be supported. Throughout this book we have explored how different we all are, so by this time you probably know that it is unrealistic to expect our loved ones to know the right words. By writing a response letter and sharing it, you give your partner a chance to express love and support through the channel that will be most effective and fulfilling for you. For more information about how and why feeling letters work, read the chapter about feeling letters in *Men Are from Mars, Women Are from Venus.*

A Note from the Author

More than 25,000 individuals and couples in twenty major cities have already benefited from my relationship seminars. I invite and encourage you to share with me this safe, insightful, and healing experience. I look forward to seeing you there. It will be a cherished memory that you will never forget.

For information about seminars or any of the items listed below, please write or call:

John Gray Seminars
20 Sunnyside Ave., Suite A-130
Mill Valley, CA 94941
1-800-821-3033

TAPES, SOFTWARE, NEWSLETTERS, VIDEOS, AND BOOKS BY JOHN GRAY

Secrets of Successful Relationships
Recorded live from John Gray's Relationship Seminars.

Healing the Heart
Recorded live from John Gray's Heart Seminars.

Private Session
Computer software for exploring and healing feelings.

What You Feel, You Can Heal:
A Guide for Enriching Relationships

Men, Women and Relationships:
Making Peace with the Opposite Sex

Men Are from Mars, Women Are from Venus:
A Practical Guide for Improving Communication and
Getting What You Want in Your Relationships

Beyond Words Publishing, Inc.

Our Company Mission:

Inspire to Integrity

Our Declared Values:

▲ We give to all of life as life has given us.

▲ We honor all relationships.

▲ Trust and stewardship are integral to fulfilling dreams.

▲ Collaboration is essential to create miracles.

▲ Creativity and aesthetics nourish the soul.

▲ Unlimited thinking is fundamental.

▲ Living your passion is vital.

▲ Joy and humor open our hearts to growth.

▲ It is important to remind ourselves of love.

Our Promise to our Customers:

We will provide our customers with the highest quality books and related products that meet or exceed their expectations. Our customers will be satisfied with their purchase and receive their orders promptly, or we will refund their purchase.

To Order or to Receive a Catalog Contact:

Beyond Words Publishing, Inc.
13950 NW Pumpkin Ridge Road
Hillsboro, OR 97124
(503) 647-5109 or Toll-free: 1-800-284-9673

Other Books from
Beyond Words Publishing, Inc.

STRAIGHT TALK WITH YOUR GYNECOLOGIST:
How to Get Answers that Will Save Your Life
by Eddie Sollie, M.D., OB/GYN, with Sara Steinberg,
$12.95 softbound

Written in a conversational style, this how-to guide empowers women to become equal partners in their health care. Emphasizing the value of open communication, *Straight Talk* provides guidelines for choosing the best doctor for you, questions to ask your doctor before, during and after the exam and instructions for reading your own pap smear report. This book gives women the tools to take responsibility for their personal health and to ask the questions that can save their lives.

RAISING A SON: Parents and the Making of a Healthy Man
by Don and Jeanne Elium, $18.95 hardbound, $10.95 softbound

This conversationally-styled, "how-to" book, written by family counselors, is a guide to assist both mother and father in the parts they must play in the making of a healthy, assertive, and loving man. It is suitable for parents, professional-care providers and educators.

AIDS-PROOFING YOUR KIDS: A Step-By-Step Guide
by L. E. Acker, Ph.D.; B. C. Goldwater, Ph.D.; and
W. H. Dyson, M.D., Ph.D., $8.95 softbound

The first and only collection of the most practical teaching strategies currently available for educating teenagers about responsible sex. This timely book was written by three doctors who specialize in family psychology, social learning, medicine, biochemistry, and AIDS prevention. They lead parents, step-by-step, through AIDS-proofing exercises with their kids. The book gives the crucial facts on the disease and offers strategies to parents for teaching both abstinence and/or condom use.

TRIUMPH OVER DARKNESS:
Understanding and Healing the Trauma of Childhood Sexual Abuse
by Wendy Wood, M.A., $12.95 softbound

A book geared toward understanding and healing the trauma of childhood sexual abuse. In this collection of powerful commentaries on incest, rape and abuse, women and men share their varied experiences through poetry, prose and personal accounts. The reader learns that there is hope and a path toward wellness. Author Wendy Wood, M.A., is the founder of a nationwide networking agency whose purpose is to connect mental-health professionals with survivors of sexual abuse.

To order or to receive a catalog, contact:
Beyond Words Publishing, Inc.
13950 NW Pumpkin Ridge Road
Hillsboro, OR 97124
(503) 647-5109 or Toll-free: 1-800-284-9673

Other Books and Tapes by Dr. John Gray

WHAT YOU FEEL, YOU CAN HEAL
1 book, 214 pages, $12.95

Dr. John Gray brings 18 years of experience as a therapist, seminar leader and author to this comprehensive handbook for healing the heart. This 214-page book is the ultimate guide for enriching relationships and increasing one's self-esteem. Through practicing the simple but profound techniques contained within this book, thousands of couples have renewed their relationships while individuals have increased their self-esteem. Warmly written and whimsically illustrated, this easy-to-read and entertaining book will take you through the steps required to break through love's barriers.

SECRETS OF SUCCESSFUL RELATIONSHIPS
12 cassettes, $99.70

In this entertaining and insightful series you will:
- Learn seven secrets for creating and sustaining passionate relationships
- Understand and appreciate how men and women are different
- Discover how you unknowlingly sabotage your relationships
- Realize the eight ways to get the love you need now!
- Learn the hidden reasons why men pull away and why women get upset
- Discover how men and women react differently to stress
- Enjoy the secrets of great sex
- Learn new techniques for successfully giving and receiving love

HEALING YOUR INNER CHILD
2 cassettes, $19.95

Learn two powerful exercises for feeling better when you are upset. The first cassette contains a gentle guided process to increase self-love and heal your inner child. In the second cassette, Dr. Gray reveals how, in 20 minutes, you can free yourself from the gripping influence of negative moods. By practicing this revolutionary new technique you can heal the hurt and pain which gives rise to unwanted fear, anger, anxiety and resentment.

THE NEW HEALING THE HEART SERIES
12 cassettes, $99.70

This series provides an innovative step-by-step approach to heal the heart from the painful influences of your past and to create loving and positive attitudes. In five sessions, Dr. Gray explores how to:

- Create greater success
- Overcome fear and anxiety
- Increase self-acceptance and self-esteem
- Heal the emotional wounds of childhood
- Release resentments through forgiveness

In addition, this series contains the two *Healing Your Inner Child* cassettes and the three *Healing Your Past* cassettes.

MINI SERIES
For a taste of Dr. Gray's information, we have divided his *Secrets of Successful Relationships* complete tape series into mini sets.

1. *Understanding Men and Women*   4 cassettes, $29.95
2. *Healing Your Past*   3 cassettes, $24.95
3. *Secrets of Passion*   3 cassettes, $24.95
4. *Secrets of Great Sex*   2 cassettes, $19.95
5. *Successful Relationships*   3 cassettes, $24.95